LATIN AMERICA
IN ITS ARCHITECTURE

LATIN AMERICA IN ITS CULTURE
César Fernández Moreno, Series Editor

LATIN AMERICA IN ITS LITERATURE
César Fernández Moreno and Julio Ortega, Editors

LATIN AMERICA IN ITS ARCHITECTURE
Roberto Segre, Editor

LATIN AMERICA IN ITS ART
Damián Bayón, Editor

LATIN AMERICA IN ITS MUSIC
Isabel Aretz, Editor

Latin America in Its Architecture

Roberto Segre,
Editor

Fernando Kusnetzoff,
Editor of the English Edition

Translated from the Spanish
by Edith Grossman

HM
HOLMES & MEIER PUBLISHERS, INC.
New York / London

First published in the United States of America 1981 by
Holmes & Meier Publishers, Inc.
30 Irving Place
New York, N.Y. 10003

Great Britain:
Holmes & Meier Publishers, Ltd.
131 Trafalgar Road
Greenwich, London SE10 9TX

English translation and new material
Copyright © 1981 by Holmes & Meier Publishers, Inc.

Original Spanish edition:
América Latina en su arquitectura © Unesco 1975

This book has been published with the financial assistance of Unesco.

LIBRARY OF CONGRESS CATALOGING IN PUBLICATION DATA
Latin America in its architecture.

   (Latin America in its culture; 2)
   Translation of América Latina en su arquitectura.
   Bibliography: p. 199
   Includes index.
   1. Architecture—Latin America—Addresses, essays, lectures.　2. Architecture
and society—Latin America—Addresses, essays, lectures. I. Segre, Roberto.
II. Kusnetzoff, Fernando.　III. Series.
NA702.A5413 1980　　　720'.98　　　79-27695
ISBN 0-8419-0532-0

MANUFACTURED IN THE UNITED STATES OF AMERICA

Contents

Introduction to the English Edition

Architecture, History, and Society in Latin America

FERNANDO KUSNETZOFF
Translated by Andrew Gordon

The publication of *Latin America in Its Architecture* represents for the English-speaking reader a valuable and long-awaited contribution on the content and direction of Latin America architectural production. This work, which comprises a selection and revision of the original text, published in Spanish by UNESCO in 1975 and edited by Roberto Segre, introduces a collection of essays written by well-known experts, who in varying degree share a similar vision of architecture as the material expression of a concrete social totality. Consequently, while emphasizing the specific circumstances that have characterized the evolution of different Latin American societies and while explaining in this manner the uniqueness of their architectural production, these essays differ from those more visual discussions that view architecture as a study of the creative genius of some relevant personalities, or as something that stems from a universal and abstract process manifested in a global civilization and a succession of styles. Although considering those factors in proper perspective, in these essays center stage goes to ideological content, to fundamental reflection on the specific factors that have conditioned the architectural product.

Perhaps the above requires some additional explanation about the circumstances in which these essays were conceived and about the present edition. On the one hand, they form part of a polemic process that has been agitating the professional and academic communities in Latin America, certainly not with particular respect to architecture, but with respect to the whole of the subcontinent's cultural and material production. The polemics are a natural response to the wide area of debate over the general Latin American condition, a debate which in the preceding decade erupted with particular vigor in the field of the social sciences as a result of the depletion or failure of several social and economic development experiences. This state of questioning rapidly penetrated into the seemingly neutral world of the "arts." Architecture, the art most "contaminated" by social practice, could naturally not escape such critical examination. The task force that UNESCO called together and assembled in Buenos Aires, Argentina in 1969 in order to plan for a volume on Latin American architecture, recognized this situation at the very outset and because of it, a substantial part of the original text focused on the study of regional and urban problems. The present edition replaces those essays with a synthetic work (Segre, Chapter 2), which along with maintaining the principal themes of those studies, offers a highly valuable, up-to-date evaluation. It was considered necessary to revise the original edition because the Latin American urban-regional theme has fortunately received widespread attention from the English-language publishing world, including the translation of studies by several of the authors included in the previously mentioned first edition.[1] This has not been the case with the architectural theme, of which only few collected works and monographic essays on contemporary architects, generally from an aesthetic perspective, have been published.[2] In contrast, the works included in this edition, by referring to the conditioning framework of architecture avoid the limitations entailed in considering only exceptional stereotypes such as the Palacio de Alborada (Palace of Dawn) in Brasilia, or impressionist and folklore descriptions of conventual or popular habitat architecture, and allow for a fuller understanding. Indeed, the authors of these essays have demonstrated particular care in approaching the complexity of the Latin American world in its dialectical relationship with architecture, with its struggles and contradictions, with its particular values, traditions, and influences, with its creative innovations as well as with its puerile imitations.

In the ordering of the essays that compose this book, three themes, which in one way or another are explored by a majority of the authors, stand out: (a) a consideration of the changes in the Latin American social and historical context as an explanatory foundation for the evolution of architecture; (b) an analysis of the conditioning of architecture by its urban setting; (c) an evaluation of the production process of architecture in relation to the institutional and professional environment. These central themes have, in turn, permitted a suitable arrangement of the eight essays selected for this edition, which with the exception of the first essay by Segre, form part of the original Spanish edition. It is our belief that the collective contribution of this book clearly supports the validity of these premises raised a decade ago, and that this is probably the first work that offers the English-speaking public a dynamic, polemical, and at the same time, coherent vision of the situation in Latin American architecture.

The Social and Historical Context of Architecture in Latin America

History comes forward to greet the visitor to Latin America at every turn, and architecture, with monumental testimony about certain eras forms a preeminent part of this history. The convergence of peoples from diverse origins in the same geographic area, the sharp social and cultural contrasts visible in any metropolitan plaza, speak to us of a subcontinent which on the one hand has arrived at its present condition through a series of traumatic experiences, and on the other, still finds itself searching for ways in which to integrate its respective national societies. This is why there exists a certain official history with chauvinist streaks, which in some cases and periods is exemplified in unique works of architecture, that exists side by side together with more general processes by which Latin America has been defining, or rather accepting, its mode of insertion into the global system of nations. This second vision corresponds more accurately to the one adopted by the authors of these essays.

The preferred starting point dates to the time of the invasion of the Iberian colonizer, who in his double role as missionary and plunderer, rejected the preexisting forms of social organization, especially in the more advanced settlements, as in the cases of the Central American and Andean civilizations, and abruptly eliminated a significant part of their most valuable cultural manifestations. In certain instances over the ruins of technically elaborate constructions, the *conquistador* precipitously imposed a new formal language, reflecting the new distribution of power, a distribution that was maintained without variation until after the political emancipation that occurred at the beginning of the nineteenth century. This extensive colonial period, that lasted more than three hundred years, produced different effects within the core of Latin American societies. Geographic factors as well as differences in the degrees of submission and survival of the indigenous population encouraged development around certain viceroyal capitals, and the relative abandonment of vast rural regions. At the same time, the social structure was consolidated for the benefit of the dominant elite of Peninsular origin, who imposed their needs and architectural tastes.

This situation, the emergence of an architecture that had its basic symbolic and functional meaning defined by a variegated Iberian minority of captains, sacristans, and merchants, is extensively discussed by several of the essayists. In the initial chapter, Darcy Ribeiro[3] opens the debate with an excellent investigation of the conditioning factors for cultural and artistic creation in colonial America. In his criticism of the notion of cultural relativism, Ribeiro maintains that the dominant society eradicated the native cultural forms and established in their place a transplanted European cultural universe, that was inauthentic in that it lacked real meaning for the overwhelming mass of the population:

> In fact, throughout most of our colonial history, we do not find an educated class that expresses its nation's cultural creativity. What we do find is a transplanted elite, which mimics the cultural gestures that belong to another context, gestures that mean nothing to their own population and are unsatisfactory as well for the native educated class, which suffers the dislocation of its

double role: local agents of a superior culture which they are proud to represent, and members of a subordinate society whose way of life mortifies them
(Ribeiro, p. 27–28).

Such inauthenticity, however, did not inhibit a certain degree of local
creativity, even if essentially it was merely a reiteration of European stylistic
trends. Thus, the imposition of baroque variants is explained, notes Ribeiro,
as the style of the principal colonial architectural works of a public, religious, and private character. The Church, in particular, appeared as the
ruling institution in cultural life, and because of this, its representatives, born
or educated in Europe, displayed a sensibility in tune with the dominant
metropolitan centers. For an evaluation of architectural expression during
that period, the essays by Gasparini and Cetto (chapters 3 and 4) bring
material together for a clearly open-ended debate on the relative value and
degree of originality in those vestiges of the long colonial period.

Gasparini reassumes Ribeiro's concern for the cultural influences on
Latin American colonial architecture, in order to vigorously attack two
tendencies that he considers equally invalid: the "Hispanicism" of certain
Spanish historians who attempt to accentuate the cultural singularity of
Spain with respect to the rest of Europe; and, the nationalist emphasis of
certain Latin American authors who seek to "Mexicanize," "Peruvianize,"
or "Mestizoize" the manifestations of colonial art. Gasparini leans toward
an interpretation based on the idea that the imposition of metropolitan culture
allowed only for "differential specificities," in accord with the regional and
provincial character conceded by the Spanish crown to its possessions. Consequently, there were similar elements of architectural production in distant
regions that did not harm the variation or expressive differences, which in the
case of South America included non-Iberian contributions. On the other
hand, Gasparini discusses the indigenous contribution and concludes that it
was only valued for its manual labor which was directed toward the execution of nonnative motifs that accounted for its paltry character and estrangement from the pre-Colombian tradition. In his detailed study of the
Brazilian colonial situation, Gasparini confirms the repetitive modality, in
this case of the Portuguese model, itself initially somewhat less significant
than the Hispanic model, perhaps on account of a weaker apparatus of domination. However, with the emergence of Bahía as the seat for colonization,
the direct transmission of the Portuguese model, which arrived already
influenced by various other European expressions, was guaranteed. In this
manner, as in the religious architecture, we encounter the use of imported
building materials—often used as ballast in transport—offering surprising
results such as the Concepción de la Playa (Conception of the Beach)
temple, "another church that was prefabricated in Portugal out of *lioz* rock
and which arrived in Brazil in separate, numbered pieces." In conclusion, the

author defines the colonial period as "neither absolute originality nor total reproduction."

As for Max Cetto, in his essay on the external influences upon colonial architecture, he offers a dual level of architectural and urbanistic analysis in order to call attention to what he labels, "an internal reelaboration of European typologies." An interesting case, which illustrates his position, is that of the so-called Indian chapels, or open chapels. By permitting the celebration of open-air masses and by extending the ceremony to a large indigenous population, the chapels contributed functionally to the ambitious missionary enterprise begun in the sixteenth century.

The relative unity that the colonial period imposed on Latin American architecture, particularly in those public and religious buildings that are still preserved, yielded to rapid and confusing stylistic diversification when the system of Spanish domination collapsed and was replaced by independent political regimes at the dawn of the nineteenth century. New ruling classes now found ideological sustenance in the more dynamic countries of the European world, where bourgeois revolutions imposed formal languages on the cultural environment, expressing the essential character of capitalist societies on the rise. Certainly beyond the scope of this introduciton is the mention of those modalities through which the incipient Latin American republics would develop in a framework of subordinate relations to the growing economic powers of European capitalism. These relationships have been intensively explored by that community of social scientists whose interest lies in defining the process in terms of "dependent relationships."[4] We only wish to reiterate that on the material level the architectural practice reflected the objectives and interests of the struggling social sectors during the difficult period of republican consolidation which characterized the nineteenth century. Recently we have begun to observe the accumulation of architectural evidence imposed both economically and politically by the ruling class, an accumulation that is in this phase characterized by a clearly eclectic stylistic complex.

Vargas Salguero and López Rangel in chapter 5 and Segre in the second and in the final essays of this book extensively analyze the neoclassical period of Latin American architecture. Its historical proximity, in addition to the complexity of its dominant political and social structure, explain the abundance and variety of architectural production that had definitively abandoned the baroque language at the formal level. The new replacement was the *"neoclassicism that would become the civic expression of those power elites who, by means of rationalist-mechanistic ideology of classical European canons, were manifesting their conception of the economic and cultural destiny of our societies."* (VS and LR p. 123). What is indicated here is a deliberate separation from the colonial world's religious and absolutist limitations and its replacement by a group of civilian societies which sought to modernize themselves in their practices and institutions. Along with the penetration of foreign capital came a new division of labor and consequently, a construction activity that could materially support it. Banks, legislative palaces, academies, buildings for spectacles, and huge mansions were indiscriminately added to the traditional symbols of colonial power, especially in the more prosperous republics of Mexico, Brazil, Argentina, and Chile:

> Buildings of monumental character were erected even in the central areas of the cities; their pompous classicism expressed the ideology of an oligarchy that was trying by all means possible to maintain a precarious internal peace, and that through *positivism* was concerned with presenting an image of prosperity and culture in a world where the masses had been made marginal by the privilege of the ruling class. In this way architecture and city planning played their ideological-political role in our countries, representing the equilibrium that the oligarchs were trying to maintain, during the so-called period of independence. [Vargas Salguero and López Rangel, p. 127].

In the case of Latin America, this eclectic period corresponded to the historical fluctuations originating from the European model. There the arrival of the twentieth century brought with it the exhaustion of the neoclassical language, leveled by a rationalism which sought to confront with new technical resources a scheme of social relations in which the middle and proletarian sectors' demands increasingly intervened and were difficult to ignore. Europe and the United States gave birth, in architecture, to the functionalist movement, which experienced a widespread acceptance by the Latin American professional elites. At this point, to the antiacademic attitude toward formality was added an attempt to connect architecture with the social processes in progress, which in the cases of Brazil, Mexico, and Venezuela produced a kind of "architectural populism," to use the terminology of the above-mentioned essayists.

The reading of these essays, as well as those by Segre, Cetto, and to a certain extent, Bonsiepe (chapter 6) allows us to identify a characteristic situation in the development of Latin American rationalist architecture, that being the interaction of the professional elites with the various structures of the State apparatus. During the 1940s, with variations, Latin American governments were able to instill a social sense into the most representative architectural works. For that period, this reflected the predominant political game of the State, the need to establish the State as the apparent mediator between the dominant economic interests and the new rising classes. On the one hand, the State financed architectural public works that symbolized its increased participation in those modernization processes in progress—ministries, universities, and hospitals. On the other hand, the State initiated ambitious programs for low-income housing as a response to the rapid urban and metropolitan expansion taking shape during those years.

World War II brought a brief abeyance, which would open the door for a new age of architectural experimentation, involving a change from the simple, rigid adoption of the European avant-garde architectural schemes. A period of sustained economic development, which continued through the early 1950s and was supported by an intensive industrialization process, permitted the growth of an environment of relative optimism for Latin American social and economic development. Architects took advantage of opportunities to carry out large projects that reflected the combined interests of a State intent on development and of national producers. It was the time of spectacular housing complexes—the Monobloques in Caracas, or Pedregulho in Rio de Janeiro—where formal and constructive variations were elaborated and relatively integrated into the local surroundings. They began to be admired as the possible prototypes for a new urban habitat. Nevertheless, the structural limitations of the development models utilized in Latin America have shown over the past two decades a decrease in the rate of growth, sharply contrasting with the rapid demographic concentration in the principal cities. This situation has put into question both the feasibility and validity of those architectural solutions. The short-lived illusion of the State's capacity to finance programs of a social content, such as low-income housing, gave way to other expenditure and accumulation priorities within an uncertain capitalist system. In this manner, we reach the most recent period, where the State, aware of its limitations, has partially abandoned its building impulse while the private sector, in service to the affluent classes, has turned to real estate speculation making explicit its disdain for "social interest housing." Under these conditions, improvised housing, built by millions of squatters who remain marginal both to the market mechanisms and to the limited governmental programs, proliferates in the metropolitan areas of Latin America. Summarizing this review of the cited essays, a dominant convergence is noted in the interpretation of an architecture which has essentially been conditioned by the inherent contradictions of social development, and which has ultimately resulted in huge agglomerations. The singularity of this urban phenomenon throughout all of Latin American history happens to constitute a second and important condition for understanding architectural production.

The conditioning of Latin American architecture by its urban environment.

In contrast to the formative process of other societies, Latin American societies have favored the forms of urban life since the moment they were first incorporated into the "Western" world, in spite of the fact that a substantial portion of the population, until recently the majority, resides in the vast rural areas. In the preceding section, we have mentioned the historical circumstances that determined this evolution. In fact, from as early as the sixteenth century, the implantation of the majority of Latin American cities had already been defined.[5] Consequently, erudite architecture, in the words of Ribeiro, developed in the urban centers, with the notorious exception of the patronal mansions or the *latifundios.* In contrast, the rural environment reflected for more than four centuries the particular production relationships existing in the countryside, where an overwhelming majority of the rural population had lived and continues to live in poverty conditions. Housing rarely consisted of more than precarious and unstable dwellings. Even for those societies in which agricultural exploitation permitted higher-density settlements, as in the cases of regions with indigenous, rural communities, the predominant architectural expression reflected the general poverty of the rural people. For this reason, we question the fascination that overcomes the visitor from the a city in his sporadic and brief incursions through the countryside. Apparently, he is charmed by the tranquility and simplicity of a small country village or settlement. Perhaps this is the result of a subjective and psychic reaction against the tensions of a metropolitan life-style. Certain exceptional circumstances would be necessary, such as some agrarian reform experiments taking place in only a handful of Latin American countries, so that changes in the processes and relations of production might, in turn, stimulate a rise in the architectural and environmental level of the rural area, as has been achieved in Cuba.

Yet more than four centuries of urban settlements constitute a formidable accumulation of construction, whose material inertia is difficult to alter. It is in this preferred urban environment that the evolution and contradictions of Latin American architecture clearly appear, and reveal the changing life-styles of the different social groups, as well as their conflictive power relationships. From the beginning, two urban, spatial characteristics have survived unaltered by time: on the one hand, the distinct hierarchy of public spaces that have symbolized the political and economic functions of the State; and on the other hand, a well-defined spatial segregation of the component social classes of urban society.

Consequently, we need not assume deterministic extremes of a physical or ideological character in order to recognize that, beginning with the generalized application of the grid-plan in the Spanish Latin American colonial cities, a two-fold symbolic and practical intention was manifested. This involved grouping around their Plaza Mayor or Plaza de Armas (main town square) those functions and buildings that constituted the power structure, giving, during the colonial period, a monumental physiognomy to those public spaces.[6] This was followed by the introduction of a new spatial language of extensive avenues and parks that corresponded to the republican stage of development, which in the nineteenth century signified connecting the direct expression of the growing and ostentatious power of the national bourgeoisies to the traditional functions of the central State. Only during the last decades have we appreciated the concerted efforts of these bourgeoisies, in conjunction with governmental bodies, to preserve the use, not only of some privileged spaces, but also of all of the central areas required for their vital functions. In this manner, and by eclectically gathering the urbanistic doctrines in vogue in Europe and the United States, the Latin American metropolises have witnessed complex attempts to revitalize their central areas. In many cases, this has meant disturbing the preexisting environmental conditions, by yielding to intensive land and real estate speculation, a situation which according to Segre, implies that, 'The structure of the city was subject to national bourgeois interest that controlled the center and its areas for expansion, segregating the space occupied by the petty bourgeoisie and the proletarian zone, defined by the direct relationship of habitat-production" (chapter 2, p. 55).

In this manner, the predominant architecture of the central areas came to represent a tenuous compromise between the governmental agencies and their bureaucratic demands for internal expansion, and the business and financial groups who needed the same areas for the pursuit of their economic activities. In many cases, the combined pressure from both sectors involved sacrificing certain spaces and buildings of unquestionable social or historical value. This occasionally produced reactions which Segre discusses in his first essay (chapter 2, pp. 37–76). In the central areas, the opportunity was then available to experiment frequently and indiscriminately with the most recent and costly technological innovations in architecture and urban design from the developed world. Without having to consider initial or maintenance costs, these experiments relied on the enthusastic participation of talented architects in search of their self-fulfillment. Here, as in its original environment, recent architecture has displayed from time to time achievements of a high technical caliber—analyzed by Escobar Loret de Mola (chapter 7)—and sporadically of social character, along with numerous cases of a simple modernizing eclectism, imitative and mediocre. But more important than discussing the relative value of certain specific works of architecture in this urban environment is the consideration of the immediate and future consequences of this ambiguous bureaucratic-capitalist pact on the economic, environmental and functional crises of the cities' central areas, as well as its effects on the rest of the urban surroundings. Not only do the central areas of larger Latin American metropolises—such as São Paulo, Mexico City, Caracas, and Buenos Aires—contend with critical situations in matters of infrastructure, transportation and circulation, environmental pollution, and real estate speculation, but intermediate-size capitals and cities such as Tegucigalpa, Guayaquil, and Valparaíso have already exhibited similar problems. However, the aforementioned pact members have reacted to the mounting problems by allotting huge sums of money, taken from national revenues, to hurriedly and superficially correct situations, for which the fundamental causes have remained unchanged.[7]

At the same time that the central areas were deteriorating, there was also a housing crisis of increasing proportions, which served to expose the fact that the metropolitan economy functions so as to exclude an important segment of the population from its benefits. In the previous section, the efforts by the public sector to tackle the housing problem were mentioned. Massive construction programs were instituted, although they have invariably turned out to be insufficient for satisfying the staggering pace of metropolitan growth. We also mentioned the gradual governmental acceptance of the spontaneously erected shelters and shantytowns that had previously been the target of forcible removals and demolitions. In fact, once the official and academic sectors got over their initial fear of the possible insurgent character of this "marginal" sector of the population, they began to use a new approach. Basically, this attitude, with some variations, has attempted to legitimate the persistence in Latin American cities of vast residential areas characterized by poorly built housing (generally erected by the residents themselves) and a general lack of provisions and basic services for both family and collective living. This new attitude is partially supported by the vague hope that in the future the anticipated development of national economies will enable those sectors to be fully equipped, as much through that population's own efforts, as by the institution of public programs. In both of his essays, Segre criticizes this idea by discrediting the implicit economic, cultural, and ideological justifications of resident-built housing when it occurs in an exploitative environment that prohibits a real and decisive level of popular participation in the determination of these processes, and, ultimately, an authentic social transformation.[8] On the other hand, when the peripheral metropolitan dweller meets to some degree his basic need for shelter, the city loses an important way of rationally ordering its growth and of creating real sources for economic and occupational activity. It loses the option, possibly of greatest value, of establishing models for social integration which until now have seemed to need as a prerequisite a radical change in the conduct of Latin American societies, and this by means of attending to the basic needs of the majority of their populations.

The persistence and growth of these two situations, disorder and inefficiency in the urban center along with precarious conditions in shantytowns and low-income housing, have confronted the Latin American architect with the unavoidable necessity of judging his own conduct in the generation or consolidation of these problems. What was a vague, initial utopianism rooted in the rationalist doctrines of the modern movement of architecture, has given way to a better understanding of the complex nature of the contradictions that characterize, with especial intensity in the principal cities, the societies of Latin America. This consciousness-raising process, more strongly felt among young professionals, in the architectural schools, and by their students, constitutes a third theme of this book.

*The Production and Educational Processes of Architecture in Relation to
the Institutional and Professional Environment in Latin America*

To begin this section, it is of major interest to note the essay by Guy
Bonsiepe (chapter 6) on the practice in Latin America of industrial design,
a field related to, but different from, architecture, where, nevertheless,
formalist and consumer deviations similar to those prevalent in architectural
practice are found. The author critically points out the concern for attaining
an acceptable formal level in product design, a "good design" that behind its
elitist and advanced appearance, is generally hiding a marketing purpose
imposed by interests that seek the promotion of a product in a scarcely
innovative market. The author compares what he calls "the transfer of
designs" with the processes of transfer of technology and goes on to discuss
product policy in the developed world. This policy, which is directed toward
increasing supply, is, as the author points out, of little relevance to societies,
such as those in Latin America, in which its feasibility is limited:

> It is precisely this proliferation of products that should be questioned—an
> indispensable first step in establishing and creating an alternative design. The
> supply of consumer products in the central nations is created subliminally by a
> principle of microsocial organization: the division of society into acquisitive
> families composed of individual consumers of individual products [Bonsiepe,
> p. 151].

This logical determination of the industrial product by the predominant
conditions of a market system is generally considered alien or improper in the
case of architecture by a vast sector of the community of architects, professional organizations, and certainly by a majority of the centers of education of the discipline. These sectors have persistently displayed an argu-
mentative attitude that attempts to present architecture as a discipline of
superior character in a culturalist and universal vision through which the
architect appears to be acting neutrally on behalf of abstract entities such as
"man" and "society." The well-known fact that a good portion of architectural practice is communicated in publications and magazines plagued with
commercial advertisements for the real estate sector and the construction
industry does not seem to greatly affect the theoretical position of those
singular humanists.

Nevertheless, and particularly in relation to architecture schools after the
1940s, the basis for the meaning of architecture was supplied by the stylistic
rebellion carried out against the neoclassical formalisms and expressed
through the doctrinal language of modern architecture and technological
possibilities. Undoubtedly, this became insufficient for the generations of
architects and students who now recognize in this profession a deeper state of
crisis, one that is related to the alienation of its activity from the social

transformation processes that they perceive to be necessary for the countries of the region. This critical attitude displayed by certain architects is partially derived from two simple pragmatic considerations: the realization that their professional possibilities have increasingly been restricted—the majority of work in the private sector is concentrated in the hands of a limited number of professional firms, closely linked to financial and real estate circles—and on the other hand, their employment by institutions in the public sector often saddles architects with bureaucratic and routine functions, nothing like the illusions of creative activity instilled during their periods of apprenticeship. Sooner or later, these frustrations have surfaced in architecture schools where, during those periods and instances of relative democracy in Latin American political life, a reflection on the profession's crisis has been articulated in the discussion of the structural characteristics of national development. In many cases, professors and students of architecture have thus been in the vanguard in the processes of university reform in Latin America. They have advocated not only the the urgently needed establishment of updated educational systems, but also the placement of these institutions in a leadership position in the service of sincere processes for social transformation. Such has been the tradition of certain architecture schools in Mexico, Brazil, Uruguay, Argentina, Chile, and Ecuador, with dramatic fluctuations dependent on regressive periods in the political life of some of these countries. The testimonies of Escobar Loret de Mola and Segre concerning the experiences of Cuban architects in an environment that emphasizes equalitarian social priorities, are encouraging reports of possibilities opened to the Latin American architect in service to the community.

The outcomes produced by those rebellious attitudes of members of the architectural community in confrontation with a type of social development considered unjust, have placed the Latin American architect, save for a few exceptions, in a difficult and inevitable position. On the one hand, as a professional, it is clear that the architect, a member of a limited intellectual elite, can not aspire to produce or influence decisively the course of the structural processes affecting society. Paraphrasing Bonsiepe, it can be said that architecture is a corollary, not a protagonist, of social change. The escapist refuge into private activity, which as pointed out above is denied anyway to a considerable number of professionals, does not therefore attract the architect imbued with social conscience. Instead, he turns to and to some degree becomes part of those sectors and currents that support transformations that would modify the general conditions of underdevelopment in his society. In certain circumstances, this type of involvement has meant his direct participation in the national political life, sometimes under dramatic conditions. But generally this has not been the case. The objective conditions of the social situation make virtually impossible any direct transition to a transcendent political practice. Sometimes because of his professionalized training and the limitations of his social class identification, the architect does not clearly perceive his possible participatory role. Does this then mean that only a resigned attitude of watchful waiting will be appropriate until the time that circumstances on a national level truly change in the desired direction?

The answer to this dilemma will naturally depend on the specific circumstances confronting the architect in his society. However, there are at least two options that every architect should consider: first, the character of the development of Latin American societies continues to generate new forms of relations, whose spatial content may be conducive to elevating the level of social conscience. The limitations of the State's apparatus, its inability to satisfy the numerous needs and demands of the population concentrated in large metropolitan areas leaves a considerable margin for the direct initiative of the affected communities. It opens ample paths for practices of integrated living and sometimes of survival in terms of work, education, and housing, to which the architect can and should contribute from his own discipline, while at the same time participating in the organizational and self-assertive activities of such communities. Certainly this means new roles and functions, different from the limiting technical and planning capabilities acquired during professional training. More than approaching, it means integrating ourselves into the daily social and political life of the population majority in order to understand and contribute to the physical living environment of their communities. It means simultaneously to break away from elitist, traditional influences as well as from bureaucratic paternalism. And this requires a realistic evaluation of the conditions surrounding this type of liberation, beginning with an inevitable process of self-definition.

A second consideration, this time at the national and continental levels, is that at the beginning of the present decade, some prospects of movement in the direction of transformations necessary for social development seem to be opening once again for Latin America. While exhausting the traditional models of formal democracy that had ignored the abandoned masses' plea, the changing character of Latin American political processes reflects both the weaknesses and contradictions of the forms of authoritarian replacement, which because of exclusion and repression might have appeared unshakeable. It will be the task of each society, in accordance with the character of its historical experience to reiterate past experiments or to test its own innovative ones for social and integrated development. What appears most evident is that for the immediate future, the type of institutional stability so precious to certain social theorists will be rather an exception in the Latin American region. If we consider the prevailing interpretation which unfolds upon reading the essays of this book, assuredly neither the architects nor their material achievements will be absent from these processes. It will then be the duty, once more, of new generations of Latin American architects to suitably interpret the sense of the changes in progress, thus contributing concretely to the production of environments and buildings in accord with a society on the rise.

Notes

1. The Latin American urban-regional bibliography is quite extensive. Here we will only cite a few representative works: Jorge E. Hardoy, *Urbanization in Latin America,* Doubleday 1975; F. Rabinowitz, F. M. Trueblood, V. Cornelius, and R. Kemper, editors, *Latin American Urban Research,* vols. 1–6, Sage, 1971–1978; A. Portes and H. L. Browning, *Current Perspectives in Latin American Urban Research,* University of Texas Press, 1976; B. Roberts, *Cities of Peasants,* E. Arnold, 1978.

2. For example: Leopoldo Castedo *A History of Latin American Art and Architecture,* Praeger, 1969; Francisco Bullrich, *New Directions in Latin American Architecture,* Braziller, 1969; and the now venerable book by H. R. Hitchcock, *Latin American Architecture Since 1945,* The Museum of Modern Art, New York, 1955. To this, studies can be added on the work of architects such as Niemeyer, Mindlin Villanueva, and Zabludovsky and de León.

3. The article by Ribeiro contained in this book corresponds to Part 3 of his introduction, which appeared in full in the original Spanish edition. The ideas of his introduction are fully detailed in his book, *The Americas and Civilization,* E. P. Dutton and Co., 1972.

4. The recent publication in English of *Dependency and Development in Latin America,* by Fernando H. Cardoso and Enzo Faletto, University of California Press (1979), is a significant contribution to the generation of the dependence concept in Latin America. Also consult *Latin American Perspectives,* nos. 1, 4, 11, 21 (1974–1979), CMS, Riverside, California.

5. See in J. E. Hardoy, *Urbanization in Latin America,* "Two Thousand Years of Latin American Urbanization," pp. 22–30. Also see the collection of articles edited by R. P. Schaedel, J. E. Hardoy, and N. S. Kinzer, *Urbanization in the Americas from Its Beginnings to the Present,* Mouton, 1978.

6. The significance of the *Plaza Mayor* for the ruling governments continues to be a subject for debate, in which some of the essayists of this book have participated. Recently the polemics have been reopened with the provocative text by Miguel Rojas-Mix, *La Plaza Mayor—El urbanismo, instrumento de dominio colonial* (The Main Square—Urbanization, Instrument for Colonial Rule), Barcelona: Muchnik Editores, 1978. Criticism on the work, reviewed by Cortiñas Pelaez, has appeared in the Mexican journal *Vivienda,* January 1978, INFONAVIT.

7. The problem affecting the principal Latin American metropolises contrasts with the North American experience in that the much commented "fiscal crisis" of New York City implies a relative antagonism among the federal government, situated in another city, and the state and city governments. In Latin America, with the exception of Brazil, the national capitals are simultaneously the seats of government and the principal metropolises. For this reason, the national authorities have taken an interest in accumulating "ransom" funds for their central areas.

8. A variety of literature discusses the potential conflict arising from "marginal" Latin American populations, starting with Joan Nelson "The Urban Poor: Disruption or Political Integration in Third World Cities," *World Politics* 22, 1970; Wayne Cornelius, "Urbanization as an Agent in Latin American Political Instability," *American Political Science Review* 63, 1969; and Alejandro Portes, "Urbanization and Politics in Latin America," *Social Science Quarterly* 52, 1971. The prevailing criteria during those years attributed a habitually conservative and/or passive attitude on the part of the low-income population with respect to their

degree of political participation. This has been subsequently revised by the above-cited authors and directly questioned by others such as, Howard Handelman, "The Political Mobilization of Urban Squatters," in *Latin American Research Review* X/3 1975, who investigates the Chilean experience, and Manuel Castells, "Marginalité Urbaine et Mouvements Sociaux au Mexique," in *International Journal of Urban and Regional Research,* 1/1, 1977. Regarding the utilization of energy by the Latin American squatter who erects his dwelling within the prevailing metropolitan environment, a line of argument proposes the viability of such practices, beginning with William Mangin's article, "Latin American Squatter Settlements: A Problem and a Solution," *Latin American Research Review* II/3, 1967 and the well-known books by John Turner, *Freedom to Build,* Macmillan, 1972, and *Housing by People,* Pantheon, 1976. The limitations of this approach are revealed by several authors, among them D. J. Dwyer, "Self-Help Housing Possibilities," in his book *People and Housing in Third World Cities,* Longman, 1975, and Rod Burgess, "Self-Help Housing: A New Imperialist Strategy?" published in ANTIPODE 9/2, 1977.

1 / Civilization and Creativity

> Like the rest of the world we live a decisive, mortal moment, orphans of the past, and with a future still to be invented. World history is our common task. And our labyrinth is that of all men.
>
> Octavio Paz

The study of the manner and circumstances in which cultural creativity is practiced in the Americas demands a preliminary critical examination of several concepts, especially the notions of cultural relativism, authenticity, and functionalism as they are habitually used by anthropologists.

In its generally accepted meaning the concept of cultural relativism refers to the idea that cultures, being individual and unique entities, have singular qualities which make them unsusceptible to judgmental comparisons. To juxtapose one tribal culture to another or to a more advanced civilization, or to compare two different civilizations, is like comparing a rabbit with a chicken, or both of them with a rhinoceros. None of them can be considered better or worse than the others; value judgments are not appropriate.

This argument is acute because real qualities emerge from the cultural constructs, and it is generous because it elevates simpler cultures in relation to more complex ones; to the deep-seated enthocentrism in every human society it opposes a unifying, equalizing understanding. But, unfortunately, it is also questionable, because it concludes that cultures are neither superior nor inferior but simply different, when, in fact, on the basis of objective criteria, they can be either more or less developed.

The arguments used to sustain the theory of cultural relativism are based on the impossibility of making evaluative comparisons among different religious rituals, culinary tastes, artistic styles, norms of behavior, and so forth. The anthropologists, however, are so insistent upon demonstrating the impossibility of comparing the components of a culture that they forget that it is perfectly feasible to do so in some areas, for example, the economic efficiency of the techniques of production. They also forget the complex but undeniable connections among the stages of development of technology and productive capacity, the forms of social organization, and the degree of rationality in the world view.

This delicate blend of subtle observation, generous appreciation, and blind spots makes of the notion of cultural relativism a means of creating conformist attitudes. In effect, the defense of the inalienable right of the simplest societies to maintain their cultures becomes, through this ideology, a diletantist appreciation of the archaic and a nostalgic defense of human values that flourish only in dependent and backward societies. The same occurs with other notions related to cultural relativism, for example, the concept of the singularity or originality of cultures and civilizations.

A more critical attitude toward these questions would have us consider the fact that cultural development is not as relative and unsusceptible to comparison as is believed. On the contrary, throughout all of human history we find concrete societies set in specific socioeconomic formations—that is, at certain stages of evolutionary progress. Such formations can be compared with each other and can be objectively classified as equal, superior, or inferior in terms of the efficiency of their adaptation to nature in order to provide subsistence, the breadth of mutual relationships within the social structures in which different groups are integrated, and the degree of rationality in their symbolic interpretations of the world.

Besides explaining more, this approach is also more dynamic. It admits that the position in which a society finds itself does not correspond to its innate qualities or the immutable characteristics of its culture, but to circumstances that can be changed. When these circumstances are changed, any society can experience periods of accelerated progress if it successfully incorporates into its culture elements of the store of information concerning production technology that, rather than being characteristic of any single culture, forms part of what is today the common patrimony of human knowledge. With this point of view we can seek explanations for a culture's level of development in its way of life and in the conjunctures at which a people relate to the rest of the world and experience the influence of actual civilizing processes, rather than in its supposedly unique cultural characteristics.

However, we need to retain the critical position of cultural relativism with regard to present forms of civilization. Indeed, nothing is more absurd than to consider them as finished or terminal forms of human development, or as conditions that are desirable in and of themselves—the more modern and advanced, the better. They are not finished forms: they represent stages in the long process of human and cultural self-transformation that continually operates in time. They are not intrinsically desirable: they represent vicissitudes in a comparatively spontaneous process rather than the realization of rationally conceived objectives.

The civilizing process is essentially a continuing oscillation between alienation and integration, in which society pays a high price for its conquests yet inevitably advances, setting new goals for itself which in turn become both alienating and integrating. In fact, any civilization contains residues of the past and larval forms of new cultural constructs that are not yet mature; they can either betray or promote human ideals. Even if one believes that ideals cannot be defined because of their transitory nature, they can often be evaluated, at least negatively. In other words, abstract human ideals cannot be programmed, but we can specify which modes of behavior, interaction, and feeling are clearly inhuman or antihuman, and recognize that no civilization has been free of them.

THE AUTHENTIC AND THE SPURIOUS

As we search for a critical understanding of culture as it exists in Latin America, another theoretical task is imposed on us—that of elucidating the notions of the integration and the purity of cultural constructs. It cannot be denied that cultures have a certain capacity for integration or internal organization that is achieved through the continual interaction among their component parts and that confers a certain functionalism on the whole. It is undeniable as well that cultural constructs present a certain degree of authenticity and harmony. That is to say, beyond the functional correspondence among its parts, the whole exhibits physiognomic traits that distinguish one culture from another, and stylistic traits that are imprinted on the personalities of its members as well as on its creations, making them unique and distinctive.

These judgments, however, are often generalized. They are inspired by specific qualities of autonomous tribal cultures, and imply that all cultures—even the most complex—are eminently genuine and authentic. At this point we are confronted by subtle preconceptions that are filtered through the notion of cultural relativism, according to which each culture is a singular entity in which the life of a people is crystallized and, for that reason, all of its parts are worthy of respect as genuine creations. But this point of view disregards the fact that each culture is the product of vicissitudes that necessarily deform it since they function as obstacles to fully creative and autonomous development.

One would suppose that a people existing in isolation would have greater possibilities for developing an integrated body of culture. But even under these conditions negative cultural constructs can be produced. On the other hand, it is well known that when a culture develops under conditions of internal or external oppression, it tends to generate contradictory and often negative characteristics. Since most societies never experience the conditions of isolation and equality that would protect cultural authenticity, but are almost always obliged to create and recreate their cultures in situations of competitive interaction with other societies and antagonisms among their own constituent groups, we must admit that in any culture there exist as many elements affirming authenticity and creativity as elements that are deleterious to and restrictive of not only the autonomous development of that society, but even of the formation of its members as balanced personalities.

Certain socioeconomic conditions represent such extreme cases of limitations on cultural creativity that the society subjected to them is deformed, oriented in directions opposed to affirmation and survival. In these circumstances the society itself frequently disappears, not through the physical extermination of its members, but by their subjugation to the oppression of a foreign group that views them as enemies, and can therefore exercise a despotism more fanatic than would be possible within a homogeneous society. This is the case in the process of loss of culture in which a population, or a part of that population, is subjugated and used by another sector of society as a mere source of energy for its system of production. Torn out of its context, that population loses its culture as a necessary condition to its integration into a new cultural construct. The first result of confluence with the dominant society is the eradication of the original culture; later a new and inauthentic cultural construct—a spurious colonial culture—is created.

Most frequently, for those peoples involved in great civilizing movements, cultural creativity occurs under these deforming internal and external pressures. And the result is a culture that of necessity is weighed down with spurious content born not of the urge toward self-expression and growth, but of the effort to survive under the most adverse conditions. These considerations force one to accept the fact that cultural constructs should be examined and judged either as instruments that stimulate and affirm creativity and the autonomous development of a people, or as misfortunes that mitigate against any efforts at renewal—and to admit as well the possibility of restoring the authenticity of a culture by eliminating its spurious content through self-constructive processes.

In all likelihood cultural restoration constitutes a natural process whereby societies try to avoid their own deterioration. In this, as in many other cases, however, the natural processes sometimes need to be stimulated and encouraged through rational intervention aimed at achieving objectives defined as desirable. The indispensable requirement for achieving renovation is precisely this—to admit that the culture contains as many spurious elements as authentic ones, that in its spontaneous development both are generated, with this additional irritant: when it confronts adverse conditions it generates more spurious components than genuine ones. The more general of these adverse conditions are associated with the interaction between societies, when rather than meeting on a basis of equality and mutual benefit, one society exploits the other. They are associated as well with the interaction among a society's social strata, when instead of being mutually favorable to the general development of the society within a specific civilization, it depends on exploitation and, as such, impedes harmonious development and a prosperity than can be generalized to include the total population.

CULTURAL VICISSITUDES

Culture, viewed critically, constitutes a conceptual model of the world constructed by each human community as the very condition of its being and existence. This model reflects the previous experience of the society as well as its structural characteristics. Thus the stratification of classes, conditions of dependence, or the heterogeneity of social or regional development, appear as differentiated variants of that culture. Only in the case of a society that is ideally homogeneous, and for that reason simple and rudimentary, does culture take on the configurations of a coherent and uniform entity. In all other cases, and especially in advanced civilizations, cultures are always complex entities, differentiated and made dynamic by intense, traumatizing processes.

Since its inception social stratification has implied the bipartive division of culture into a high component dominated by the educated, and a vulgar, popular component. The conditions of colonial or neocolonial dependence correspond to the cultural alienation which by justifying that domination helps to perpetuate it. Many of the elements that contribute to self-affirmation and authenticity in the central nations are detrimental in the peripheral areas. Social or regional heterogeneity has its corresponding imbalances: conditions of archaism or modernity in certain regions or social strata, rootlessness among the elite and marginality among the masses.

These contingencies may affect large portions or even the majority of the population, in which case who they are (for example, the black, the Indian, the mestizo) and what they are (for example, slaves or the marginal groups in modernized production systems) may contrast flagrantly with the ideal patterns of that society, with the result that these groups experience the frustration and unrest of not conforming to dominant expectations. In other cases, such as isolated peasant or shepherd populations, unbridgeable gaps may be established between their mentality and that of the integrated and modernized sectors of society; occasionally this gives rise to serious conflicts.

However, under ideal conditions of autonomy, the division of culture into high and popular, and the educated constraints under which works of science and the arts are produced, does not necessarily prevent them from being genuine creations. The possibility of this happening under conditions of cultural dependence is greatly reduced.

One can only speak of the culture of the Latin American peoples in the sense of a complex and fluid entity that corresponds not to any given form but rather to a tendency to search for an authenticity that has never been achieved. Although one might also say the same of any past or present civilization, clarification of how these changes occurred in Latin America is indispensable to an understanding of our cultural creativity.

In fact, throughout most of our colonial history, we do not find an educated class that expresses its nation's cultural creativity. What we do find is a transplanted elite, which mimics the cultural gestures that belong to another context, gestures that mean nothing to their own population and are unsatisfactory as well for the native educated class, which suffers the dislocation of its double role: local agents of a superior culture which they are proud to represent and members of a subordinate society whose way of life mortifies them.

This inauthentic state corresponds, culturally speaking, to the exogenous condition of the consular ruling classes, who were established here to direct the colonial enterprise. For a long period of time artistic creativity flourished in the culture of this elite as a transplant that established itself in a world that was formless—it had lost its faculty for self-expression due to the non-existence or eradication of the educated class of the subjugated society. As the centuries passed, and as the result of enormous efforts at reconstruction, a new society and a new culture emerged, different from and even opposed to that of the mother country, but shaped along lines that derived from it. Since that time creativity has become more genuine; now it no longer obeys the rules and values of the past, but follows the styles of the new civilization within which the new growth struggles to express itself.

In the sphere of popular culture—the culture of the common people—creativity also underwent the same changes. The old, authentic forms of self-expression disappeared because they were no longer viable, and the new production aimed principally at distant markets did not offer the worker or artisan any opportunity to affirm his individuality; gestures were repeated mechanically in order to produce objects and tools appreciated only for their commercial value. Only in minor activities, such as the pattern of a straw roof, does a weaving technique survive that once found expression in baskets, or in clay pots that still retain, for the trained observer, forms of a lost style.

Despite these difficulties, we find a higher degree of creativity and cultural authenticity in the area of popular, folkloric culture. In effect, the basic adaptive forms that guaranteed the survival of colonial implantations were elaborated and fixed on this level. The Indian, before being exterminated, taught those who were going to replace him the names of the plants and animals of the new land, hunting, fishing, and farming techniques, the skills needed for the manufacture of goods and tools. On the basis of this patrimony of knowledge and artisanry developed over the centuries, the new societies were able to satisfy the material necessities for survival. Even today this inheritance allows large portions of the Latin American population to continue to survive. Also on this level, multiple forms of interaction and association are developed which provide the solidarity of human community beyond the compulsive norms imposed by the ruling classes. Finally, on this level, one finds myths and legends that explain the world and man's place in it and that even today make it possible to love life as it really is.

The ruling classes of Latin America, and their educated component, exercised what was essentially a managerial function in the sphere of economy and production, a controlling one in the sociopolitical field, an innovative one in the field of scientific technology, and an indoctrinating one in the area of ideology. That is, they instigated or stimulated a series of changes in the modes of production with the help of technological revolutions that occurred abroad and, at the same time, they modernized the forms of government and commerce, either copied from or inspired by models that were developed in some of the central nations.

As modernization progressed in technology and production, in social institutions, and in ideology, artistic creations were also redefined and renovated. This almost always took place at a more rapid pace in the high culture than in the popular one, which could only adjust to modernization with considerable lags. Consequently, the people could rarely understand the language of the artists and intellectuals who supposedly expressed their way of life.

These vicissitudes that deform cultural creativity, although present in all the historico-cultural configurations of the Americas, have been more apparent in some than in others. The *transplanted peoples,** intrinsic segments of European societies transplanted overseas, could absorb without significant harm the various ideological content of Western tradition. This has not been true of the *witnessing peoples* or the *new peoples*. For example, assimilation of the European ideal of the human figure in which the image of the white man was identified with the beautiful, the noble, and even the normal, and the diffusion of that ideal to peoples of a different racial type, alienated them, making them conceive of themselves in terms of an image that was offensive to them. It should be added that because the artistic creations of the witnessing peoples of Latin America were visibly different from European canons, they were treated with contempt. Only by means of a deliberate attempt to recover their cultural authenticity could those peoples judge the creations of their ancestors as beautiful and valuable. As for the new peoples, their situation as racially mixed societies born, as it were, at the trading post, made them seem inferior in European eyes. The internalization of this idea by the native ruling classes, and its diffusion to the mass of the population, has added to their alienation.

Only in recent years have critics' efforts to reintegrate, to lift the weight of prejudices designed to foster the Latin American peoples' resigned acceptance of their backwardness as something natural and necessary, begun to

---

*Translator's note: In an earlier portion of the essay not included in this volume, Ribeiro classifies modern non-European cultures as follows:

(1) *witnessing peoples,* represented by survivors of high civilizations with whom Europe came into contact during its expansion after 1500. Included in this group in Latin America are Mexico (Aztec), Guatemala (Maya), and Bolivia, Peru, and Ecuador (Inca);

(2) *new peoples,* who emerged from the fusion of ethnic matrices—African, European, and Indian—forming an ethnic group different from the original component matrices. In this grouping in Latin America Ribeiro includes Brazil, Venezuela, Colombia, the Antilles, and parts of Central America. Chile, Paraguay, Uruguay, and Argentina were originally new peoples, but historical circumstance moved them into different categories;

(3) *transplanted peoples* include modern nations created by the migration of European populations to new territories where they established societies essentially identical to the ones they had left. Canada, the United States, Argentina and Uruguay are examples.

bear fruit; due to unchanging causes, the delay in reintegration can be explained, in large part, by the fact that the very disciplines that study these problems were, until very recently, unable to provide more effective or challenging explanations of Latin American reality.

The pioneers of the new way of thinking, less involved with the ruling classes and more capable of exploiting the possibilities of a heightened consciousness, were the first, in fact, who dared to be Latin Americans intellectually, dared to face objectively our ways of being and living and, with that as their starting point, to plan for social and cultural change. This was true of the Cuban José Martí, the Peruvian José Carlos Mariátegui, the Brazilian Euclides da Cunha, among many others. Yet they were pioneers whose followers have only recently matured sufficiently to design Latin America's new self-portrait.[1]

Thus a new critical consciousness has come into being, opposed to the old ingenuous consciousness and capable at last of rethinking the world on the basis of the Latin American experience, of looking at what exists as problematical and susceptible to planned, rational change. In the light of this critical consciousness more lucid and realistic analyses of Latin America are beginning to be formulated. It is clear that underdevelopment is not the prelude to development, but rather its counterpart, whose continued existence perpetuates a situation in which poor and backward peoples pay for those who are wealthy and advanced, and in which the protection of minority interests is invariably in collusion with the forces that cause the underdevelopment.

STYLE AND CIVILIZATION

Up to this point we have focused on some distinctive characteristics of cultures and the changes they are subjected to under conditions of dependence. Now it is appropriate for us to explore how these conclusions help us understand the intellectual and artistic life of Latin America.

We should indicate at the outset that despite the instability of their cultural life, the Latin American peoples—particularly the social strata that dominate high culture—share not only a certain vigor but also an evident homogeneity in their intellectual and artistic creations. Any attentive traveler who visits the monuments of colonial architecture in Latin America, or any analyst who has at his disposal good documentation concerning accurately dated works of art, can observe the flowering of successive waves of creativity, each of which is notoriously and uniformly the same throughout the continent. The same is true of the plastic arts and of literature, which have also flourished in waves, but always homogeneously.

It would be impossible not to observe, however, that the uniformity discernible in these artistic creations is not the product of endogenous processes, but rather the reiteration, in American territory, of successive artistic forms developed in Europe. That is, although one can distinguish local character-istics, it is not a question of national arts, but of arts created in America with unique but essentially European qualities.

The forts that were the first great works of architecture, the churches and cathedrals that followed, the great public buildings, the private palaces, as well as the sculpture and paintings that decorated them, could, in many cases, have been located in Europe, or at least in the Iberian Peninsula, without attracting too much attention because of their singular qualities. The same could be said of other artistic genres, although literature, by its very nature, is more impregnated with local color and more marked by provincialism.

These statements postulate the need for careful examination of the nature of stylistic currents within the body of civilizations. We believe it possible to state that style is a form of significant and expressive communication within the educated sphere of a culture—in other words, it is a language that is fully intelligible only to a circle of initiates.

One can therefore affirm that style is a function of culture, of civilization. An attribute of civilization is that it marks the creations of its artists with certain modal characteristics that distinguish these from the works of other cultures or civilizations. Although a civilization may not develop a unique style that impregnates all artistic genres, the styles that succeed one another within the temporal, historical period that corresponds to the life of that civilization are coherent languages. It is true that at times two or more styles coexist, and that different styles within the same genre can predominate for long periods of time. The tendency, nevertheless, is—or has been—the uniform stylization of all contemporaneous creations of a given artistic genre produced during the life of a civilization.

Style as a uniform esthetic quality is a coherent formal mode that places works of art within a given category. Thanks to its specificity, style permits one to place, with complete precision, a cultural creation whose stylistic form in time and space is the result of this quality. When one speaks of a piece of Chavín ceramic, for example, or of an Impressionist painting, no specialist doubts what it is, and is rarely deceived in its classification. What guides him is a peculiar conformation, a special expressiveness imposed on the colored clay or the painted canvas that does more than any external documentation to place it historically.

The expressive power of style as the language of civilization marks not only the creations of the artistic centers of the central nations, but also impregnates the works of all societies subjugated by them. Consequently, following the traumatization of the native American cultures and the eradi-cation of their educated upper class, a drastic paralysis of the original esthetic impulse as expressed in native artistic styles left little room for works that conformed to styles brought over from Europe. From that time on no real line of creativity or style emerged, or could emerge, at the level of high culture.

Even at the level of popular culture, technique deteriorated and style fell into decline. At the level of high art the situation was even more drastic. The American peoples, colonized and forcibly incorporated first into a mercantile civilization and then into an industrial one, could only express themselves in the language of that civilization which, against their will, had become their language. When European artistic styles, as well as other elements of that culture, were transplanted to the Americas and adapted to the new reality, they acquired some local peculiarities, but remained essentially unchanged in their basic structure. Since then creativity could be manifested here as well as in Europe, although it was affirmed only through repetition and insofar as its expression was achieved within those same *formae mentis.*

Literature, painting, sculpture, architecture, and music flourished on both sides of the Atlantic, shaped according to the same patterns, though cruder here because our society was more modest, more dependent, and poorer. The apparent lack of originality is due to the fact that after being integrated into the civilizing European current that engendered them, American societies expressed themselves in that civilization's terms; these became as imperative as the tribal style was for each member of the tribe. Since the European nations were in the midst of the Counter-Reformation, whose style was the baroque, that determined the forms of the churches built in America. Here and there the weight of the ancient cultural tradition guided the hand of the native artisan, periodically producing peculiarities that today can be classified as Mexican baroque, Andean baroque, or Brazilian baroque—but they are always baroque. They deviate no more from the basic norm than the variations on the baroque inside Europe.

CULTURAL CONFLUENCES

Beauty is not the product of wealth, certainly, but only in rare cases does it flourish in abject poverty. High art is usually associated with prosperity. Only prosperity can make and needs to make a visible display, permitting itself luxury and objects of art and honoring those who can create them. It is not surprising, therefore, that expressions of high artistic creativity in Latin America occur during periods of prosperity. It is the prosperity of the very few, it is true, and it is founded on the penury of the masses, but it is sufficiently wealthy to devote a part of the economic surplus to churches, palaces, and objects of art and, consequently, to the designers, artisans, musicians, and painters.

For this reason there is a period of artistic flowering associated with the mining of gold and silver, another with sugar, cotton, and coffee plantations and, most recently, with the smokestacks of industrialization. The arts do not flourish in the mines, the plantations, or the factories, however, but in the urban networks that are built with the wealth that these produce. By the same token they flourish with greater frequency in the distant European nations than in colonial cities.

It must be added that art is never associated directly with the people involved in production, not even with the owners of the farms and mines, who are usually too lacking in culture, too concerned with the management of their wealth to divert energy to cultural refinements. Demanded by and cultivated by social parasites more than by producers, the arts flourish not only far away from, but also turned away from, their material foundations. The priests, the rulers, the bureaucrats, the financiers are the ones who need to see their divine and human glories exalted by the hand of the artist. Urbane, cultured, and in the case of colonial Latin America, European-born and educated, they were people who felt like exiles in their own countries. The art they valued and required was an art based on European standards. Occasionally an American-born artist, nourished in the local traditions, managed to leave the singular imprint of his sensibility on the work entrusted to him. But such boldness was looked upon as a defect, and was only consented to when it was impossible to discipline the creator according to European canons so that he would be faithful to the ideal models. Moreover, the educated artist himself avoided these deviations; he too considered them to be impurities and imperfections.

The colonial cities of Latin America—the setting where art flourished—were widely scattered; they grew chaotically in rhythm with the development of different areas of production. They were always administrative and commercial centers, most of them established on ports, but some built in the mountains or in the interior. The first cities were fortified trading posts, like those built in the Antilles in the beginning of the sixteenth century, or encampments for the conquistadors, like San Vicente and Porto Seguro on the Atlantic coast of Brazil, or Asunción in Paraguay, in the heart of the continent. None of them was wealthy enough to squander money on the ostentation of art.

The civilization based on gold and silver saw the birth of the first colonial metropolises: Mexico City, built over the former capital of the Aztecs; Cuzco, on the ruins of the Incan capital; Lima, on the Peruvian coast; Quito and Potosí-La Plata, in the interior—all built according to plans that were seen as the affirmation of European and Spanish domination of the conquered pre-Columbian world. To an even greater extent the same was true of the urban networks created in turn by these metropolises.

In Brazil, a century later, another wave of gold and diamond mining also produced its urban network, whose cities were Ouro Preto and the port of Rio de Janeiro. Bahía, Olinda, and Recife had been built earlier: their display was based on the wealth arising from sugar production. Later the cotton plantations would produce San Luis. The extraction of rubber in the tropical forest would give birth to Belén and Manaos, and coffee would build São Paulo.

In Spanish America, after the depression provoked by the mines running out, the urban network was revitalized by a surge of economic prosperity that renovated the old cities and created new ones. Thus the sugar plantations activated Havana; wheat and cattle were expressed urbanistically in Buenos Aires and Montevideo; the harbor and the mining of nitrate gave vitality to Valparaíso and Santiago de Chile; oil converted Caracas into a modern city. And most recently, the industrialization of Latin America, although it did not end its dependent status, reactivated numerous cities—Mexico City, São Paulo, and Buenos Aires, for instance—and created many others.

However, there is no urban or artistic record of any of these branches of production in the cities they nurtured. The colonial metropolises of gold and sugar were not mining towns or farming centers; Buenos Aires was hardly a cattle town, or Manaos a lumber town, or Caracas an oil town. They were and still are today European cities built overseas, cities whose esthetic styles are an expression of Western civilization.

Brasília, the last of these great cities, built one thousand kilometers inland in order to populate the empty interior of Brazil, could as easily have been built elsewhere. It is not the city of the Brazilians—it is a city of contemporary man in an emerging civilization.

Western civilization was expressed for almost five centuries in this constellation of American cities. They were established as the West's enclaves in the first impulse of agrarian and mercantile expansion, and they prospered because of a proletariat recruited in the colonies. In a second movement stimulated by the industrial revolution they were revitalized, enlarged, and modernized to serve as nuclei of a polycentric civilization that was still European and Western in spirit. In our own time the great cities of the New World, like all vital metropolises, are beginning to free themselves from their former servitude so that they can be the focal points of a new civilization whose forms we cannot even predict.

A review of the succession of styles indicates that Late Gothic, Mannerism and, finally, the Baroque shaped the plastic arts in Latin America. This was inevitable: the Church was the major patron of the arts and only the styles adopted by it were allowed concrete expression. Renaissance Europe, attempting to rediscover itself through the restoration of Greek and Roman archtetypes, was often parodied in Latin America. Nonetheless, in the fine arts, particularly in architecture and sculpture, original creations did flourish in America, some indeed as expressive as those of Europe. At first these works followed the designs of European artists, many of them non-Iberian, who contributed elements from other countries that crystallized here into extraordinary forms. Later they were designed and executed by American-born artists to whom we owe some of the highest artistic creations in Latin America. Shaped according to baroque patterns that were interpreted more and more freely, they were visually compelling works, overwhelming in their coloration and exuberant in their sculptural forms and movements.

With the decline of agrarian-mercantile civilization and the first impulses of industrial capitalism, the fine arts in the central countries were oriented toward neoclassicism, while the literary arts leaned toward romanticism. These waves of change soon reached the Americas, where they became associated with the exaltation of the struggle for independence. Their efforts were contradictory. In the visual arts a visible decadence prevailed, perhaps because the Church, an institution solidly associated with colonialism, an institution that exercised exclusive control over all education, and functioned as sole teacher of the arts, began to decline. When independence was won, the Church became only one voice among many; it was no longer the richest or the most powerful. The great buildings were no longer churches but governmental buildings and the houses of the bourgeoisie, which adhered to a vapid neoclassicism and were adorned with painting and sculpture that became increasingly academic. The artists, in the service of new patrons as demanding as they were ignorant, became more sycophantic and conventional than ever.

Coinciding with the simultaneous growth of urban life and the increase in the number of educated people who broadened the artists' public, the possibility was created for the spread of new, libertarian ideas to wider circles, who felt solidarity with the lower classes and were motivated by a critical attitude toward the power structure and its representatives.

The final *formae mentis* of the nineteenth century never achieved the strength of the baroque or of early romanticism. They were styles and languages prescribed by a conventional esthetic expression, but they were already out-of-date: the spiritual unity not only of Europe but of the various focal points of Western civilization had been broken. It was now polycentric and sought to express the unique qualities of each of its components in individual, national forms.

Since that time the artist has been witness to the world, a witness who invents his own vision. He knows that it is as viable as any other, neither better/or worse, and he speaks, from his circumstance, to all men.

This is the world in which we are learning to live, subject to a dizzying rhythm of change that transforms and questions everything. Certainties that once appeared absolute, seemingly undeniable values, judgments that were once beyond doubt—all are being questioned. This inquiring boldness that leaves nothing intact can only be compared to the prodigious changes that mark the dawn of a new civilization.

And, indeed, a new civilization is in the process of being born. All that we know of its culture is that it will be more uniform everywhere in the world and that it will be based increasingly on explicit knowledge and rationalism. As it develops it may well bridge the gap between high and popular culture, and break down the last barriers behind which provincial cultures could still flourish.

There is something terrible in the idea, with its implicit risks, of intentionally producing the new culture, the new life, the new man. The alternative, however, is their casual, haphazard production. There have been times when social life could no longer be ruled by the residues of cultural creativity crystallized in traditional models of conduct. These are times of great transformation, like the Renaissance—of transformations that are, perhaps, even more radical because previously everything was changed in order to focus on new models, styles, and patterns. Now, perhaps, a time is beginning without any possible patterns. The old formulas are used up, and although the fountains of inspiration may not be dry, it will no longer be possible to canonize them; while tradition can dignify a norm by making it appear to be the only one possible, reason must counter with alternative solutions. This means that we are not only living on the level of an old civilization's collapse but at the dawn of the new civilization's emergence.

This supposes that within the limits of this new civilization of universal dimensions—it will make each man heir to the entire human patrimony of knowledge and art—there will no longer be room for the stylistic peculiarities that for centuries have marked artistic creativity. Art, through the millennia, has been torn by devotion to itself as a unique, individual expression, by the pressures of a refined audience, and by the contingencies of mechanized production. Now it is finally returning to its original and constant purpose: to provide each man with the conditions for loving and dignifying his existence by means of his capacity for communicating spiritually with other men through his own creations.

Note

1. Critical bibliographies of these intellectual movements can be found in W. Rex Crawford (1966), Martin S. Stab (1969), Pedro Henríquez Ureña (1960), and Mariano Picón Salas (1950) for the Hispano-American writers, and in Joãb Cruz Costa (1956) and Nelson Werneck Sodré (1965) for the Brazilians.

2 / The Territorial and Urban Conditioning of Latin American Architecture

ROBERTO SEGRE

Translated by Andrew Gordon

TOWARD AN ENVIRONMENTAL APPROACH TO ARCHITECTURE

Architecture and the Urban Context

In 1955, when Henry Russell Hitchcock published his book on postwar Latin American architecture, he could still refer to a group of isolated works that synthesized the dominant tendencies of the 1950s for the principal countries of the continent and the Caribbean.[1] If the grave problems that would affect Latin America on both territorial and urban scales were already visible on the horizon—the profound economic and social contradictions, the rapid population growth, the migration from the rural areas to the cities, the minimal construction activity on the part of the state, the predominance of speculative building—architecture, in the interpretation of the critics, preserved its autonomy and primacy with respect to the urban and rural contexts. Each country expressed itself clearly through a limited number of creators and works: in Argentina, Amancio Williams' bridge house or the apartments of Kurchan and Ferrari Hardoy; in Uruguay, Julio Vilamajó's College of Engineering; in Brazil, the Ministry of Education by Costa, Niemeyer, and Le Corbusier in Rio de Janeiro; in Mexico, the Ciudad Universitaria (University City) by Pani, Del Moral, Arai, and O'Gorman; in Venezuela, Carlos Raúl Villanueva's Ciudad Universitaria in Caracas; in Cuba, Antonio Quintana's Retiro Médico (Medical Retreat).

At that time, Latin America had 188 million inhabitants; Buenos Aires, 4.7 million; Rio de Janeiro, 3 million; São Paulo, 2.3 million; Bogotá, a half million; Mexico City, 3 million; Lima, 1 million; Caracas, a little more than a half million.[2] What happened thirty years later on the threshold of the 1980s? Latin America's population approached 400 million: Buenos Aires at 11 million; Rio de Janeiro at 10 million; São Paulo, 14 million; Bogota, 5 million; Mexico City, 15 million; Lima, 5 million; Caracas surpassed 4 million.[3]

What do these cold, quantitative figures indicate about the population growth? The logarithmic increase, not only of the urban population and the metropolitan areas, but also of the social conflicts, economic problems, the discord between city and countryside, the strained disarray of the metropolitan technical infrastructure, the deterioration of the lower-class habitat, the offensive luxury of the centers of consumption in the large cities, and the vast anonymous expanses of the Latin American "megalopolis."[4]

Is it still valid to isolate architectural works from their surrounding context to define the character of the built space? The answer is negative. Conceived as a cultural representation of a historically determined society and as a coherent, functional response to the universal necessities of the population, architecture sheds its primacy—as communication preconceived in values of meaning—to a shapeless mass of construction. For the most part, buildings have been promoted but not utilized by the bourgeoisie who frame the orbit of life for the majority of people on the continent. The contrast between the scarcity of architecture produced by "designers" and the abundance of speculative building underscores the antagonisms inherent in the dependent capitalist system, the socioeconomic structure for the majority of countries in the region.

From the Habitat of Vancouver to the Charter of Machu Picchu

The awareness in the 1970s of the accelerated crisis of the built environment in Latin America (i.e., that part of the environment built by people) and of the impossible differentiation between architecture and context are reflected in the statements of progressive creators,[5] and affect even those designers who defend to the ultimate consequences the autonomy of architecture with respect to its objective determinants; economic, social, and technological.[6]

The problems that have been cited are not Latin America's alone; rather, they belong to the countries of the so-called Third World. For this reason, in the past decade, a strong denunciation and a penetration of the factors that condition the environmental systems were produced, promoted by international bodies, the designers—city planners, architects, industrial designers—and in certain cases by national governments.[7] While some world events, organized by the United Nations, counted on significant Latin American participation—the Stockholm Conference on the Environment (1973), the United Nations Program on the Environment (1975), and Habitat: United Nations Conference on Human Settlements (Vancouver, 1976)—others took place on the continent, crystallizing the specific problem of this hemisphere: the International Exposition on Housing (VIEXPO, Santiago, Chile, 1972), the United Nations Conference on Water (Argentina, 1977), and the Thirteenth Congress of the International Union of Architects (Mexico, 1978), dedicated to the theme of "Architecture and National Development." To those we can add a declaration of the principles on the organization of physical space—the Charter of Machu Picchu—conceived as an "American" response of universal validity to the environmental problems that affect the major part of the world population.[8]

There is a close connection between the themes contained in the conclusions of these cited events and the public policies in different countries: the

Mexican Law on Human Settlements, the Mexican Declaration of the Thirteenth Congress of the International Union of Architects, the Plan of Action from Vancouver, and the Charter of Machu Picchu. The alarm produced by the ecology, energy, and food crises, tacitly recognized as social and economic crises in the capitalist countries, brings about the necessity for national controls on natural resources, the treatment of the environment, and the configuration of urban structures. All of these policies agree that the way a society expresses itself physically upon its territory should be coordinated by interdisciplinary work teams, in order to establish an equilibrium among the esthetic, socioeconomic, and technical objectives and to guarantee the "quality of life" for the masses of urban and rural population.

According to the Charter of Machu Picchu, "The objective of the planning process, including economic planning, urban planning and design, and architecture, must be to interpret and respond to human needs. It should result in the provision of urban services, facilities, and forms appropriate to the needs of the people in the context of available resources and cultural values. To achieve these ends, the planning process must be based on systematic and continuous interaction between the design professions, city dwellers, and their community and political leadership." Furthermore, the Plan of Action from Vancouver establishes in its first two chapters[9] the necessary state control on socioeconomic development and the organization of physical space: "(1) Each country, as a matter of urgency, must establish a national policy on human settlements that encompasses the population distribution and the connected social and economic activities in the national territory; (2) each national policy for social and economic development must have as an integral part a national policy on human settlements and the environment."

Besides state intervention and the important role played by the technical experts, the theme of popular participation in the configuration of the environment is emphasized, just as it is expressed in Recommendation 49 of the Plan of Action from Vancouver: "Popular participation should be an indispensable factor in human settlements, especially in the planning of strategies and their formulation, application, and implementation; it should be influential at all levels of the government for the process of adopting decisions intended to stimulate the social, economic, and political growth of human settlements."

Although the series of formulations provided in these documents constitute a step forward in the awareness of the close connections existing between socioeconomic development and the configuration of the environment, they still possess a degree of generalization and abstraction with regard to the concrete solutions of the problems. They do not denounce the causes from which they originate nor do they suggest the means to overcome them within concrete historical circumstances. Why is the capitalist state not planning a coherent action for its territory that would eliminate the urban-rural contradiction? Why does it not stop the harsh land speculation and the dominance of the laws of supply and demand imposed by private ownership on urban land? Why is the integration of community participation in the politics of State human settlements not insisted upon? Is the State not the executor of the popular will?[10] Why does the State possess insufficient means to provide infrastructure for cities and housing for those segments of the population most in need of assistance? Why, in the words of the Charter of Machu Picchu, "do the potential benefits from planning and architecture not reach the great majority of people?" Why does the State not establish basic 'human' standards for housing and why does it instead accept those set forth by the so-called 'marginal settlements' as the only solution to the housing problem?[11]

The need to find objective answers to these questions motivated at the forum of Habitat a series of precise statements in the "Third World Charter of Declaration on National Politics of Human Settlements."[12] On the one hand, popular participation is not only conceived in terms of habitat, but also "in the decision-making process concerning all aspects of a country's economic, political, and social life. . . ." On the other hand, socioeconomic changes precede and determine the possibility of acting on an environmental scale: "A national policy on human settlements that attempts to satisfy the popular needs will only be effectively established on the foundation of a profound transformation in societal structure." It appears evident that, without euphemisms, it becomes a question of a change in the political, social, and economic system, especially when one attests to the impossibility, within the capitalist system, of achieving the desired environmental cohesiveness as an expression of a global social culture.

In this respect, documents such as the Charter of Machu Picchu prove to be ineffective, mere theological statements that even hide some of the objective aspects of environmental reality. If fifty years ago, in 1933, the Charter of Athens could pass over, for lack of knowledge, the achievements of the October Revolution, in this decade, an authentically Latin American architectural proclamation can not ignore the environmental gains that were achieved in twenty years in socialist Cuba, overcoming a great part of the limitations prevailing in the majority of countries in that area, or the fragmentary attempts initiated in Chile or Peru, concurrent with the beginnings of structural changes. Let us now consider how in both rural and urban Latin America the distance separating desires, proposals, and feasibility either shrinks or expands, according to the actual configuration of the territory.

HUMAN SETTLEMENTS IN RURAL AREAS

Architecture and the Physical Environment

The natural environment of Latin America has not been propitious to the development of architecture. The equilibrium maintained by primitive American civilizations—Inca, Maya, and Aztec—among the human settlements, the ceremonial centers, and the physical context, and the integration of nature into their architectural creation, began to deteriorate with the Spanish and Portuguese conquest of America.[13] The spatial separation between colonizers and natives—the exploiters and the exploited—and the concentration of accumulated wealth in the port cities and the capitals of the vice royalties by European civil servants and the incipient local aristocracies served to differentiate the culturally elaborated architectural codes from the "spontaneous" constructions that developed in the rural areas. During the colonial period, the country became the region where even into our day patterns of popular culture, folklore, and traditional construction methods were preserved, from the Caribbean *bohíos* (shacks) to the stone dwellings almong the mountain ranges of the Andes.[14] When the Latin American countries achieved independence, they began to subject themselves economically to the industrialized nations of Europe—England, France, Germany—or to the United States. In order to supply the metropolitan centers, the large-scale extraction of mineral, agricultural, and livestock resources was carried out toward the end of the nineteenth century by scientific methods requiring the presence in the countryside of technicians and administators in service to the ruling class.

While traditional folklore progressively degenerated in the habitat of exploited field workers on large landed estates or of those expelled to arid lands, where they were reduced to minimum subsistence on tiny parcels of land, the landowners or the agents for the European and North American firms introduced the new environmental components determined by the development of industrial production. There continued, however, some cultural impurities both in the traditional folklore and in the codes of European "high" bourgeois culture. In Brazil, the big property owners' homes—the *fazendas,* described by Gilberto Freyre—define, within the colonial architecture, the typology of the rural mansion, built of local materials and in harmony with and tempered by factors of ecology and landscape of the physical environment. In Argentina, the cultural dependence of the landowning oligarchy on England and France served to transform the mansion of the *estancias* (ranches), isolated in the vastness of the Pampa, into replicas of Tudor or Victorian castles—in some cases totally imported from Europe—of small castles from the Loire, or of diminutive, eclectic, Parisian palaces.

Major impact on the rural landscape has been made by the operating plants of mining, land, and cattle companies in Chile, Peru, Argentina, or on Caribbean plantations, which organize the intensive extraction of natural resources. The "company towns" of saltpeter and copper built in the Andes by Anaconda, Kennecott, and Cerro de Pasco, and the railroad system constructed by the British to transport agricultural products to the port of Buenos Aires, spread the use of prefabricated steel elements throughout the entire country and were being utilized in railroad stations, factories, warehouses, bridges, *galpones* (barns), and silos at the docks or in slaughterhouses and refrigeration facilities of the Swift and Armour companies.[15] These structures were superimposed on the traditional rural architecture and expressed the dependent productive-extractive system of the southern cone of Latin America. In Central America and the Caribbean, the plantations of the United Fruit Company and the giant sugar-producing centers built in Cuba during the 1920s established the stratification of architecture by social class in the *bateyes* (cabins) and the wood-constructed "balloon frames" imported from the United States, with a typology ranging from the salaried workers' shacks to the plantation administrator's luxurious mansion.[16]

Economic Determinants in the Rural Areas

During the 1930s the specialization in primary production of the majority of Latin American countries was firmly established as a function of the needs of the metropolitan centers. Central America exported the tropical crops; Cuba and the Caribbean, the sugar; Venezuela, oil; Colombia and Brazil, coffee; Chile, copper; Argentina and Uruguay, wheat and beef. Once the wave of European immigration, which had brought the labor force that was utilized in part for the agricultural and cattle exploitation of some regions had ceased, the rural Latin American landscape experienced no qualitative changes with regard to new functional structures, which would have meant an elevation in economic standards or living conditions for the rural population. On the contrary, the polarization of economic development in the urban areas produced the stagnation and deterioration of rural communities, which rapidly disintegrated after World War II as a result of the migratory wave to the cities.

For the twentieth century, it becomes impossible to speak of a "rural" architecture in Latin America that does not coincide with the representative signs of exploitation and underdevelopment. The two typical forms of land ownership—small farms and landed estates—do not permit overcoming the strict pragmatism of functional, "modern" structures, indispensable for the extraction of natural wealth (in some exceptional cases, "designed," within the architectural canons of the Modern movement), nor the precarious structures of the rural community, in which, from generation to generation, a miserable existence is eked out. These figures portray the aforementioned duality: in 1960, 1 percent of all the agricultural enterprises controlled 62.5 percent of the total rural surface on the continent; this 1 percent consisted of large landed estate holdings of more than a thousand hectares (1 hectare = 2.47 acres). At the same time, 76.4 percent of all properties accounted for only 4.5 percent of the land.[17]

In spite of the rapid Latin American population growth—close to 400 million in 1980—[18]the rural territory remains an empty space, with an average population of fifteen inhabitants per square kilometers.[19] (A square kilometer equals approximately 0.3861 square mile.) Twenty-four percent of the inhabitable surface still has less than one person per square kilometer.

The continent constitutes a vast unrealized food reserve, a status imposed by the developed nations by means of economic controls and vast rural properties. This explains why out of 570 million hectares of arable land, only 120 million, or about 21 percent, are utilized.[20] While the growth of the gross industrial product during the last ten years has been 6.7 percent annually, agriculture barely tops 2 percent. The population dedicated to primary productive tasks—120 million in 1974—has rapidly declined in relation to the urban population: from 54 percent in 1960, it was reduced to 40 percent in 1973. In this process, precarious living conditions are also a factor: it is estimated that in 1970 there were more than 17 million underemployed workers, to which can be added the elemental subsistence conditions for 9 million small-scale farmers.

In spite of talk in the world at large about a "green revolution" and the increase in the productivity index due to the application of new technologies, the contribution of agriculture in Latin America to the gross industrial product has declined from 20 percent in 1960 to 15.7 percent in 1970. The impossibility of satisfying internal needs has required the importation of food from abroad; in the past decade, the figure of 450 million dollars annually has been reached, which represents 12 percent of the total imports.

Throughout this century, Latin American countries with major contradictions in their rural areas have tried to implement agrarian reform projects by distributing land among the rural population. This method was considered the most suitable for attenuating the severe class conflicts in the rural areas without changing the capitalist economic and social base. Applied for the first time in Mexico and Bolivia, as a consequence of the participation of the peasants in the political struggles of the national bourgeoisie, agrarian reform was later put into practice in other countries under the auspices of the Alliance for Progress.[21] Eighteen agrarian reform laws have been passed and recognized on the continent but their effectiveness has been minimal because in actual practice the "redistribution" amounted to a limited distribution of small parcels to the rural population for subsistence farming, and did not affect the vast estates situated on the richest farm lands.[22] There are exceptions, such as the attempts made in Chile, Peru, and recently in Nicaragua, countries in which the dismembering of productive larger units is avoided by the formation of cooperatives and state farms. Only in Cuba, where change has been made possible by the economic and political system, has there been integral agrarian reform.

The Beginnings of Spatial Planning

In global terms, the Latin American situation is unfavorable for the planning process, if one thinks of it as the best organization of space for the majority of the population. From the point of view of the monopolistic and oligopolistic enterprises, linked to and favored by the State and the privileged groups who control the productive aparatus, one can then speak about territorial "planning." One must conclude as Rofman affirms, that Latin American planners "do not plan, either for planning or for social change."[23]

After the world crisis of 1929, when a political economy known as "import substitution" resulted in industrial development, the first attempts at spatial planning in Latin America were also initiated. The location of industries and the related plans for the development of depressed regions or those affected by natural catastrophes determined the characteristics of the first initiatives and the formation of specialized organizations in various countries through the 1950s. Wiener and Sert designed the Cidade dos Motores (Motor City) in Brazil and Chimbote in Peru; in Chile, CORFO (National Development Corporation) was created in 1939, as a result of the earthquake that had struck the country. Others include the Commission for the Balsas River in Mexico; the Corporation for the Valley of Cauca in Colombia; the Superintendency for the Development of the Northeast (SUDENE) to counteract the negative effects of droughts in the northern part of the country in Brazil. Central planning organizations were established in other countries: in Venezuela (1958), the Central Office for Planning and Coordination; in Cuba (1955), the National Council for Planning; in Ecuador, the National Council for Planning and Economic Coordination; in Nicaragua (1952), the Office of Planning.[24]

During the 1960s, planning reached a chill point in Latin America. The triumph of the Cuban Revolution brought to light the explosive contradictions contained in the continent's socioeconomic system, at the very moment in which multinational North America firms were investing heavily in the region.[25] In order to avoid the repetition of a similar revolutionary process, the United States and Latin American governments carried out a "developmental" economic policy based on a strong expansion of industry, accompanied by State action geared toward the modernization of the administrative apparatus and the creation of urban infrastructures with funds obtained through loans from North America or from international organizations. The Conference of Punta del Este in 1961 constituted the start of this action and was supported by the Alliance for Progress, the Bank for Interamerican Development (BID), the Interamerican Social and Economic Committee, and the technicians of the system, that were trained by the Organization of American States (OAS) and the Economic Commission for Latin America (ECLA), in conjunction with the Latin American Institute of Economic and Social Planning (ILPES), created in 1962. The implementation of some regional plans—the founding of Brasilia and the city of Guyana, the Bahian *Recóncavo* in the central region of the state of Bahía, the industrial development of Concepción (Chile) and Monterrey (Mexico), and the application of the "development pole" concept—did not stimulate positive results in the rural zones. Their transformation required more radical measures than the simple decentralization of industrial enclaves. Between 1960 and 1968 in northeastern Brazil, six hundred industrial projects were carried out, but failed to alleviate the high unemployment rate in the country-side or generate a modernization of the agricultural infrastructure.[26] A summary of the period appears in a report from ECLA: ". . . at the end of the decade, the Latin American colonies are far from having established the basic institutions and structures that will assure more stable economic and social progress." In other words, the economic and spatial policy was oriented by transnational enterprises that were constructing hundreds of light industries in the cities—producing durable consumer goods and not capital goods—to satisfy the bourgeoisie's demand for products. Furthermore, the construction programs of the state and of private enterprise basically ful-filled the middle-class demand for housing. While in the rural areas there was no improvement, the marginal neighborhoods of the cities grew rapidly as a result of the mirage caused by the short-lived prosperity generated by "developmentalism."[27]

Planning Objectives of the 1970s

In the past decade, the sharpening of the social, economic, and functional contradictions in the region, as indicated by the irreversible process of "hyperurbanization," has stimulated governments of different political ten-dencies to search for some valid rules on a national scale that would inter-connect economic and spatial planning. We can summarize five objectives that are basic to most of these recent plans.

• *Regional interrelation between the Metropolitan Centers and the Surrounding Area.* Integrative plans between urban centers and the surrounding region have come about in order to avoid the continuing undifferentiated "oil slick" growth of the cities. Mexico City, Quito, São Paulo, Buenos Aires, Caracas, and other cities on the continent are among those with regional organizational schemes.

• *Decentralization and Strengthening of Industrial Locations.* In Mex-ico there exists a plan to establish twenty-six average-size industrial cities, with populations of twenty-five thousand to fifty thousand throughout the entire country, which has been divided into nine regions by the National Commission for Regional Development.[28] In Colombia, the National Plan for Development, "The Four Strategies," supported by the Agency for International Development (AID) is attempting to strengthen medium-size cities in order to attract the population overflow from the agricultural areas.[29] In Argentina, the plan for industrial decentralization is connected to the studies of the Buenos Aires Metropolitan System currently executed by the National Program for the Concentration of the Habitat and Territorial Regu-lation (CONHABIT).[30] In addition, there are plans for the development of industry and tourism in certain provinces of the Patagonia region: in Puerto Madryn the largest aluminum-producing plant in Latin America has been built.[31]

• *Utilization of Natural Resources.* During the 1970s, restrictions placed on oil consumption and the resulting energy crisis particularly affected the highly industrialized nations. Foreseeing the intensification of these difficulties during the coming decades, some Latin American countries have begun important infrastructure work in order to take advantage of the energy-producing capacity of water resources. While Argentina is in the process of completing its Chocón dam, the countries on the Plata River basin are carrying out a project for two large-span dams: the Itaipú dam in Saltos del Guayrá in the border zone between Paraguay and Brazil, and the Salto Grande dam on the Uruguay River on the border between Argentina and Uruguay. The latter project affects an area of 28,000 hectares, with a population of 358,000 inhabitants. A detailed urban plan has been drawn for one of the first examples of a "new town" in Argentina, Federación, which will replace a city that will be covered by the waters of the lake.[32]

• *Road Systems and Placement of Settlements in Virgin Land.* Since the 1950s, Brazilian politicians have shaped the progressive transformation of the country's populated coastal settlements by developing uninhabited space in the interior. The founding of Brasília was a first step, the colonization of the virgin lands of Amazonia, a second. With a surface area of five million square kilometers, which constitutes two-fifths of South America, Amazonia has prodigious natural resources. It is hoped that the exploitation of these will not alter the delicate ecological equilibrium of the region, especially since it is considered to be the "green lung" of the continent.

The colonization of Amazonia has three purposes: first, the utilization of mineral and agricultural resources. For this, the Brazilian government has allowed a Rockefeller enterprise to intensively exploit the forests and cattle, while the extraction of iron and manganese deposits, raw materials which are later processed in foreign metropolitan centers, is handled by Bethlehem Steel and the U.S. Steel Corporation.

The second purpose of colonization is settlement of the unemployed rural population, originating from the Northeast. In 1964, SUDENE moved one thousand families to sixteen colonies in Amazonia, but the lack of services and communication resulted in the failure of this first attempt. In 1970, Garrastazu Médici's military government issued the National Integration Plan, which reiterates the importance of new lands to absorb the unemployed labor force and curtail migration to the cities. The National Institute for Colonization and Agrarian Reform (INCRA) attempted to settle one hundred thousand families between 1971 and 1974. During this period, it was only able to relocate four hundred families, a clear indication of the failure of the operation. Consequently, the urban system, which had been planned along the new highways, did not materialize. The new system was to be based on a scale of settlements—the minimum unit, *agrovilla,* every 7 kilometers; the *agropolis,* every 20 kilometers; and the *ruropolis,* every 140 kilometers. These were to be equipped with different levels of services.[33] For now, however, there are only precarious wooden settlements situated arbitrarily along the highways.

The third purpose of colonization is to connect Brazil and its bordering countries by means of highways. The construction of the Transamazonic highway, spanning a distance of 5,400 kilometers, and the subsystem of interrelated roads will connect Brazilian cities with Surinam, Venezuela, Peru, Colombia, and Ecuador. Highways already exist that link São Paulo with Paraguay and Bolivia.[34] The network of highways has two basic purposes: economic and military. Brazil needs to export its excess industrial products to bordering countries, as it does with Bolivia and Paraguay, and to compete in the markets of the continent's other industrialized nations, such as Mexico and Argentina. On the other hand, the "subimperialist" position adopted by the military governments requires a system for rapid communication with the rest of Latin America, in anticipation of future regional conflicts. Until now, the colonization of Amazonia has not had positive results. Social conflicts, for example, the extermination of indigenous populations, and ecological alterations caused by the indiscriminate felling of trees—an irreversible destructive force in the functioning of the ecosystem— have been created.[35]

• *Planning as a result of natural disasters.* During the 1970s, Latin America was struck by several earthquakes that caused thousands of deaths and considerable damage. In Peru and Chile vast areas suffered extensive damage and reconstruction required a process of regional planning. In Central America, the consequences were more serious. In 1972 Managua, Nicaragua's capital, was almost totally destroyed: 10,000 dead, 57,000 homes destroyed, 95 percent of commerce and light industry leveled, as were schools, hospitals, and markets. In 1976 in Guatemala City, a similar phenomenon occurred: 22,000 dead, 76,000 injured, 50,000 homes destroyed.

The planning offices of both countries established proposals for regional development, the decentralization of the urban center, and architectural solutions for the reconstruction of residential neighborhoods and public service infrastructures. But the conflict of interests among landowners and the venal character of the governments involved confined the reconstruction to the needs of the middle and upper bourgeoisie, prolonging miserable living conditions for the majority of the population.[36] The recent political changes that occurred in Nicaragua have opened a new hopeful perspective for urban and regional planning and for a change in the environmental framework of the community. Shortly after the revolutionary victory, the National Institute for Agrarian Reform was created and expropriated 250,000 hectares of the best land to establish state agro-industrial complexes and farming cooperatives. After the foundation of a solid national economic base is established, the necessary means will be available for urban reconstruction, not only of Managua, but of all the towns destroyed by dictator Somoza's bombings. It is expected that the major plans, carried out with the technical assistance of the OAS, will permit radical changes in the population's spatial localization and the infrastructures of services.

The Experience of Peru and Chile

In Peru and Chile, regional plans included not only designs of physical structures for the territory, but also proposals for the new social and economic relations that attempted to radically change the standard of living of the rural population. The major innovations appeared on the social level, forms of participation and self-management for the rural communities; in the system of services, education, public health, and culture; and in the creation of functional infrastructures, road and irrigation systems and technological equipment. However, the Chilean military coup in 1973 and the change of direction in Peru given to that military government after 1975 by a new political leadership, have curtailed the radical processes of social, economic, and consequently, territorial transformation in both countries.

In 1968, Peru began the nationalization of its coastal agro-industrial complexes and the integration of rural communities into productive structures. It was hoped that by implementing agrarian reform, the limits of individual subsistence farming, inherent in the system of *minifundios* (very small land parcels), would be broken. For this purpose, priority areas have been established that, subdivided into minor geographical units, express their homogeneity in terms of ecology and physical infrastructure. The Integral Projects for Rural Settlement constitute the basic cells for bringing together the rural population. Dimensions vary according to location: on the lower or middle part of the coastal valleys and the inter-Andean or the Andean high plateau, where they become extensive in size, the parameters for agriculture under irrigation vary between 5,000 and 15,000 hectares, while the extensive cattle-raising of the Puna reaches unit sizes of 200,000 and 300,000 hectares.[37]

The Integral Projects for Rural Settlement group together the Agrarian Production Cooperatives (CAP), an integration of small land parcels sharing communal services, and the Agricultural Associations of Social Interest (SAIS), which comprises in its initial stage of development 2.5 million hectares and more than 100,000 rural families.[38] To the north of Lima, an agrarian production cooperative, Andahuasi, has been established, with a population of more than 2,000 inhabitants, covering an area of more than 1,000 hectares. The project complies with the criteria set forth by the community on the characteristics of the town and its components.[39]

On the political and social level, the farmers' participation has been guided by the National System of Support for Social Mobilization (SINA-MOS), whose objective is to organize the population into dynamic units, both territorial and functional, of a communal, cooperative nature. There has also been an attempt to structure a regional planning system through levels of decision and consultation that would allow for grass roots participation and for decentralization in planning.[40] The local bourgeoisie's control of the productive structure and the presence of foreign capital have turned out to be limiting factors for the realization of planning with social content.

In Chile, the government of the Popular Unity tried to correct in the course of its three years such imbalances inherited from previous bourgeoisie planning as the excessive development of the central macrozone of Santiago. The newer plan called for territorial, functional, and economic role of the cities, towns, and villages to be defined in accordance with size, so that the *regional systems of population centers* might be included in their policies of *integrated developing geographical areas.* The essential goal was a balanced evolution of the national territory by means of the so-called *concentrated decentralization* of social activities.[41]

The objectives proposed by the National Office of Planning (ODEPLAN) can be summarized by the following nine points: (a) to readapt the economic-spatial structure of the country; (b) to decentralize population growth; (c) to create in each region sources for agricultural and industrial work; (d) to mobilize idle and poorly employed resources; (e) to accelerate the development of industry on a regional level; (f) to increase the average productivity of each region; (g) to engage popular participation at each stage of the planning program; (h) to cut down on the degree of the rural population's dispersion by concentrating it, when possible, in areas endowed with the necessary services for its inhabitants and for production activity; (i) to introduce urban elements into the agrarian physical and social structure, for the purpose of reducing the differences between the cities and countryside.[42]

In the countryside, the Popular Unity government was able to rectify the counterproductive tendency of Christian Democratic policy which, while turning over separate units of land to a smaller number of farmers, took apart and disassembled certain historically constituted cultivation practices.[43] In 1971, the Centers for Agrarian Reform (CERA), in order to provide economically viable units, created interconnected settlements that served to break the fragile autonomy of the isolated properties. This constituted progress in terms of the socialization of production and the democratization of cooperative management. In this manner, the government attempted to integrate the rural structures into the process of consolidation of urban properties in the urban centers, so as to form a collective network of productive structures on a national level. Coinciding with this economic organization, there were also some projects which introduced new types of urban organization and interior arrangement in houses carried out for rural communities.[44]

The coup by the military junta radically destroyed the gains achieved during the brief period of the Popular Unity government. The new military government's submission to the interests of imperialism, multinational enterprises, and the oligarchy of landowners demonstrated once again the external conditioning of the Latin American national bourgeoisie. A few short months after the coup, the military government abolished the agrarian reform law and returned 2,644 farm properties of the total 4,700 expropriated beforehand. Besides the indemnity paid in foreign currencies to the copper enterprises— Anaconda and Kennecott—the CORFO proceded to return all the nation- alized enterprises to the private sector. In June 1974, a majority of the 480 firms under the control of CORFO had already been given to the private sector, and almost all of them were denationalized.[45]

Cuba: Urbanization of the Rural Areas

Since the victory of the revolution, the changes that have occurred in rural Cuba have carried as their principal objective the replacement of the private ownership of land and production facilities with national ownership and the establishment of new social and economic relationships. This has required complex organizational changes in terms of production, the system of current cultural and social values, and a restructuring of the territorial base, which is to be completed in evolutionary successive stages. Two agrarian reforms constitute the starting point for the concentration of land into the hands of the state. The government gained control over 76 percent of the cultivable areas, once the lands of the bourgeoisie were nationalized. In order to avoid breaking up the territory into small properties, which would have blocked the development of integral plans and the organization of production in terms of high technology and output, these areas were organized into sugar farms and people's farms.

The National Institute for Agrarian Reform (INRA)—now the Ministry of Agriculture—established the country's agricultural policy and controlled the process of marketing, the creation of infrastructures, and the distribution of equipment. In turn, the rural communities organized themselves into the National Association for Small Farmers (ANAP) and locally into the twenty-eight zones for Agrarian Development and the corresponding branches for the different forms of collectivization. This territorial subdivision was replaced in 1968 by the directed and comprehensive plans which corres- ponded to a superior level of agricultural planning, and coincided with preparations for the large *zafras* (sugar crops) that began in 1970.[46]

During the five-year period 1970 to 1975, the accelerated integration of technology and agriculture, especially in the cultivation of sugar, developed parallel to the regional integration of agricultural plans and the policies for new settlements. This culminated in the change in the political-adminis- trative structure instituted in 1976. The work of rural and urban planners has played a fundamental role at this stage. Based on a series of premises that have determined the reorganization of productive and functional structures, the regional projects have made their mark from the urban level to the assimilation of small farmers in the state's specialized rural areas.

The first premise essential to economic development is the predominance of agriculture during the decade of the consolidation of technical and organizational infrastructures (1965–1975). During the following five years (1976–1980), industrialization was stimulated, linked in great part to the processing of agricultural products.

The second premise is a consequence of the first: with the primacy of agriculture, the territory must be dealt with as one region, and not in terms of separate poles of development; it must be equipped with an urban skeleton and not with isolated urban nuclei. It becomes a question of creating conditions in order to begin reducing the imbalance in size, population, services, and standard of living between the large cities—Havana, Santiago, Camagüey—the medium-sized ones, and the minor nuclei that make up the urban system. By this process, the 150 sugar centers distributed throughout the country become points of articulation in the region and the essential base for agro-industrial linkage. The new political administrative division, which replaced the six traditional provinces with fourteen of smaller size and greater socioeconomic coherence, allows, within the political structure, for closing the distance between leadership and the rank-and-file on decision-making matters.

The third premise consists of concentrating and rationalizing the agricultural units of production, while slowly changing the arbitrary diversity of crops and reorganizing the parcels inherited from the former capitalist private ownership system of land subdivision.

The fourth premise involves the creation of rural infrastructures that would balance the inherited deficiencies and would establish the necessary foundations for introducing population and technology into the rural areas. A national highway and its secondary road system have been planned, a hydraulic system has been designed—dams containing four billion cubic meters of water—composed of predams and microdams, located in diverse regions of the country. The construction of a group of dairies and technical installations for specialized agriculture has also been planned. To these functional infrastructures, human settlements are added to create a system of towns and services. Linkage among all of these components requires the execution of detailed territorial planning, with the same degree of exactness that traditionally corresponds to urban planning. In this respect, the Cuban planners are "urban" designers of the countryside.

The social value of agricultural labor constitutes the fifth premise of the process for transformations in the Cuban territory. The change in the productive structures and the intervention of architects and planners are not sufficient factors in themselves to change the rural areas qualitatively: it is also necessary to change the social relations. This has been achieved by means of employing young technicians and university specialists in the scientific processes of agricultural development; the formation of youth brigades of workers—the Youth Labor Army; the participation of urban workers in voluntary labor; the fusion of manual and intellectual labor on the part of students in the secondary school system—the creation of the Basic Rural Secondary schools and the placement of these learning centers within the agricultural plans for diverse regions of the island; and finally, the insertion of the life-styles and components of urban culture into rural towns. This has prompted the use of prefabricated multifamily housing units in new rural towns such as Jibacoa, Valle del Perú in Havana, Triunvirato in Matanzas, the systems of towns in Escambray—La Yaya, El Tablón, La Parra—and Jimaguayú in Camagüey. Of 323 rural settlements, 120 were constructed between 1971 and 1975. There are now under construction more than 115 new towns with a total of 38,000 dwellings.[47] In summary, the designer who conceives homogeneous environmental structures for the region in accordance with the economic, functional, and cultural needs of the Cuban people as a whole is involved in an experience unique in Latin America.

THE TRANSFORMATION OF URBAN AND METROPOLITAN STRUCTURES

Mexico, Argentina, and Brazil: The Creation of the "Megalopolises"

On this "empty" continent, as Jorge E. Hardoy defines it, the most rapid process of urbanization and metropolitanization in ths so-called Third World takes place, in spite of still apparent ups and downs.[48] While some countries' total population is 60 to 70 percent urban, others, like Honduras or Haiti, do not exceed 20 percent.[49] The primitive coastal cities, founded by the Portuguese and Spanish, have maintained their particular stability, as the majority of them evolved into large contemporary metropolises. Ports of entry for various human groups and an infinity of goods, and ports of egress for the continent's basic riches, they acquired a particular cosmopolitan character. Urban primacy over the rural context is a definitive indication of modern culture in Latin America, whose accelerated and multifaceted growth overwhelms the static patterns of rural folklore. It is not a matter of an antagonistic culture, but of a synthetic one, forged by the different human groups that successively mixed with one another in the cities. During the twentieth century, the migratory movements, first external and then internal, as well as the social stratification that coexists within the urban territory—from the landowning oligarchies to the subproletariat of rural origins—make the modern city a sociocultural kaleidoscope, where at present the authentic expression of Latin American culture is forged.[50]

Let us take a look at some of the figures that characterize the urbanization process. The rate of urban population growth has been greater in these last decades than the general index for Latin America: 5 to 6 percent annually in comparison to the average of 2.7 percent. Between 1940 and 1970, the population residing in centers with a population of more than 10,000 increased from 30 million to 130 million; the increment in cities of more than 100,000 inhabitants was also greater during the same period: from 19 million, it surpassed 90 million inhabitants.[51] But the most impressive factor has been the concentration of the population in metropolitan areas. In thirty years, the population of Buenos Aires has grown from 4.7 million to 11 million; São Paulo from 2.3 million to 14 million; Rio de Janeiro from 3 million to 10 million; Mexico City from 3 million to 15 million; Caracas from 500,000 to 4 million. This means that 30 percent of the entire Latin American urban population lives in seventeen metropolitan areas of more than 1 million inhabitants.

According to Hardoy, the urban concentration of the population on a limited surface area of the continent will continue to increase up to the year 2000; in that year, out of a total population of 600 to 700 million inhabitants, 400 million will be city dwellers. At that time, 80 percent of the population will be concentrated in the cities. There will be one metropolitan area with more than 20 million inhabitants (São Paulo); two with more than 15 million (Mexico City and Buenos Aires); possibly four with more than 10 million (Rio de Janeiro, Lima, Bogotá, and Santiago); and a total of between thirty and forty with more than 1 million.[52]

These statistics are not surprising if they are compared to the similar evolution of urban centers in developed capitalist countries. But the figures, accompanied by their social, economic, infrastructural, and cultural characteristics, then acquire a pessimistic dramatic character, which contradicts the accepted theory of the increase in standard of living associated with urban development. The localization of industry plays an important role in the characterization of urban problems, in view of the fact that it is not distributed evenly throughout the region. Concentrated in the larger capitals, industry takes advantage of the proximity of the port-entryway for raw materials, the greatest resources for infrastructures and labor, and the centers of bourgeois consumption. Their dynamic role in the economic "development"—rather than "growth," which signifies a positive incentive for the standard of living for a majority of the population—turns out to be restrictive on account of two factors that condition industrialization: (1) dependence on external capital; (2) the predominant production of consumer goods for the bourgeois strata. During the period 1960 to 1970, one billion dollars entered Latin America annually, headed for industrial investments. While in 1960 the North American capital that participated in industry corresponded to 18 percent of the total, in 1973 it reached 44 percent. Brazil, Mexico, and Argentina received 71 percent of all direct private investment in industry: 34 percent of this went to Brazil. Production has centered around food, textiles, automobiles, light equipment, and electrical household appliances. Consequently, as a result of the Brazilian "miracle," workers' real wages from 1960 to 1970 were reduced by 33 percent. The participation of 80 percent of the country's active population in the distribution of the national income decreased from 44 percent in 1960 to 36.2 percent, while 5 percent of the population increased its share from 26 percent to 37.8 percent.[53]

Despite State plans for decentralizing industry, the excessive concentration of large agglomerations persists. More than 90 percent of the region's industrial production and public services is concentrated in forty-one cities, but 70 percent of this is located in only ten urban centers.[54] In the so-called river-industrial axis of Argentina, which consists of the coastal zone between the cities of La Plata and Rosario—including Buenos Aires and a stretch of land 400 kilometers long—and which corresponds to 2 percent of the nation's surface area, 46 percent of the Argentine population (11 million in 1970) as well as 72 percent of the nation's industrial work force, is found concentrated in 74,000 industrial establishments. Similar phenomena can be found in São Paulo and Mexico City and to a lesser degree in the so-called "corridors of development": Caracas-La Guayra, Santiago-Valparaíso, Valencia-Maracay.

The metropolitan centers attract a population that outnumbers the available industrial jobs. The immigrating rural population, expelled from *latifundios* and attracted by the supposed opportunity for employment in the large cities, constitutes the mass of unemployed and underemployed who on the one hand, as expected by Marx, make up the "industrial reserve army," and on the other, enter small businesses and service occupations. This social group of rural people, subproletarians and proletarians—incorrectly referred to as "marginal" since together they make up the working class—along with the petty bourgeoisie employed in administration and commerce, give the Latin American cities their "hyperurbanized" character and are functionally defined by their tertiary activities. These "megalopolises," not economically self-sufficient, and lacking minimum levels of services and technical and administrative infrastructures, do not permit popular participation in planning decisions. They constitute a body whose growth dynamic is determined, not by centralized decisions from the state, but by the pressures from the financial and industrial interests, by land speculators and foreign capital. Therefore, we agree with Hardoy when he affirms: "Given the political and power structure that subsists in the countries of South America, it is improbable that a real incorporation of the large masses of rural and urban workers into the national economic effort and its political life can be carried out."

The Characteristics of the Metropolitan Center

The formal and spatial structure of the Latin American city has gone through three distinct phases: (1) the regular gridiron plan established by the Laws of the Indies for colonial Latin American cities or the irregular layout of medieval origin of the first Brazilian urban centers; (2) the application of Haussmann's principles, during the second half of the nineteenth century in Mexico City and at the beginning of the twentieth in Buenos Aires, Montevideo,

Havana, which monumentalize and arrange the central areas hierarchically, representing the functions carried out by the state and the new national bourgeoisie. Urban planners of European origin carried out the first master plans and superimposed a system of focal points and radical avenues on the colonial gridiron—Forestier in Havana, Agache in Rio de Janeiro, Maillart in Montevideo; (3) the modernization of the urban form, in accordance with the change in scale that the metropolitan dimension promotes and the presence of new social functions. Foreign and local designers produced master plans for the old cities and for some new centers that would be stimulated by industrial development. Le Corbusier with a group of young Argentine and Colombian architects conceived the master plans for Buenos Aires and Bogotá. Wiener and Sert devised the master plans for Havana, Chimbote, *Cidade dos Motores,* and Medellín. Doxiadis prepared a proposal for Rio de Janeiro; North American and British planning firms—the Joint Center of the Massachusetts Institute of Technology (MIT) and Llewelyn-Davies, Weeks, Forestier-Walker & Bor—worked on Ciudad Guayana, El Tablazo, and Tuy Medio in Venezuela. Lucio Costa conceived the pilot plan for Brasilia. Simultaneously, municipal planning offices were created to carry out the master plans for a majority of the Latin American capitals.

Have these initiatives succeeded in granting coherency and continuity to the formal configuration of the Latin American city? According to Alejo Carpentier, the Cuban novelist, it is the very absence of these attributes characteristic of European cities that gives a unique personality to our urban centers: "Our cities *do not have style.* However, we now begin to discover that they have what we could call a *third style*: the style of things which have no style."[55] In reality, it is not a question of a conscious esthetic of *anti-style,* rather there are objective factors that determine the failure of master plans and the arbitrary and chaotic form of the Latin American city.

Its history was not forged by planners, urbanists, and architects, but by land speculators, construction firms, and private initiative, with their popular and "high" culture attributes. After the nineteenth century, with the formation of the suburbs, the colonial gridiron began to expand arbitrarily with the distribution of building plots, neighborhoods, or communities. The structure of the city was subject to the interests of the national bourgeoisie, which controlled its center and its areas of expansion, segregating the territory occupied by the petty bourgeoisie. The proletarian zone was characterized by the direct relationship of habitat-production. This separation of social groups is repeated in all of the cities on the continent, showing similar formal and spatial characteristics: the colonial center was replaced by eclectic public buildings during the 1920s; in the decade of the forties, the massive blocks of ministries and offices, which correspond to the "monumental-modern" codes appeared; finally, beginning with the fifties, first steel and glass skyscrapers and later the "brutalist" buildings that conformed to the parameters of modernity appeared in the metropolitan centers as a result of the centrally located functions.

Within the heterogeneous amalgam that forms the superposition of functions, some structuring attempts on the urban configuration have appeared. Construction of major infrastructural works has been undertaken by the State in order to guarantee the activities that meet the needs of the bourgeoisie, for example, the ownership of the individual automobile and the easy access from residential neighborhoods to the central areas. Almost all of the Latin American cities have constructed peripheral and inner-city highway systems, which brutally invade the urban texture and cause the dislocation of the poor populace from the affected areas.

Caracas has a series of highways that transverse the city lengthwise along the valley. In Mexico City, an alternation of peripheral rings has been constructed, in addition to a series of intersecting highways, superimposed on the checkerboard. In Buenos Aires, the traditional Avenida 9 de Julio crosses the city on its north-south axis, with a width of 120 meters, and required for its completion the demolition, not only of modest housing in the *Sur* district, but also of luxurious apartment buildings in the *Norte* district. The peripheral ring, Avenida General Paz, with a stretch of highway along the bank of the Plata River, has been completed. Rio de Janeiro has been linked to Niteroi by means of a bridge—a sophisticated work of engineering—that crosses the Bay of Guanabara. In Quito, work will be begun on the modern and complex Terminal Terrestre, planned and to be constructed by an Israeli firm. To these systems, arteries of superhighways between inland cities and the ports can be added: the technical display of the São Paulo-Santos viaduct and the Caracas-La Guaira and Santiago-Valparaíso highways. The hundreds of millions of dollars invested in these costly road projects have not solved the circulation problems nor have they helped to lessen the environmental pollution caused by automotive vehicles. For this reason, during the 1970s plans were conceived and construction begun on subway systems for Mexico City, Santiago, Caracas, Quito, Rio de Janeiro, and São Paulo. Buenos Aires was already the first city to employ a subway at the beginning of this century.

Another structuring element for the urban form, appearing recently in various cities, is the commercial center, assimilated from the North American model, or the creation of an administrative-cultural-commercial center, connected to an international financial district and to middle-class neighborhoods.[56] It then becomes a question of the creation of the so-called "city within a city," islands inaccessible to the majority of the population, which satisfy a desire for consumption or for services, comparable to those in the developed countries, and utilized by a limited elite. In the majority of cases, these centers become autonomous components that do not project themselves onto urban space as generating elements with polyfunctional connections. One exception was the redevelopment project for downtown Santiago, Chile, promoted by the Popular Unity government in 1972. In its sixteen blocks, there was a polyfunctional articulation of housing; administrative, commercial, and cultural buildings; and ample space for pedestrians.[57]

A radically opposed idea is demonstrated by the "Central Park" complex in Caracas. On ten hectares of centrally located area, a population of 16,000 inhabitants—with a density of 1,500 inhabitants per hectare—is concentrated in three forty-three-story residential buildings, which will be accompanied by a fifty-four-story office tower. The ground level contains a network of services on a metropolitan scale. The inhabitants of the complex can carry out all of their commercial, recreational, and cultural activities without crossing the Cyclopean concrete walls which delimit the interior spaces. As the publicity slogan confirms, one feels there "that nothing is like the past"; only the landscape of the surrounding hills covered with thousands of shanties reminds one of the past, capable of being transformed into a dangerous future.

The same introverted character can be found in some commercial centers, which were conceived as interior cities, surrounded by vast open spaces for automobile parking. Although the pioneering example in this series failed during the 1950s, with the attempt to create in Caracas, La Roca Tarpeya, a commercial "city" on a vehicular scale, others were then erected: in Mexico City, Satellite City Center; in Bogotá, Unicenter; in Santiago, the Centro Caracol (Snail Center), a copy of Wright's Guggenheim Museum; and in Lima, the Civic and Commercial Center. The sophistication of the architecture and the elaborate treatment of interior spaces change these urban, architectural complexes into artifacts alien to their surroundings, demonstrating an esthetic-figurative ritual that regulates the function of consumption in bourgeois society.[58]

Treatment of the Historic Foundations

For four centuries, Latin American cities maintained a homogeneous and balanced growth that conformed to the unity between the layout of the habitat and the symbolic system of the "monuments." In less than a century, the eruption of the models imposed by contemporary technological civilization, manipulated by interests without scruple and foreign to the indispensable and necessary relationship between social culture and the urban physical environment, destroyed the first model of the settlement, in some cases, definitively. Fortunately, "progress" did not arrive in all of the continent's cities with the same impact, and it is still possible to recover on an urban scale, in some countries, the very same cultural values identified with the homes, palaces, churches, and public buildings left by colonial society, and even some structures built by earlier American civilizations.

The 1933 "Charter of Athens" denounced the systematic destruction of the historical inheritance, that has been condoned by state bureaucrats and carried out by land speculators and builders, under the pretext of improving living conditions for the population which was forced to crowd together in the central areas of European cities.[59] In reality, this becomes a policy of appropriation of the center by the bourgeoisie and the expulsion of the proletariat in the disguise of a philanthropic modernization of urban social functions. These "remodeling," plans which were carried out in different capitals during the 1950s, were theoretically justified in a book from CIAM (International Congress of Modern Architecture), *El corazón de la ciudad* (*The Heart of the City*). In Latin America, the application of the precepts of the modern movement appear in the projects realized by Le Corbusier or Wiener and Sert. The master plan for Havana (1958) is an example of the destruction of the historic center by the invasion of automobiles and the recreation-commercial structures that were adapted for tourism. The new master plan changed the authentic formal and spatial values of colonial tradition into a "Hollywood" set, conforming to kitsch requirements of the transnational firms that manipulate the so-called tourism of the "masses."[60]

Fortunately, after World War II a conscious attitude was developed toward the cultural value of the cities and the necessity of preserving the inheritance left by previous generations. This is not only a product of the reaction against the anticultural mechanisms of capitalism, but also of the impact caused by attempting to erase every urbanistic and architectural vestige—a cultural expression of genocide that was carried out by the Nazis in Poland and in the Soviet Union since 1939.

The creation of the United Nations and UNESCO permitted the realization of several theoretical and practical initiatives that would have an impact in Latin American cities as well. Under the auspices of UNESCO, a series of world and regional conferences was held on the subject of the conservation of monuments and historic centers. During 1957, the First International Congress of Architects and Monument Specialists was convened in Paris and ICOMOS (International Council of Monuments and Sites) was founded. At the Second Congress, held in 1964, the "Charter of Venice," which extended the cultural projection of monuments to both rural and urban levels was adopted.[61] In 1967, the Conference on the Conservation and Utilization of Monuments and Historic and Artistic Points of Interest focused on the subject of Latin America and conceived the "Quito Regulations," which were valuable in connecting cultural problems with those of economic development, in addition to questioning the renovation processes for the historic center that benefit the dominant elite and necessitate the expulsion of the poorer people to the fringes of the city. On the other hand, the regulations also dealt with the connection between historic sites and their use for tourism, so as to insure a just balance between cultural preservation and economic profitability.[62]

During the 1970s, the problem of the historic center has become increasingly important in Latin America. Several international meetings have been held on the subject, and concrete plans were begun in some countries for conservation and renovation. In 1972 the Mexican government passed the "federal law on monuments and archaeological, historic, and artistic zones," which defines the limits and norms imposed on urban areas that contain valuable sites, as much in architectural terms as in those of national historical significance.[63] During the same period, the Commissions on Monuments were formed in Cuba (1963), national commissions from ICOMOS were created, and research centers in universities were established to carry out surveys and studies on the national architectural and urbanistic patrimony.[64]

In 1973 the First Regional Latin American Seminar on Conservation and Restoration was held in Mexico (The Churubusco convent) and was linked to a series of specialized courses on restoration techniques, both sponsored by UNESCO. In 1976, the UNESCO General Conference in Nairobi designated the city of Quito as a patrimony of universal interest. The Ecuadorian delegation joined the World Council of Exceptional National and Cultural Patrimonies. In 1977, the preamble of the "Charter of the Machu Picchu" addressed the integration of past and present within the urban context. At the same time, in view of the growth of modern cities, this was also the basic theme for the "colloquium on the preservation of historic centers," held in Quito and organized by UNESCO and the Regional Project for the Andean Cultural Patrimony. On this occasion, Latin American experiences were evaluated. Emphasis was put on the necessity of popular participation in these initiatives, and the interdisciplinary participation of environmentally committed experts.[65] Related to the Thirteenth Congress of the International Union of Architects, was the convening in Mexico City in 1978 of the "Interamerican Symposium on the Conservation of the Artistic Patrimony," which emphasized in its final resolution the problems of historic sites as an integral part of national and regional physical, economic, and cultural planning.[66] Finally, the "Intergovernmental Conference on the Cultural Policies of Latin America and the Caribbean," held in Bogotá, highlighted the necessity of tackling the housing problem in the historic centers "so that its effective revitalization permits the permanence of its inhabitants and the harmonious and balanced development of diverse social and economic functions."[67]

Putting into practice the ideas conceived in resolutions at the international events is no easy task. In the majority of Latin American countries, the State is unable to control the invasion of private initiative, commercial interests, land speculation, or the pressures exercised in the modernization of both the road system or the administrative infrastructures, which all generally affect or destroy the colonial structures.[68] Necessary means to eliminate the "slum conversion" of the historic zones do not exist nor does socioeconomic planning that addresses the problem of relocation—and not the definitive expulsion—of the inhabitants and new labor pools that must be centrally located. In some cases, the possibility of obtaining funds from the tourism industry necessitates the construction of cold monumental complexes, distorting stage sets of past reality, or refined environments for the moneyed elite.

With the financial assistance of UNESCO and PNUD, two principal works are nearing completion on the continent: the remodeling of the historic center in Quito and the ambitious plan for restoration of monuments and creation of tourist infrastructures on the 500-kilometer-long Cuzco-Machu Picchu-Puno axis. Loans obtained by the Peruvian government from PNUD for 500 million dollars and from the Bank for International Development (BID) for 72 million dollars comprise a regional initiative that should have not only cultural and technical impact, but also a strong influence on the economic and social development of the most visited monumental area in Latin America.[69]

Some fragmentary projects have been carried out in the centers of Mexico City, Santiago, Bogotá, and Córdoba. At other, smaller sites in Santo Domingo, San Juan in Puerto Rico, Valpraíso, Popayan, and Ouro Prêto, historic monuments as well as the homogeneity of culturally significant urban areas have been restored. Also of note on the regional level are the historic centers in northwestern Argentina, the Guaraní Jesuit missions, and the small settlements of northeastern Brazil.

Since the victory of the revolution in Cuba, the disappearance of private ownership of urban property has eliminated the obstacles that had hindered state action on the historic sites. During the 1960s, the National Commission on Monuments concentrated its efforts on the restoration of colonial buildings. Its work did not reach a city-wide scale, however, because of the channeling of available economic resources into the construction of new dwellings and social works. With the country's political institutionalization process and the formation of the Popular Powers (elected assemblies), which facilitate community participation on the provincial and municipal levels, there has been a new impetus to the prospect of remodeling historic centers. Already in the socialist constitution, adopted in 1976, the subject of monuments is given consideration: in article 38, it states: "The state, in its educational and cultural policies, protects national monuments and notable sites for their natural beauty or for their recognized artistic or historic value." In 1977, one of the first laws of the National Assembly of Popular Power referred to "National and Local Monuments" and defines the concept of the historic center: "An Urban Historic Center is understood to be the complex formed by buildings, public and private spaces, streets, plazas, and geographical or topographical particularities which structure and shape it and that during a specified historic moment have had a distinct, unified physiognomy, representative of an individualized and organized social community." In 1978, a resolution from the National Commission on Monuments established fifty-seven new sites and national monuments, including the first seven towns founded by Diego Velázquez during the sixteenth century: Baracoa, Bayamo, Santiago de Cuba, Camagüey (Puerto Príncipe), Sancti Spíritus, Trinidad, and Havana. A plan for urban remodeling in Trinidad has been carried out and studies begun on perspective plans for the colonial foundation in Havana. In summary, the integration of old urban structures and new developments controlled by the collective interests of the community will permit the preservation of particular national traditions and the consolidation, on an urban scale, of the cultural identity of Latin American countries.

Antithesis Between Plans for State Housing and Self-help Housing Construction

Twenty years ago, the United Nations organized a seminar on the urbanization of Latin America, for the purpose of analyzing the existing problems in the cities.[70] The general speaker, Philip M. Hauser, suggested with a certain optimism the possibility of improving the living conditions for the region's urban population through adjusting social and economic development. The passing of time has only demonstrated the continual decline in the standard of living for the mass of population with scarce resources. Of those factors that illustrate this, housing ranks among the first. Jorge E. Hardoy estimates the actual housing shortage at 25 or 30 million units. The breakdown by country gives the following figures for the 1970s: Argentina, 2 million; Brazil, 10 million; Mexico, 4 million; Venezuela, 800,000; Chile, 600,000; El Salvador, 176,000; Nicaragua, 209,000; Uruguay, 150,000.[71]

Consequently, a high percentage of the population—on the continent, an average of 20 to 30 percent of the total urban population—inhabit shantytowns, known as *villas misería, favelas, callampas, campaimontes, problaciomes, salvages,* etc. Hardoy pessimistically predicts that if there is no change in the socioeconomic structure, between 130 and 150 million people will inhabit shantytowns by the year 2000. During the 1970s, the percentage of people living in "marginal" settlements was as follows: Rio de Janeiro, 27 percent (900,000 inhabitants); Bogotá, 60 percent (more than 1 million); Lima, 36 percent (1 million); Caracas, 35 percent (556,000); Maracaibo, 50 percent (280,000); Guayaquil, 49 percent (363,000); Recife, 50 percent (520,000). In Mexico City, one marginal settlement, Ciudad Netzahualcoyotl, on Texcoco Lake, has a population of almost 1 million inhabitants. This phenomenon has also appeared in the new cities of Brasilia and Guyana, and accounts for an average of almost 40 percent of the population.[72]

During the 1960s, the governments and international bodies still considered it possible to resolve the housing problem by implementing state plans and creating new towns. With the economic assistance of the Alliance for Progress, a great number of "Kennedy" neighborhoods were created on the outskirts of Latin American capitals. The limited effect of these initiatives necessitated a radical change in orientation for the 1970s. It was accepted tacitly that no government in the region was capable of assuming the investment for housing the majority of the population, who themselves had insufficient resources. In view of this reality, the only solution appears to be to help the settlers to gradually transform, using their own labor and some support from the State or international agencies, their dwellings of tin and cardboard into permanent homes of masonry and concrete, without upsetting the understanding that marginal settlements are inherent to the urban context.[73]

This planning clearly expresses the importance of housing within the capitalist system: instead of being conceived of as a basic community service, like education or public health, it constitutes a commodity determined by the laws of supply and demand which govern private ownership. According to Emilio Pradilla, state-constructed housing has always been subject to the traditional means of financing, contracting labor and private construction firms, fixing rental fees in relation to the cost of the project, and the amortizations applicable within the capitalist system.[74] By fulfilling these requirements, state housing then carries a cost that is beyond the means of the proletariat and subproletariat. Does this mean that it is impossible to construct minimal housing in accordance with international standards for the needy population? In reality, what becomes evident is the inability of the "system" to resolve this problem, due to limitations imposed by (1) the venal character of a good number of the administrations of Latin American governments; (2) the complex bureaucratic structure, whose expense makes an impact on the cost of housing; (3) the impact of land costs; (4) the profits obtained by the construction firms; (5) the banking system which regulates the interests, the financing, and the amortization; (6) the carrying out of the projects by professionals connected to the administration, and not by each country's best architects; (7) the delivery of the units to persons connected to the group which holds political power—administrative, military, or political office holders.

To this, we can add the opposition toward the architectural and urbanistic results of blocks of state housing. English-speaking authors—Turner, Mangin, Alexander, Land, Oliver, Blair—do not accept the solution of high-rise housing and even criticize some of the best examples constructed in Latin America, such as the Venezuelan projects "23 de Enero" and "Cerro Piloto" in Caracas.[75] Their questioning arises from the verification of the existing social problems in the aforementioned complexes: the lack of identification of the users with the project; the impossibility of expanding the dwellings; the interior and exterior deterioration caused by vandalism; the lack of maintenance for the buildings; the precariousness of services. Their questioning turns out to be erroneous since the deficiencies do not lie in the architectural and urbanistic solutions—blocks of housing, the typology commonly utilized in all socialist countries—but in the absence of complementary factors that would establish a support system of relations with the housing, the integration of the inhabitants into stable jobs, the educational and cultural enrichment of the community, the existence of social services, the political organization of the social group and its participation in the administrative operation of the housing, in economic production, etc. When not part of a global system that would change the inhabitants' living conditions housing, isolated in itself, becomes problematic. This creates the appearance, then, that the only alternative remaining for mass housing is do-it-yourself construction and the improvement of shantytowns.

This attachment to "do-it-yourself" solutions to the mass housing problem stems from a limited conception of social and economic relations as based on the capacities of the isolated individual and his nuclear family, a conception that represents the ideals and ideology of the petty bourgeoisie. The emphasis placed on private home ownership, on its introverted character, on the possibility of carrying out as many functions as possible in its interior, the rejection of any urbanistic connection to social life beyond the private home, respond to a model that attempts to retain in Latin America the characteristic attributes of colonial housing; it is the magnification of the *"casa-patio"* (courtyard-house), which has been employed in some recent projects.[76] The step-by-step solutions to the substandard housing problem emphasize the correspondence of each step to an increase in the residents' income—increases that in general do not come to pass due to the effects of continuing inflation upon real wages. They also emphasize that housing takes on cultural value in so far as it becomes a direct expression of the aesthetic aspirations of each resident. Yet are we dealing with a true culture or with the expression of a subculture? Don't the esthetic values turn out to be falsified in the mythology of current architectural movements? In other words, the aesthetic tendencies of "high" architectural culture and the political-ideological objectives of the dominant class play a role in the valorization of these solutions. On the one hand, popular participation and expression, coincide with the current rejection of rationalist canons and the emergence of "postmodernism," "naturalism," or "folklorism." On the other hand, there is a desperate attempt on the part of the bourgeoisie to extinguish any collectivist spirit among the settlers of the shantytowns which might lead to an awakening of class consciousness and their integration into the organized political struggle carried out by the urban proletariat.[77] This explains why the work of John F. C. Turner has been widely propagated within the "system." At the Thirteenth Congress of the International Union of Architects in Mexico City, he was awarded the Sir Robert Matthew prize, because "he has actively helped new communities acquire their autonomy in the building of their environment."

These alienating and mystifying points—economic, ideological, and esthetic—cannot hide the obvious reality and ominous consequences of the urban development of Latin America that lie in the stabilization of marginal settlements, as well as in the prolongation of precarious living conditions for the large masses of population, in a context lacking basic services, green areas, infrastructures, and social spaces. Moreover, the fragility of the foundation that justifies this course of action is apparent when the afore-mentioned settlements pose a threat to the bourgeoisie's living environment and are brutally removed with the aid of the military. In Brazil and Argentina, the *favelas* situated on the hilltops in the center of Rio de Janeiro or Copacabana and the shantytowns set up on lands reclaimed from the Plata River and along the Palmero-Retiro railroad line were eliminated and their inhabitants resettled into individual dwellings in anonymous outlying neighborhoods.[78]

During the 1970s, there was some construction of housing complexes that possess an experimental value and point in the direction of continuous urban structures that break with the persistence of the traditional checkerboard and low-density habitat. In Argentina, Lugano I/II for forty thousand inhabitants, located on the fringes of the federal capital, adapts Sheffield and Grenoble's plans for continuous circulation with fourteen-story buildings. A variety of typological projects were elaborated by the office of Flora Manteola, Javier Sánchez Gómez, Josefina Santos, Justo Solsona, and Rafael Viñoly during the period 1970 to 1977. The 1,500 dwellings in San Isidro, the 5,000 in Villa Tranquila, Avellaneda, and the 2,100 that make up the Piedrabuena Habitational Complex in Matanzas demonstrate the persistence of the housing block organized with different spatial articulations that individualize and differentiate the urban environments. Along the same lines, Staff Studio, directed by Jorge Goldemberg, planned the low-cost housing centers of Morón, La Matanza, and Ciudadela I/II in Buenos Aires for an estimated population of twenty thousand inhabitants.

In Chile, during the popular Unity government, plans for row housing, high-rises, and blocks were developed in an attempt to eliminate the typological identification with the economic status of each social group: the high-rise, architecturally elaborated for the bourgeoisie, and the anonymous housing, of infinitely repeated blocks, for the lower middle class and the proletariat. The state organizations CORMU (Corporation of Urban Renewal) and CORVI (Housing Corporation) studied several planimetric schemes—for example, duplex housing—and urban groupings that were integrated in the center of the city—San Borja—as well as in the bourgeoisie's exclusive suburbs by attaching to them proletarian residential nuclei: the San Luis grouping—eleven thousand inhabitants, located in the Las Condes district in Santiago, Chile, and assigned to inhabitants of substandard housing, who had settled as squatters in that zone.

In Venezuela, the stimulus given to the construction of housing by the Banco Obrero (Workers' Bank) during the 1950s permitted the completion of the complexes planned by Carlos Raúl Villanueva—El Paraíso, Cerro Piloto, 23 de Enero. Unfortunately, this activity has ceased and the level of design did not persist, but degenerated into purely repetitive constructive schemes. However, some architects—Henrique Hernández, Carlos Becerra, Mauricio Poler—investigated new construction techniques, systems of unit layout, and urban design that were realized in Caricuao, a satellite city of Caracas, and in the prefabrication technologies employed by "Viviendas Venezolanas" (Venezuelan Housing).

Mexico is one of the countries that executed major housing plans during the 1960s and 1970s with a variety of projects that range from groups of individual houses to apartment blocks.[79] The integration of these first complexes into the urban center—the Presidente Alemán and Benito Juaréz units, and the Tlatelolco-Nonoalco urbanization—has not been continued into the 1970s, when low-cost housing was forced into the outlying areas. While in Ciudad Sahagún the schematic model of the isolated dwelling persists in the habitational unit "Vicente Guerrero" (8,850 units) five-story apartment blocks and two-family semidetached houses of one or two floors were used. The rigidity of this plan has been improved upon in three new complexes: "El Rosario" and "Iztacalaco," promoted by Infonavit (National Trust for Workers Housing Institute), and "Ermita Zaragoza" (4,500 units) in Mexico City. With these, the high-rise with elevator, such as Tlatelolco, is definitely abandoned. "El Rosario" represents the most successful urban structure, with a system of connecting buildings, pedestrian paths on different levels, and distinct spaces in which the services, crude and insufficient in relation to the density of the population, are located. "Iztacalco" is characterized by the brutalist style of its buildings with terraces, while "Ermita Zaragoza" represents a regression from the experimental thrust of certain residential prototypes: the individual house with slanting roof and exposed brick, repeated on a large scale, reproduces the model of the petty bourgeois house of the speculative commercial developments. The effect is of an infinite and compact superimposition of cottages, equipped with minimum public utilities. Retail trade and small artesan shops become difused and diluted over the whole neighborhood, because each dwelling has a space to be used as a workshop, thus fomenting the practice of "cottage industry," self-employment in isolation that allows only minimum survival for the individual.

In Cuba, housing is considered a public service, which is offered for rental to the population at a cost equivalent to 10 percent of the total family income. In the cities, individual houses have disappeared, and apartment blocks and high-rise housing of from five to twenty stories has made its appearance. Since 1970, an average of 25,000 to 30,000 housing units have been constructed annually, still short of the required minimum needed to meet the inherited shortage and the vegatative growth of the population. With respect to the other Latin American countries, the development of the habitat in Cuba possesses the following characteristics: (1) various models of housing units based on construction and technology exist, which do not affect any change in the standards or area assigned to each inhabitant; (2) building craft is carried out with popular participation, through a system called the "microbrigade" that integrates agricultural and industrial workers; (3) the development of prefabricated construction systems has been realized, with industrial plants distributed in different areas of the country; (4) the developments are equipped with services that vary in accordance with the dimensions of the complex. In some cases, light, nonpolluting industry is incorporated into the residential area; (5) plans for housing are distributed throughout the country in agreement with the needs established by population growth, linked to agro-industrial productivity plans.[80] Socialized ownership of the land provides ample freedom for localizing housing, although priority is given to the direct relationship between housing and employment. Finally, the designer's total control over new urban planning will permit the still visible contradictions, inherited from the capitalist city, to be overcome. The foundation has been laid for coherent and expressive environmental surroundings for the new society.

Contemporary Evaluation of Ciudad Guayana and Brasilia

As we conclude this analysis of the territorial and urban structures of Latin America, we cannot forget the two model cities that during the 1960s represented the most advanced experiments in Latin American urban planning: the industrial city, Ciudad Guayana, and the symbolic, administrative city, Brasília. However, at the close of the 1970s, the end results of both endeavors are not favorable, or, at least, they do not constitute a model for new urban planning to be carried out in the region. In short, what are the contradictory aspects of both cities?

Although both Brasília and Ciudad Guyana contain new formal concepts, on the social and functional level conflicts similar to those existing in traditional cities were repeated. Neither has been able to project its concepts beyond the city limits on a regional scale, nor has it been effective in achieving a symbolic context or in endowing daily life with the authentic values of the complex and multifaceted Latin American culture.

Ciudad Guayana, designed by experts from the universities of Harvard and MIT—the Joint Center for Urban Studies at MIT—is a productive, industrial center, that had its origin in the processing of iron ore found in nearby deposits. The mining, before nationalization in 1975, was in the hands of Bethlehem Steel, U.S. Steel, and the Orinoco Mining Company. Its prospect, still unachieved, was to become a center for heavy industrial growth of the region surrounding the pre-existing center, Ciudad Bolivar. Its population reached 50,000 in 1961; 150,000 in 1971; 211,000 in 1975; and an estimated 213,000 in 1980.[81] Although the planners assert that the promoting organization, the Venezuelan Corporation for Guayana, did not permit them to go beyond the strictly economic guidelines or to devote much attention to the sociological aspects, the urban plan maintains rigid segregation of social classes, which is indicated not only by territorial placement, but also by the type of housing provided which depends on the resident's level of income. It seems likely that similar policies will be followed in nationalizing the country's natural resources, but until now, there has been very little development of the central zone, including Caracas, Maracay, and Valencia.[82] In addition to these limitations in the productive base, there is the scarcity of services, the instability of the population, and the high percentage of population living in precarious dwellings. Therefore, no new ideas have arisen from this example that could give a different impetus to urban growth other than that linked to productivity. As an alternative we cite the creation of a university center or technical schools, based on the industrial specialties of the area. Ciudad Guayana with its one-dimensional, functional base becomes a modern and more elaborate version of the nineteenth-century company town.

Brasília is more contradictory, on account of its symbolic character, not only of a supposed new Brazil, but also of urbanistic creativity on the part of Latin American planners. It was barely inaugurated in 1960, after a race against time—it was supposed to be in operation before the presidential term of Juscelino Kubitschek came to an end. Overcoming the greatest technical and material adversities that have ever been confronted in the construction of a city—the basic structures built in thirty-six months, without access highways and with materials having to be transported by airplane—Brasília was seen as the concrete representation of the "Brazilian miracle." When an international symposium was held with famous architectural critics from developed countries, the discordant voice of Max Bill was heard among the praise, questioning the schematicism and formalism that had been substituted for the authentic Brazilian architectural tradition, which had been continued until the 1950s.

This criticism caused a negative reaction among the local planners, who saw at that time, beyond the formalism in Brasília, the expression of a democratic and free country that was rediscovering its nationality in the conquest and colonization of vast interior territories. Furthermore, if the principles of the "Charter of Athens" have never been fulfilled in an integral form, now the validity of Le Corbusier's statements would be demonstrated in America, interpreted by his two disciples, Lucio Costa and Oscar Niemeyer, in the creation of this "city for free men." These were principles that even the master was unable to fulfill. When planning Chandigarh, he fell into the subtle webs of stratification by caste of the Hindu society.

Brasília, on the other hand, constituted the palpable demonstration of "Latin American democracy," with its urbanistic expression realized in the homogeneity of the habitat, whose typological unity—the apartment blocks of the master plan, grouped into residential units (the super-blocks, inspired by the Le Corbusier dimension)—offered no possibility of manifesting a hypothetical stratification of social classes. Even the monumental quality of its axial layout was not considered to be an alien factor in the evaluation of the political structures of bourgeois "democracy," with the urban composition culminating in the Plaza de los Tres Poderes (Plaza of the Three Powers), the supposed symbol of the popular will manifested in the expansive plaza situated at the base of the pregnant forms of the Senate and the House of Deputies, designed by Niemeyer. It was not foreseen, at least by the designers, that the plaza would remain empty of people, and would be the surrealistic stage for "torrid" military parades.

Twenty years later, carrying this questioning to the limit, the "demopolis" has been transformed into a "necropolis."[83] Brazilian architects have reconsidered Max Bill's valid and severe criticisms. Democracy has long been lost, the symbols have changed meaning, rationalism and the "Charter of Athens" have been definitively buried. The young designers who once blindly admired Costa and Niemeyer as the champions of Brazilian architecture now perceive that Brasília did not constitute an "all-inclusive," "integrative," or "participational" experience. The search for "harmony," achieved through the now obsolete rationalist canons, required a closed experience, from which the majority of young architects were excluded.[84] Besides, the continuity of the spatial and environmental tradition, forged in colonial time and now recovered by the artistic vanguard, which constituted one of the most original aspects of the symbiosis between local traditions and the postulates of the modern movement, is absent from the urban environment of Brasília.

The actual functioning of the city presents an endless number of functional, technical, and sociological problems, clearly pointed out by Epstein.[85] But the best demonstration of Brasília's own internal contradictions, a direct reflection of those already existing in the country, is the social, functional, spatial, and formal contrast between the Pilot Plan and the ring of proletarian satellite cities, whose population is three times greater than the central area (approximately a hundred thousand inhabitants): Ceilandia (120,000 inhabitants); Taguatinga (80,000); Sobradinho (26,000); Gama (40,000); Núcleo Bandeirante (26,000); Vila do IAPI (17,500 inhabitants).[86] In order to preserve intact the original form of Lucio Costa's plan, the presence of substandard housing was prohibited in the area of the Pilot Plan. The beginnings of some such housing that were formed on the fringes of the city were removed by the military and relocated. In this manner, the objective of the ruling class was achieved, that of maintaining their living environment socially uncontaminated. The *favelas* on the hills, still visible from luxury residences in Rio de Janeiro, have disappeared from the vast plain of *Planalto*. The manual laborers, who with their efforts constructed Brasília and make its functioning possible, are excluded from architectural and urbanistic symbols controlled by the military-political system. As Pastore affirms, "while the *Plano Piloto* is called the stellar city of the twenty-first century; the satellite cities constitute residue from the nineteenth century."

In summary, the current urban and territorial panorama of Latin America, with isolated exceptions, proves dismal and disheartening for planners, urbanists, and architects who aspire to place their knowledge at the service of the population as a whole rather than of the limited and sophisticated ruling elite. Each year, thousands of environmental designers graduate from universities with no prospect of realizing their new ideas for transforming the space of Latin America. However, our faith in the progressive advancement of social, economic, and cultural change, in spite of momentary difficulties, gives us confidence that in the long run, the necessary environmental transformations that will physically express the hopes of the people, their cultural identity—their active participation in Latin American society—will occur when the decisions are made by the people themselves. And this will for action, this will for justice, this will for humanized environments, has already concretely materialized and indicates the path to follow.

Notes

1. Henry Russell Hitchcock, *Latin American Architecture since 1945,* New York: Museum of Modern Art, 1955.

2. CELADE, *Boletín Demográfico,* No. 15, year VIII, Santiago, Chile, January 1975, p. 7.

3. Ligia Herrera and Waldoziro Pecht, *Crecimiento urbano du América Latina.* Santiago, Chile: Banco Interamericano de Dasarrello, Centro Latinoamericano de Demografia (CELADE), 1976, p. 348.

4. The conditioning of the architecture in countries of the so-called Third World was defined at the beginning of the 1960s by the architect Fernando Salinas, general speaker for Seventh Congress of the International Union of Architects, held in Havana. See the proclaimed twelve points in: Fernando Salinas, "La arquitectura revolucionaria del Tercer Mundo," in *Ensayos sobre arquitecture eideología en Cuba revolutionaria.* Tecnología, Arquitectura, series 4, No. 2, Universidad de La Habana, May 1970, p. 18.

5. In a recent book still employing traditional terms, the autonomy of the individual artist and his work, expressed in interviews with the "great" architects is filtered, however by the contradictions of the Latin American environmental framework: on one side, photographs taken by Paolo Gasparini, ranging from the "antagonistic" environment to "refined" architectural works; on the other, the weight of conscience on the contextual system and its determinants, which is reflected in the replies of Rogelio Salmina, Fernando Salinas, or Pedro Ramirez Vázquez. See: Damián Bayón, Paolo Gasparini, *Panorámica de la arquitectura latinoamericana.* Barcelona: Blume/Unesco, 1977.

6.   We refer to the "evasive" tendency with respect to the contraditions that mark the development of an authentic Latin American architecture, developed by certain young Argentine architects—Diana Agrest, Mario Gandolsonas, Rodolfo Machado, Jorge Silvetti—who recognize, however, the determination imposed by the urban context. "Our perspective is based on the recognition of the necessity to establish in any physical intervention in the city a positive relation with the context." "Arquitectura como puesta en secuencia," in "Arquitectura critica—critica arquitectonica," *Summarios,* No. 13 (1977), Buenos Aires, p. 25.

7.   Different governments have created ministries and bodies that attempt to address globally the environmental problems: in Argentina, the Department of State for Natural Resources and the Human Environment and the Office for Human Environment; in Mexico, the General Law for Human Settlements was passed in 1976, and created the Department of Human Settlements and Public Works; in Cuba, the Group for Community Development (now CECONDEVI) is in charge of the planning and control of new urban and rural settlements from the social, economic, cultural, and formal points of view.

8.   The Charter of Machu Picchu was conceived in 1977 by a heterogeneous group of specialists—architects, city planners, and critics—from Latin America and the United States, assembled at the Universidad Nacional "Federico Villareal" in Lima, Peru. The only European in attendance was Bruno Zevi. This document, which attempts to modernize the "Charter of Athens" (1933) was awarded the Jean Tschumi prize in Mexico by the Thirteenth Congress of the International Union of Architects, plus a recognition from UNESCO. The members of the work group, who by our criteria did not constitute an appropriate representation of the existing architectural and theoretical tendencies in the hemisphere, were the following: Fernando Belaunde, Hector Velarde, Félix Candela, Leonardo J. Currie, Jorge Glusberg, Fruto Vivas, Pablo Pimentel, Felipe Préstamo, George Collins, Luis Miró Quesada, Dorn McGrath, Oscar L. de Guevara, Santiago Agurto, Francisco Carbajal, Alejandro Leal, Reginald Macolmson, Mark T. Jaroszewicz, Bruno Zevi, Manuel Ungaro, Oscar Alvarez, Elisabeth Carrasco, Guillermo Poyot, Carlos Morales, and Carlos A. Vargas Beltrán.

9.   *The Plan of Action from Vancouver.* The Sixty-four Recommendations for National Action approved in Habitat: United Nations Conference on Human Settlements, Vancouver, Canada, May 31 to June 11, 1976.

10.   The obvious answer to this question is that the state represents the interests of the ruling class. This concept was clearly defined by Engels, Marx, and Lenin: "The state is the product and manifestation of the *irreconcilable* character of class contradictions. . . . According to Marx, the state is an instrument for class domination, an instrument for the oppression of one class by another . . ." and finally Lenin affirms: "That the state is an instrument for dominating a particular class, which can now be conciliated with the opposing class, is something that the petty bourgeois democracy will never be able to understand." V. I. Lenin, *El Estado y la Revolución.* Havana: Editorial de Ciencias Sociales, 1971, p. 5. Also see: Friedrich Engels, *El origen de la familia, la propiecad privada y el Estado.* La Habana: Editora Política, 1903.

11.   Akin L. Mabogunje, R. P. Misra, Jorge E. Hardoy, "Aspectos ambientales de los asentamientos humanos: estándares y criterios en la provisión de alojamiento." *Revista Interamericana de Planificación,* No. 39, September 1976, p. 45. In this essay, presented at Habitat in Vancouver, the following "radical" conclusions were reached to impede land speculation, adapt technology to the precarious material conditions of "underdevelopment" and attenuate the social stratification by convincing "the wealthy classes to subsidize the poor." Euphemistically considered as an expression of the "cultural standards" of the masses, the substandard dwellings were finally accepted with fatalism. The escapism with regard to realistic solutions that would change the habitational "standards" for society's exploited strata was clearly discernible.

12.   Rafael López Rangel, "Asentamentos para el sistema o asenlamientos para los pueblos? Una reseña política de la conferencia y el Foro de Vancourvet." *Cuandernes da*

Arquitacetura Latinoamericana, 2/3, May 1977. Departamento de Investigaciones Arquitectónicas y Urbanas, Universidad Autónoma de Puebla, México, p. 51.

13. Jorge E. Hardoy, *Ciundades precolombinas.* Buenos Aires: Ediciones Infinito, 1964.

14. *Tipos predominantes de vivienda natural en la República Argentina.* Vr. 2/IVV, 4. Institute Nacional de Colonización y Régimen de la Tierra, Instituto de Investigaciones de la Vivienda. Facultad de Arquitectura y Urbanismo, Universidad de Buenos Aires, n.d.

15. Federico F. Ortiz, Juan C. Montero, Ramón Gutierrez, Abelardo Levaggi, Ricardo G. Perera, *La arquitectura del liberalismo en la Argentina.* Buenos Aires: Editorial Sudamericana, 1968.

16. An architectural and urbanistic study on the productive structures created by United States monopolies in Latin America has yet to appear. In Cuba, historic and economic research only peripherally touches upon the theme. See: Oscar Zanetti and Alejanoro García, *United Fruit Company: un caso de dominio imperialista en Cuba.* Havana: Editorial de Ciencias Sociales, 1976; Manuel Moreno Fraginals, *El ingenio, complejo económico social cubano de asúcar,* Tomos I/II/III. La Habana: Editorial de Ciencias Sociales, 1978.

17. Ismael Morera, "Crecimiento económico y equidad social: escenario de futuras sociedad es en América Latina." Report for the conference held under the auspices of the German Foundation for Developing Countries, Bonn, RFA, 1972 (mimeo, Havana).

18. CEPAL, *Desarrollo humano, cambio social y crecimiento en América Latina.* Santiago, Chile: Cuadernos de la Cepal, 1975, p. 17.

19. Jorge E. Hardoy, *Las ciudades en América latina,* Buenos Aires: Paidós, 1972, p. 90.

20. Pedro Cuscó, *Balance Crítico, Balance de la economía latinoamericana, 1959–1974.* La Habana: Editorial de Ciencias Sociales, 1978, p. 11.

21. Orlando Fals Borda. *La revolucienes inconclusas en América Latina* (1909–1968), Mexico: Siglo XXI, 1968.

22. Experience has proven that the bourgeois governments' programs for modifying land ownership under such forms as selling on credit to the rural population or colonization plans for the wilderness and insalubrious zones do not resolve the agrarian problem. On the contrary, they have become fruitful businesses for the landowning bourgeoisie and the imperialistic monopolies and maneuvers for halting the struggles for authentic agrarian reform. Declaration of the Communist Parties of Latin America and the Caribbean, *Granma,* June 16, 1977, La Habana, p. 2.

23. Alejandro B. Rafman, "Resultados obtenidos en el proceso de planificación en América Latina." *Revista Interamericana de Planificación,* No. 38, Vol. X (June 1976), Bogotá, p. 72.

24. Rigoberto García, "El proceso de planificación en Latinoamerica." *Revista Latioamericana de Planificación,* No. 44, Vol. XI (December 1977). Mexico, p. 5.

25. Pedro Cuscó, *Balance Critics,* p. 6. Between 1947 and 1973, direct capital investment in Latin America totaled 9.239 million dollars. During the same period, the branches returned 21.765 million dollars.

26. Walter B. Stöhr, *El deserrollo regional en América Latina. Experiencias y Perspectivas,* Buenos Aires: Siap, 1972, p. 167.

27. After the 1960s, progressive inflation began to affect every Latin American country, with the major consequences falling most heavily on the rural and proletarian populations. The nations' debts with the exterior also continued to climb: from 2 billion dollars in 1950, they rose to almost 30 billion dollars in 1975. See Pedro Cuscó, *Balance Crítico,* p. 6.

28. José Antonio Marillo. "Las ciudades industriales de México. Una experiencia latinoamericana en el desarrollo urbano." *Revista latino-americana de Planificación,* No. 37,

Vol. X (March 1976), Mexico, p. 73. In the same issue see: Luis Unikel, "Ensayo sobre políticas de desarrollo regional en México," p. 54.

29.   This plan clearly establishes the links between the national bourgeoisie and the foreign monopolies by fomenting light industries and urban building, as well as by the expulsion of the rural population in order to expand the large landed estates and modernize the productive structures. See Ramiro Carmona, editor, *Colombia: distribucion espacial de la población.* Bogota: Corporatión Centro Regional de Població, 1976, p. 234; and Emilio Pradilla Cobos, "La política urbana de Estado colombiano," in Manuel Castells, compiler, *Estructura de clases y política urbana en América Latina.* Buenos Aires: Ediciones Siap, 1974, p. 76.

30.   Sistema Metropolitano Bonaerense," SUMMA 113 (June 1977), Buenos Aires, p. 42.

31.   See the special issues "Patagonia I y II" in the journal *SUMMA,* No. 90 (June 1975) and 91/92 (July/August 1975). Also the "Plan Integral para el desarrollo del Turisio en la provincia del Chubut, *SUMMA,* No. 63 (June 1973), Buenos Aires.

32.   Hector Echechuri, Marta Balderiote, Carlos Adlerstein, "Aspectos de planeamiento ambiental en el proyecto de Salto Grande," *SUMMA* 106 (November 1976), p. 23.

33.   Martin T. Katzman, *Cities and Frontiers in Brazil: Regional Dimensions of Economic Development.* Cambridge, Mass.: Harvard University Press, 1977, p. 80.

34.   Jean Pierre Monnet, "L'Amazonie est à vendre," *L'architecture d'aujourd'hui* No. 172 (March/April, 1974), Paris, p. 5.

35.   Betty J. Meggers, *Amazonia, un paraísc ilusario.* Mexico: Siglo XXI, 1976, p. 221. In some zones where the jungle has been cleared, other problems have arisen: land erosion, accelerated loss of vegetation, changes in the rain cycle, increase in the surface temperature.

36.   Gonzalo Yánez Diaz, "Consideraciones sobre el desarrollo urbano y regional en Centro América." *Cuadernos de Arquitectura Latinoamericana,* No. 1, June 1976, Departamento de Investigaciones Arquitectónicas y Urbanas. Universidad Autónoma de Puebla, p. 39.

37.   Documentos del Seminario Latinoamericano sobre Reforma Agraria (Chiclayo), Peru, 1971.

38.   Abel Núñez Ortega, "Del *Avllu* a las cooperatives agrarias do produccion." *América Latina* 3 (Moscow), 197, p. 84. Counting only the CAP and the SAIS—the two most important cooperatives—472,000 hectares are currently cultivated, or 22 percent of the country's total surface area of existing agricultural land.

39.   J. P. Cousin, "Andahuasi. Question sur le projet d'architect." *L'architecture d'aujourd'hui,* No. 173 (May/June 1974), p. 27.

40.   Willy Bezold, Jorge Cabrera and Helan Jaworski. "La planificación participante y la planificación de base en el Perú, *Revista Interamericana de Planificación,* No. 34, vol. IX (June 1975), Bototá, p. 5.

41.   Moisés Bedrack, *La estrategia de desarrollo espacial en Chile (1970–1973),* Buenos Aires: SIAP, 1974.

42.   Gonzalo Martner, "La estructura de un sistema nacional de planificación." *Revista Interamericana de Planificación,* No. 23 (September 1972), Bogotá, p. 13.

43.   Manuel Castells, "Reforma Agraria, lucha de clases y poder popular en el camp chileno." Documento de trabajo No. 58, CIDU, mimeo, Universidad Católica de Chile, October 1972, p. 19.

44.   *Arquitectura de la Reforma Agraria. Temuco,* Departamento de Arquitectura de la Universidad Católica de Chile, October 1972, p. 19.

45.   Bartolomé Hernández, "Chile: balance para un modelo." *Economíz y Desarrollo,* No. 30 (July/August 1975), La Habana: p. 81.

46.   José Acosta, "La revolución agraria en Cuba y el desarrollo económico," 1972.

Report of the Seventh Conference of Agricultural Economy of the West Indies. Instituto de Economía, Universidad de La Habana.

47. Sección cubana FPAA, *Cuba, la vivienda, desarrello urbano.* La Habana: Editorial Ceditec, 1975, p. 75. The construction of new towns has produced a sharp decrease in the number of shacks: from 340,000 in 1953 to 260,000 in 1970. The index in relation to rural housing has decreased from 73 percent of the total to 38.5 percent.

48. Jorge E. Hardoy, *Las ciudades en América Latina,* Buenos Aires: Paidés, 1972, p. 70.

49. John Durand and César A. Pelácz, "Patterns of Urbanization in Latin America," in Gerald Breese, editor, *The City in Newly Developing Countries: Readings on Urbanism and Urbanization.* London: Prentice-Hall, 1972, p. 178.

50. On this point, historians, writers, and technical experts are in agreement. José Luis Romero maintains that the history of Latin American urban culture is the most dynamic and representative expression of the social conglomerate, representing the different influential strata of the continent. (José Luis Romero, *Latinoamerica: las ciudades y la ideas,* Mexico: Siglo XXI, 1976.) On the other hand, Carpentier supports the original dialectical character of our cities, which distinguishes them from cities found in parts of the world: "Ours, on the other hand, and for a very long time, have been in a process of symbiosis, amalgams, and transmutations, as much architecturally as humanly." (Alejo Carpentier, "Problemática de la actual novela latino-americana," in *Tientos v diferencias,* La Habana: Uneac, 1974, p. 15.) Finally, Morese, in analyzing the development of São Paulo, is unable to obviate either Chico Buarque de Holanda or Carlos Maringhela. ("São Paulo: estudio de una metropolis industrial," in Richard Morse, *Las ciudades latinoamericanas* l. Antecedents. Mexico: Sep-Setentas, 1973, p. 125 ff.)

51. J. Anthony S. Ternent. "Hacia políticas nacionales de urbanización en América Latina." In Ramiro Cardona, *América Latina: distribución espacial de la población. Bogotá*: Corporación Centro Regional de Población, 1975, p. 322.

52. Jorge E. Hardoy, "Políticas de urbanización y reforma urbana en América Latina," in J. E. Hardoy, Guillermo Guissa, comp., *Políticas de desarrollo urbano y regional en América Latina,* Buenos Aires: Ediciones SIAP, 1972, p. 128.

53. Pavel Boyko, *América Latina: expansión del imperialismo y crisis de la via capitalista de desarrollo,* Moscow: Editorial Progreso, 1977, p. 205.

54. Yakov Mashbits, "Organización y ubicación de las fuerzas productivas en América Latina," *América Latina* No. 4 (1975), Moscow, p. 44.

55. Alejo Carpentier, "Problemática de la actual novela latinoamericana," p. 15.

56. These centers already exist in Rio de Janeiro and São Paulo. The Directorship of the Association for Centers of World Commerce has already planned for a similar one in Caracas, a city which has increasingly become a financial center in Latin America. The Bank of America, one of the world's largest, moved its Latin American division from San Francisco to Caracas. "La ciudad para el hombre. Foro en defensa de la Ciudad." Facultad de Arquitectura y Urbanismo, Universidad Central de Venezuela. *Punto,* No. 60, year XVII (May 1978), Caracas, p. 25.

57. "Area de remodelación en el centro de Santiago de Chile." *SUMMA* 87 (March 1975), Buenos Aires, p. 23.

58. An interpretative reading of the significance of these commercial centers has been developed in Silvia Arango, "A propósito de 'Unicentro,' una perspective semiológica," in Carlos Castillo, *Vida urbana y urbanismo.* Bogotá: Instituto colombiano de cultura, 1977, p. 335.

59. Congresos Internacionales de Arquitectura Moderna (CIAM). *La Carta de Atenas,* Buenos Aires: Editorial Contémpora, 1957. In this document, the emphasis is placed more on monuments than on the protection of urban historic clusters.

60.   Knud Bastlund, José Luis Sert. *Architecture, City Planning, Urban Design.* London: Thames and Hudson, 1967.

61.   Consejo Internacional de los Monumentos y de los Sitios. Carta International sobre la conservación y la restauración de los monumentos y de los sitios, Venecia, 1964. Article 1: "The notion of the monument is understood as an isolated architectural creation, as well as urban or rural site which offers us a testimony from a particular civilization, a representative phase in evolution or progress, or an historic event."

62.   Normas de Quito. Informe Final de la Reunión sobre, Conservación y Utilización de Monumentos y Lugares de Interés Histórico y Artístico. *Colegio de Arquitectos del Estado de Jalisco,* AC, No. 13 (January/February 1978), *Guadalajara,* p. 59. On those aspects cited, see chapters VII, "Los monumentos en función cel turismo," and VIII, "El interés social y la acción cívica."

63.   Ley Federal sobre Monumentos y Zonas Arqueológicas, Artísticas e Históricas (Diario Oficial, May 6, 1972). *Colegio de Arquitectos del Estado de Jalisco* AC, No. 12 (November/December 1977), Guadalajara, p. 63. Chapter IV described the characteristics and restrictions that govern the monumental areas.

64.   Some of the most important ones, for the work realized, include the following: the Institute for American Art and Esthetic Research, founded by Mario J. Buschiazzo at the School of Architecture and Urbanism of the Universidad de Buenos Aires; the Center for Historic and Esthetic Research, created by Graziano Gasparini at the Universidad Central de Venezuela; the Institute for Esthetic Research at the Universidad Nacional Autónoma de México; the Department of Conservation of the Historic Patrimony and the Department of the History of Architecture headed by Ramón Gutierrez and Ricardo J. Alexander at the Universidad Nacional del Nordeste in Argentina; the Group for Historic Research on Architecture and Urbanism, of the Department of Architecture at the Facultad de Construcciones, La Habana.

65.   *Coloquio sobre la preservación delos Centros Históricos ante el crecimiento de las ciudades contemporaneas.* Dirección Nacional de Patrimonio Artístico, Quito: casa de la Cultura Ecuatoriana, 1977.

66.   "Conclusiones del Symposium Interamericano de Conservación del Patrimonio Artístico," Instituto Naicional de Bellas Artes, Mexico, 1978, *Casa de las Americas,* No. 114, La Habana, p. 164.

67.   Sylvio Mutal, Introduccion to *Coloquio sobre la preservació*n de los Centros Históricos ante el crecimiento de las ciudades contemporáneas, p. 4

68.   Emma Scovazzi, "Una obra mayor del urbanismo sudamericano que se pierde: el Centro Histórico de Quito," *SUMMA* 77, June 1974, Buenos Aires, p. 73. In the analysis of the center, contained in the directive plan, it says: "The walls of the cloisters and convents have been destroyed so that they could be replaced by grotesque commercial imitations of colonial architecture. Stores, signs, and placards now decorate the once sober and cold walls which imposed austerity and accented the character of our severe architecture. Everything is saleable; everything is rentable. The altars are adorned with signs made of florescent lights and colored paper which hide the filigree of the original decoration. Stone floors have been covered with vinyl tiles. . . ."

69.   José de Mesa Figuero, "Un progetto per la valcrizzazione dei siti archeologici: il piano Copesco." Milan: *Enciclopedia della scienza e della scienza e della technica Mondadori,* 1975, p. 242. The author, director of the general project, shows optimism for fulfilling the proposed objectives during the period 1973 to 1978. In reality, these objectives were not realized. In the recent balance for project PER-39, the incompletion of the restoration plans, in addition to administrative obstacles imposed by the Peruvian agencies, inadequate scientific procedures in the restoration of monuments, lack of participation of the local population in the

works and projects, concessions to commercial tourism, and the authorization for the implantation of luxury hotels in the historic areas, which would destroy the environmental unity of the sites, are all verified. See Ramón Gutierrez, "Preservación en Cusco, una esperanza frustrada," *Documentos de arquitectura nacional y americana,* No. 6 (September 1978), No. 6 Instituto argentino de investigaciones en historia de la arquitectura, Resistencia, p. 84.

70.   Philip M. Hauser, *La urbanización en América Latina,* Paris: UNESCO, 1962.

71.   Rigoberto Garcia, "El proceso de planificación en Latinoamerica," p. 14.

72.   Akin L. Mabogunje, R. P. Misra, Jorge E. Hardoy, "Aspectos ambientales de los asentamientos humanos," p. 14.

73.   The idea is accepted and promoted by CEPAL as well as by the World Bank. A report from CEPAL affirms: "Governmental attention was periodically overturned on the presumably less honorable technologies, which supposed a tacit or express recognition of the legitimacy of the peripheral settlements." (CEPAL, Desarrollo humano, cambio social y crecimiento en América Latina, Santiago de Chile, 1975.) On the other hand, Robert Ronamara affirms: "Consequently, the projects for 'sites and services' stimulate self-help and enable the low-income population reside in housing in coherent and viable communities at a minimum of public expense." (Housing, Sector Policy Paper, Washington: World Bank, May 1975.)

74.   Emilio Pradilla, "Notas acerca del 'problema de la vivienda,' " *Arquitectura/Autogobierno* 7 (July/August 1977). Escuela nacional de arquitectura-autogobierno, Mexico: UNAMO. Also Emilie Pradilla and Carlos Jimenez, *Arquitectura, Urbanismo, y Dependencia neocolonial,* Buenos Aires: Ediciones SIAP, 1973.

75.   John F. C. Turner, *Libertad para construir,* Mexico: Siglo XXI, 1976, and *Vivienda, todo el poder para los usuarios,* Madrid: Blume, 1977.

76.   These ideas appear in the proposals realized in Peru at the PREVI competition, organized by the United Nations and Peruvian Bank for Housing. Christopher Alexander, Sanford Hirshen, Sara Ishikawa, Christine Coffin, Shlomo Angel, *Houses Generated by Patterns,* Berkeley, California: Center for Environmental Structure, 1969; also Peter Land, *Economic Garden Houses: High Density Development Design, Planning, Landscape.* College of Architecture, Planning and Design. Chicago: Illinois Institute of Technology, 1977.

77.   William P. Mangin and John C. Turner, "Benavides y el movimiento de las barriadas," in Paul Oliver, *Cobijo v Sociedad,* Madrid: Blume, 1978, p. 139. In this text, a distorted interpretation of objective reality appears: "In Peru, the spontaneous settlements on the margin of the law have managed to establish a satisfactory relationship with the urban surroundings, at the same time more economic and better for the soical and political morale than the current solution of government housing."

78.   John J. Harrigan, "Political Economy and the Management of Urban Development in Brazil," in Wayne A. Cornelius and Felicity M. Trueblood, *Urbanization and Inequality: The Political Economy of Urban and Rural Development in Latin America.* Vol. 5, Latin American Urban Research. Beverly Hills: Sage Publications, 1975, p. 207. "In Rio de Janeiro a major project for the expulsion of *favelas* was developed, where close to 175,000 *favelados* (hut dwellers) were relocated by the National Bank for Housing (BNH) and the agency for urban remodeling (CHISAM) between 1968 and 1971. Another 600,000 were relocated between 1971 and 1976.

79.   Rafael López Rangel, *Contribución a la visión crítica de la arouitectura.* Departamento de Investigaciones Arquitectónicas y Urbanísticas del Instituto de Ciencias a la Universidad Autónoma de Puebla, 1977, p. 115. "From 1960 to 1970, the Mexican state constructed 90,495 housing units. Presently, the program of different agencies, created for this purpose, are working on a little more than 140,000 units.'"

80.   Roberto Segre, *La vivienda en Cuba: República y Revolución,* Departamento de Cultura, Universidad de La Habana, 1979.

81.   Ligia Herrera and Waldomiro Pecht, *Crecimiento urbano de América Latina,* p. 311.

82.   Fernando Travieso, *Ciudad, región, y subdesarrollo.* Caracas: Fondo Editorial Comín, 1972, p. 1940.

83.   Massimo Gennari, "Delenda Brasilia," *Domus* 562 (September 1976), Milan, p. 9. "The consequences of the processes of structural disarticulation, which are produced in a metropolitan area in a regimen of economic and political dependence, are expressed, in fact, as a projection on a new social order, replete with prophetic symbols and unavoidable features of the necropolis."

84.   Luis Paulo Conde, Julio Katinsky, Miguel Alves Pereira, *Arquiteture brasileira apos Brasilia/Depoimentos.* Rio de Janeiro: Instituto dos Arquitetos do Brasil, 1978, p. 14.

85.   David G. Epstein. *Brasília: Plan and Reality,* Berkeley: University of California Press, 1973.

86.   There are certain divergences with respect to the total population of Brasilia. The population residing in the Plano Piloto is considered to be between 100,000 and 140,000 inhabitants. The population of satellite towns is estimated at 300,000, although a recent study (Schilling) has increased the total population of the eight satellite cities to 700,000. See Pierre Merlin, Les villes nouvelles, Paris: Presses Universitaires de France, 1972, p. 252; Jose Pastore, *Brasília: a cidade e o homem,* Companhia Editora Nacional. Editora da Universidade de São Paulo, 1969, p. 5; Paulo Schilling, "Brasília, esperanza fallida," *Prisma Lationamericano,* No. 83 (July 1979), La Habana, p. 26.

3 / The Present Significance of the Architecture of the Past

GRAZIANO GASPARINI

SOCIAL STRUCTURES AND ARTISTIC MANIFESTATIONS

In order to understand the cultural role of colonial cities it is necessary to know the level of culture of the "colonizer," and in this regard it must be admitted that the level of Spanish thought in the seventeenth century was not the best-suited for encouraging progressive influences on its colonies. Spain lived in a world apart in which "neither the values of rational logic and meticulous analysis that characterized the French in the seventeenth century, nor the worldly, concrete empiricism of the English had any value in this somewhat magical world that raised the labyrinthine construction of her theology up to heaven. For the other peoples of Europe the 'kingdom of man' had begun; Spain still wanted to be the 'kingdom of God.' "[1] Without realizing the importance of the rise of European capitalism, and with an economic structure devoted to the maintenance of parasitic social groups Spain, motivated by religious fanaticism and "convinced of her saving mission, presided over the cultural transformation of Latin America, profoundly determining the character of her colonies and condemning them to backwardness. However, without the doctrinal content as a motivation, Iberian expansion would not have had the power of assimilation that allowed Spain to live with so many different peoples on whom she imposed her cultural and religious stamp, or the ability to take action in her confrontation with them."[2]

In fact, *salvationism* can explain Spain's justification of her presence in America: the evangelizing mission aimed at winning over the Indians to the Catholic faith. It is clear that this is no more than a simple rationalization of the process of exploitation of raw materials and labor. This activity has not attracted the attention of the historians of colonial art and has almost been ignored in analyzing her profound impression on colonial society and, consequently, on its cultural manifestations. It is significant to state that "Christianity, Language and Architecture are the three great legacies that Spain left to that vast continent,"[3] without even mentioning that other great legacy—the economic, social, and cultural backwardness that ultimately permitted Latin America's underdevelopment.

Socioanthropological studies have documented the component relationships of colonial society and have not hesitated to demonstrate the contrasting conditions of prosperity and poverty, arbitrariness and subjugation that constituted the norms of life during those three centuries. On the other hand, interpretations of the fine arts and architecture of the same period give the impression that colonial art was produced in a climate of quiet serenity and well-being that permitted free, creative, and autonomous artistic activity almost completely removed from European influences. This position is the result of a traditional, partisan historical methodology based on erudition without content that inhibits a vital, modern understanding of cultural facts because it utilizes colonial art as a means of sublimating that period. It is disturbing to note that this tendency exists as much among some American historians who view colonial art as an autonomous artistic expression as it does in Spain, where that same art is considered to be an extension of the Spanish artistic sense and, consequently, is analyzed in terms of *Hispanism* and *invariables*.

Spanish historians have always tried to prove that Spanish architecture has its own exclusive uniqueness that is different from the rest of Europe, because they believe that such "differences are composed of the pure and traditional invariables [constants] present throughout the history of Spanish architecture."[4] By the same token colonial architecture has been interpreted as Hispano-American or as a provincial extension of Spain. Angulo finds that Mexican baroque architecture is only "another manifestation, albeit an important one, of the Spanish baroque."[5] The self-sufficiency theory of the stylistic and expressive autonomy of Spain has the same defects as the Mexican theory that tries to prove the *Mexicanism* of colonial art in that country. In both cases the force behind the theories is a pedantic nationalism that deforms reality.

For the same reasons it is not appropriate to analyze colonial architecture in terms of invariables. The theory of invariables, rather than critically evaluating the elements of change, proposes to emphasize the constant elements. It analyzes the work of art which, as it occurs, is always the same and never the same. It calls on this sameness to prove that Latin American architecture is the same as Spain's, and when concrete reference is made to Spain it is used to demonstrate the persistence, self-sufficiency, and indifference of the Hispanic in the face of European architectural movements.[6] The theory of the insular condition of Spain also serves to support the permanence of the invariables and to avoid the harsher theory of a state of backwardness and intellectual stasis that has its origin in the difficulty of freeing oneself from one's indebtedness to tradition.

The invariables can be related to the concept of indefinitiveness or typological generality; they are not based on the invention of forms but are derived, rather, from a series of patterns or models. The concept of the invariable is related to formal and functional analogy; it is a schema of a common, basic form-function deduced from a sum of formal-functional variants. Consequently, even when the invariables originate in the experience of artistically produced forms, they nullify the original creative value by dint of passive repetition. Esthetically, they are of limited interest because they deal with a negative, introverted phase stressing popular and traditional components. Moreover, we associate affinities, repetitions, and common traits with the invariables; they are all nonproblematical matters that join together the most general visual characteristics instead of analyzing what is unique and distinctive.

There is no denying that some colonial cities were centers that reached a certain artistic standard of quality and served as models to be followed and imitated. But it was a derivative artistic standard suited to cities that received imported cultural patterns conveniently adapted for colonial use. My basic premise is that only those cities that generated original and creative impulses radiated cultural significance and influence. For example, Rome and Florence in the past, Paris, London, and New York in the present were and are true centers of cultural influence; on the other hand, the possibility of producing autonomous, native artistic expressions did not exist in the American cities of the colonial period because of their very condition of being colonial and ruled by a system of inevitable dependence. Even in the colonial cities of a certain stature, like Mexico City and Lima, artistic activities were always derived from European models. For that reason what radiated from them was artistically of a provincial quality that would eventually be deformed when it spread to the periphery. Consequently, the colonial city, because it lacked the necessary level of culture, instead of being a center of influence that furthered the formation of artistic schools, was a center for the diffusion of selected forms and concepts that had passed through rigorous controls before being considered appropriate for divulgence.

To my mind the term *school* can be applied to an artistic activity that shows the influence of an exceptional artist, or that reveals specific formal and conceptual preferences accepted and shared within a determined area or period. In either case the school derives its expression from a series of experiences and pursuits. In the cases of colonial artistic manifestations, instead of employing the term schools, I consider it more appropriate to employ *regional expressions,* because when an artistic activity is controlled by directives and principles that inhibit the development of individual and collective experience, the appearance of critical processes and the pursuit of direct experiences is not possible. It is true that in the pictorial production of any American region a unifying and characteristic stamp has been achieved in the totality of the works as, for example, in the so-called Cuzco School, but that peculiar regional similarity, rather than deriving from principles of experience, comes from the acceptance without any other alternatives of the principles of authority.

Individual and collective experience implies a search, the rejection of the culture that expresses the system, and rebellion against the passive acceptance of schemata that express the principles of authority. It is evident that such conditions were not present in colonial culture because the authoritarian system imposed a world structure given as the one revealed by the supreme spiritual authority—the Church—which impeded any effort to discover reality and truth in the development of experience. And from this it followed that the structure accepted *a priori* as the immutable structure of truth ruled colonial thought for three centuries.

The difference between the social structures of colonial America and those of Europe also helps us understand the differences between artistic manifestations on both continents. American art achieved a distinctive specificity not only because of its provincialism but also because of the way in which the ideas that were allowed into the New World were applied and put into practice. Despite their common nexus, those ideas produced different attitudes simply because the way they were channeled was different and, as a result, they also had a different effect on those living in the colonial world. What becomes important, therefore, is the study of the ideas behind all artistic thought, and of the varied consequences that manifest themselves in artistic production when conditions appear that alter the apparently unified character of those ideas.

Since they were subject to orders from Europe the capital cities of colonial America, as Kubler has demonstrated,[7] belonged more to the category of regional capitals than to the hierarchy of capitals where power is concentrated. Although "the internal organization and functions became American and colonial rather than European,"[8] and "in practical matters they operated as true metropolitan centers with almost autonomous concentration of power and decision-making capacity,"[9] in the area of culture they never moved away from European influences and antecedents. The fact that the colonial capital cities were subjected to foreign political directives and cultural models justifies our stating that the American colonies, because they were colonies, had no true capital cities. When Mexico City and Lima are called the capitals of vice regencies, that description should be interpreted symbolically as limited to a merely administrative territorial division because, if by *capital* one understands the seat of power, it is evident that the capital of the Spanish possessions in America was Madrid.

Architecture has always reflected the supremacy and extent of power in its monumentality. The monumentality of the main square in Mexico City, the Zócalo, produces the greatest sense of the presence and strength of power; however, in comparison to the European palaces of the seventeenth century it is clear that the capital of Mexico, besides being the seat of the *power that rules,* is at the same time the seat of *power ruled* by the European capital. The palaces in America were built to a *human scale,* to the measure of administrators rather than of kings and princes. Viceroys and governors occupied high positions in colonial bureaucracy, but they still belonged to the category of those who were "in the service of the king" and they held those positions only so long as it suited the king. Spending enormous sums of money on the construction of palaces in America meant, after all, less money in the royal coffers. The viceroyal palace in Mexico City is a notable building, but it is modest when compared to the residence of any prince elector in southern Germany.

On the other hand, religious architecture enjoyed special privileges; its buildings had to demonstrate the power won back by the Church during the Counter-Reformation, make visible the triumph of Catholicism over pre-Columbian idolatry, keep the work of evangelization and indoctrination alive in the indigenous population while, at the same time, it overwhelmed that population with the exuberant opulence of its gilded alterpieces. Moreover, the wealth accumulated by the Church allowed it to carry out a vast construction activity that was easily justified by spiritual needs and the "dignity of the faith."

PERIPHERAL CULTURAL MANIFESTATIONS

The design of the colonial capitals had nothing to do with local traditions or with the persistence of pre-Columbian urban concepts. Leaving aside the exceptional cases of adaptation such as Cuzco and Cholula, the monotonous form of the checkerboard plan, imported from Europe, acquired American characteristics through the insistent repetition of this scheme in the foundation of almost all cities. The gridiron plan appeared in American cities from the first foundations and predated the regulating norms that the Spanish lawmakers dictated for urban planning. The Laws of the Indies compiled the principles of what had already been realized and expressed them in a language that had its origins in theoretical sources such as the treatise by Vegecio, the *De regimene principium* of St. Thomas, the *Crestià* by the Catalonian Eiximenis, the treatises of Alberti and of Vitruvius. In my opinion there is no essential difference between the opinions of those who interpret the checkerboard plan as a classical inheritance and those who see in it the application of modern norms, because both concepts share a continuity and persistence which, although occasionally inactive, had never disappeared totally from Western culture. It is a concept that was established in the classical period, that was kept alive among the dormant ideas of the Middle Ages despite limited usage, and that the culture of the Renaissance put into practice and modernized because the will to order and control, identified with Renaissance culture, was compatible with it. This modernism, therefore, rather than representing the application of new and original ideas, was derived from ideas that had been revived. The acceptance of the schema and its invariable repetition on American soil helped to perfect it.

The level of cultural dependence typical of colonial America imprinted the unavoidable characteristics of provincialism on its architecture. The phenomenon of provincialism is one of derivation, submission, imitation, and separation from the activities of the great centers of primary creative development. Although they did not entirely overcome the local variants that were sometimes rich in originality, in America the same aspects of provincialism were produced that have appeared and still do appear in all peripheral cultural manifestations. The concept of colonial art is inevitably related to provincialism and, in the case of America, this established her as a receptive zone linked to great centers of religious and cultural influence. Although colonial architecture is essentially repetitive, the sum total of the different regional expressions and the various contributions originating from different sources made up an expressive totality that achieved a differentiated character that was both specific and unified. The conglomerate of different contributions was not integrated into a chronological, geographical, or sociological order. This variability has favored piecemeal analysis rather than an understanding of the unifying elements contained in the diversity. The differences among levels of regional expression are undeniable, but the provincial character is uniform. Therefore, "unity in diversity" permits the formulation of a theoretical model that allows us to understand the phenomenon.

Among the different cultural areas in colonial America one can point out the presence of elements that are the same for all and, at the same time, the presence of elements that exist exclusively in certain regions. For example, while the salomonic column appears in all of Hispano-America, the *estípite* (an inverted pyramidal pedestal) is a peculiarity of New Spain and a rarity in South America. Domes resting on a drum or octagonal base are also repeated constantly in New Spain, while in South America the circular form predominates. Generally, in Mexico, the surface decoration of the facades reaches a more pronounced exuberance and has a very different character from those in South America, where more restraint in decorative enthusiasm and greater fondness for classical forms are manifested. One notices greater similarity and a more unified level of expression in examples from peripheral areas: the popular monuments in the Arequipa-Callao zone do not differ substantially from those in Cajamarca, Guatemala, and other places in Mexico. In all of these manifestations, despite distances and differences, one breathes the same familial air—dialectal, primitive, and characteristic of areas that are cut off from more advantaged artistic centers.

The reasons for the differences between New Spain and South America have their roots in cultural contacts that originate in different sources, and in the degree to which received forms were subsequently reelaborated. South America received more non-Iberian influences than New Spain, which in turn maintained closer contact with the mother country; the presence of Spanish artists like Gerónimo de Balbás and Lorenzo Rodríguez in the eighteenth century encouraged the diffusion and reelaboration of the forms introduced by them.

Foster has shown how prior acceptance of a form or architectural element can exclude the acceptance of others, so that the mere priority of an imported and accepted form can be decisive in the formal character of later activities.[10] Thus, the regional expression of a specific area reveals differences when compared with that of another because in each the preferential acceptance of characteristics thought of as models is manifestly clear. The repetition and diffusion of the model within its zone of influence, although it may undergo the inevitable changes resulting from reinterpretation and local contributions, never loses its connection with the original formal idea: it makes its presence felt in the region and establishes the formal similarities that help to underline the common traits of that regional expression. For more than a century the towers of the Cathedral of Cuzco were a regional model for areas beyond Lake Titicaca; "planiform" decoration made its influence felt from Arequipa to distant Potosí; the classicist models of Quito had repercussions in Pasto, Popayán, and Cali; the ornamentation of local plasterers also invaded the region, and the works of Gerónimo Balbás and Lorenzo Rodríguez were the models which gave impetus to the move away from altarpieces with inverted pyramidal pedestals (*estípites*) and the exuberance of altarpiece facades. Decentralization, distance, and few contacts between one zone of influence and another also fostered the formation of regional expressions.

In short, American regional expressions were the result of a process of internal transmission within limited areas and manifested themselves in variations of formal motifs derived from the models that were accepted first; it is important to point out that these models resulted from the delayed acceptance of formal elements that first appeared in important urban centers and in monuments considered to be models and that therefore initiated the series of derivative forms.

It is obvious that transmitted architectural types are better understood in important urban centers where one finds the most expert craftsmen and skilled labor; on the other hand, in their successive irradiations out toward the peripheral zone these models pass through dissimilar processes of transformation: simplification, exaggeration, lack of formal understanding, local additions mixed with deformations due to faulty interpretation, and amateurish, crude execution. Indian labor was not a factor in the changes in colonial architecture, and variations attributed to "Indian sensibility" are merely modifications and deformations of the reworking of imported forms and concepts. As for craftsmanship, indigenous labor shows different degrees of skill, from works of extreme rusticity to those that reveal a knowledge of craft in no way inferior to European labor.

This is not the appropriate time to discuss again the unpopular term *mestizo architecture*, or even worse, *mestizo style*. The discredit into which these terms have fallen does not allow us even to consider them. I think it is appropriate, however, to discuss the role in colonial art of so-called indigenous or Indian sensibility, since this sensibility is often associated with manifestations of mestizo art in order to emphasize the distinctive character of works considered to be the product of that sensibility. It is important to make clear that in almost all cases it is a matter of a controlled contribution that passively executes, with greater or lesser ability, the system of construction and the formal concepts imposed by the dominant culture. Manual labor is, in the final analysis, the great native contribution that permitted the enormous construction activity to be carried out.

When an Indian revealed artistic ability, it was exploited to increase production; instead of calling on his sensibility and free expression, his skill was utilized at low cost. The native artists who were active in colonial society were not recognized as innovators but rather as executors. Their works, rather than expressions backed by creative impulses, were limited to reproducing and recombining imported motifs. Occasionally, in areas with a great density of native population, a common imprint on regional expression and an esthetic similarity in the totality of the works were achieved. It was a group sensibility, characteristic of the executors of a specific region, that frequently highlighted the rudimentary skills of the labor force. Nevertheless, what is most evident in these works is, to paraphrase Palm, the mental distance between the model and its reproduction. The limited skills and the lack of artistry and craftsmanship manifest in most of the works produced by indigenous labor are rudimentary not so much because of lack of ability as because of immaturity. And in this case immaturity should be considered a consequence of the cultural patterns of the colonial system.

When an indigenous or mestizo artist acquired an artistic skill the nexus between his native sensibility and his artistic purposes was broken. A clear example of this are the three Cuzcan churches from the late seventeenth century: San Sebastian, with its fine retable-like altarpiece facade; San Pedro, with echoes of the Cathedral and the Compañía; and Belén, whose portico revives and exaggerates the effect of the ornamental bands (borders) applied around 1651 to the lateral portico of the Convent of São Francisco. The three examples adopt the schema of the *retalbe* altarpiece facade that contrasts with the smooth surfaces of the lower parts of the towers; the prototype is the Cathedral, and its influence is also evident in the design of the volumes of the bell towers. The names of the Indian architects Manuel de Sahuaraura and Juan Tomás Tuyuru Túpac are associated with the three churches; Tuyuru Túpac designed San Pedro with one eye on the Cathedral, whose portal he interpreted, and the other on the Compañía, whose chapels he reproduced between the inferior buttresses. The presence not only of indigenous labor but of indigenous intellect clearly demonstrates that the supposed indigenous sensibility is not manifest in these cases and confirms the utilization of the Indian artist's knowledge and ability when there is the certainty that his artistic intentions were completely European. Nothing in these works suggests an indigenous artist; ethnicity does not modify the European architectural will of the Indian craftsman. On the contrary, the poorer their knowledge and the coarser their execution, the more mestizo is the result of their work.

The homogeneity of mestizo architecture and popular architecture rests on the shared character of all peripheral manifestations. Despite distinguishing nuances among artistic expressions that result from their regional differences, these nuances do not succeed in freeing themselves from the character imposed on all colonial manifestations by contact with the dominant culture. After all, the differences are not essential, and it is always examples of minor architecture that repeat in delayed fashion the formal and inconographic schemata transmitted from major centers. They never go beyond the level of dialectal expression.

THE LUSO-BRAZILIAN RELATIONSHIP

The situation of dependence is analogous in the vast territory of Brazil that was occupied by Portugal. Although the Portuguese-dominated culture was less oppressive than the Spanish, Brazilian colonial architecture repeated with greater fidelity the Portugese models; the transmission was more direct and, above all, did not undergo the modifications caused by the intervention of non-Iberian religious orders which, though they shared the same religion, had a very different artistic education. Moreover, the Portuguese architectural patterns did not pass through the phases of reinterpretation produced by the intervention of indigenous labor as was the case in Mexico and Peru. If one compares the construction activity during the sixteenth century in Mexico with that carried out in Brazil during the same period, it is not difficult to understand the different interests that motivated the first actions of Spain and Portugal toward the American colonies. At the beginning of the sixteenth century Portugal, absorbed in maintaining control of the commercial routes to Africa and Asia and strengthening her control from the Indian Ocean to China, underestimated the possibilities of Brazil.

It is not surprising that, during the first half of the sixteenth century, the Portuguese considered the discovery of Brazil (1500) as a matter of secondary importance. In fact, her efforts to consolidate control of the coast of what is now Brazil, in the area between the modern ports of Santos and Recife, were initially a reflex action taken to prevent France and England from establishing coastal enclaves that would compete with the export of brazil wood to the Low Countries and England for use in the manufacture of wood products. Only the fear of competition on the Brazilian coast led to the prolonged occupation of the second half of the century and to the establishment of a plantation economy. The development of sugar plantations on the coastal strip between Salvador and Recife resulted from the actions of a handful of Portuguese entrepreneurs who enslaved the Indians for work on their plantations.[11]

A smaller indigenous population in comparison to the population in the areas of high Meso-American and Andean cultures, the growing demand for labor, and the constant spread of areas intended for sugar plantations motivated the mass importation of black slaves from the western ports of Africa. The Portuguese imperial system in America is different in several respects when compared to that imposed by Spain, but they are similar in the colonial process of enslavement for the exploitation of resources. "Without slaves there is no sugar, without sugar there is no Brazil" was the self-justifying argument; Brazilian sugar was for Portugal what mining in Mexico and Peru representated for the Spaniards.

The Portuguese imperial system was less systematic and rigid than the Spanish:

> but it was also less efficient. It was late in establishing itself; it suffered the consequences of the interregnum imposed by Spanish domination of Portugal (1580–1640), and then by the growing British hegemony over Portugal. Mercantile policies were comparatively more flexible and open, with a greater degree of penetration by foreign commerce, especially from the seventeenth century on, due to the alliance of Portugal with Great Britain and her submission to the latter. Social stratification was relatively more informal and was in fact less systematic and legalized. The Church had less power and the separate court of the Inquisition was not established. The religious and evangelizing motivation had a less important role and a greater degree of tolerance of and facilities for the immigration of foreigners and dissidents from the official creed were adopted. On the other hand, the exploitation of the Indians was not restrained by religious scruples or by political concerns, and thus acquired a more blatant character.[12]

The Brazilian sugar plantation (*a engenho do açúcar*) was transformed into the perfected prototype of plantation agriculture in America and into the Portuguese instrument of effective occupation and colonization. Certainly it became the most important colonial inheritance of the country.[13] In 1570 there were 60 plantations in operation in Brazil; in 1629 the number had reached 346, and in 1710, the total was 528. Nevertheless, even though the plantations belonged to the Portuguese, it was the Dutch who controlled the mercantile operation and derived the greatest profit from them. The Portuguese, in the long run, were nothing more than intermediaries. "At the end of the sixteenth century, the Dutch controlled 66 percent of the shipments between Brazil and Portugal, they owned most of the sugar exported from the colony, and Amsterdam, not Lisbon, had approximately twenty-five refineries that used semi-refined Brazilian sugar (1621)."[14] The backward economic system of Portugal could not compete with the developed structures of Holland, England, and France. Holland was a mercantile capitalist historical formation that did not base its economy on the systems of Iberian slave colonialism; on the contrary, its economic policies allowed it to mobilize

> great resources of labor, capital and ships in order to follow the Portuguese to the very source of their commerce and expel them.
> In the first fifty years of the seventeenth century the Dutch obliged the Portuguese to reduce their operations in the periphery of Asia, and in Brazil they took over Recife and held it between 1630 and 1654, thereby controlling trade in sugar if not its cultivation. The Spanish occupation of Portugal did not offer adequate resources for protecting the Portuguese bridgehead in Brazil. Although the Portuguese recovered Recife in 1654, the Brazilian sugar monopoly had been broken by the development of English and Dutch plantations in the Carribean.[15]

The agricultural policy of plantations introduced into Brazil by Portugal revealed in its operation a system of dependence and of forced submission to a developing capitalist economy. In fact, the plantation, unlike the Spanish-American hacienda, was an independent economic unit created to produce essential articles for external, that is to say European, consumption. The hacienda, on the other hand, was a large landholding for growing grain or raising cattle. Its products were consumed locally, in the mining centers or in great urban centers like Mexico City or Lima.[16]

During the whole of the sugar phase the city of Bahía was the largest and most prosperous settlement in Brazil. In 1763 Rio de Janeiro replaced Bahía as capital, since gold and diamonds had replaced sugar as the principal source of income. However, throughout the eighteenth century and during the gold epoch, Portugal was "incapable of providing the principal imports of textiles and metal products for the colony, and incapable as well of paying for domestic imports without colonial products. Like Spain, Portugal was now an appendage of her colony in America. In other words, because of Portugal's undeveloped economy, society, and capitalist political structure, Brazil was joined to the economy of Western Europe. Brazil was the economic center of Portugal."[17] The essential fact that cannot be overlooked is "that in the period from 1500 to 1700 the Ibero-Americans functioned as a peripheral segment of the expanding European economy."[18]

During the sixteenth century the Portuguese founded approximately seventeen centers on the coasts of Brazil and approximately another forty, many of them in the interior, during the following century. In the coastal centers and where topography permitted, the cities repeated the Portuguese custom of separate development of a *cidade baixa* and a *cidade alta*. Salvador de Bahia and Rio de Janeiro, the two colonial capitals, are American versions inspired by Lisbon and Oporto. Robert C. Smith claims that the Brazilian cities are replicas of the Portuguese insofar as in both cases streets were laid out irregularly around uneven *terreiros* (land parcels). I suspect, however, that the irregular design of Brazilian cities has received too much emphasis and that this irregularity has been made into one of its colonial urban characteristics. The Plan of Bahía, founded in 1549, is adapted to the platform that is its site with an aspect of order evident in the rectilinear streets which, even if they lack the obsessive pattern of the rectangular checkerboard of the Hispano-American cities, reveal a concern for doing things with a certain sense of order despite the topographical inconveniences of the site. Rio de Janeiro, founded in 1567, also adopted a regular pattern. São Luis de Maranhão, founded in 1615, had a perfectly orthogonal design. In Maurtizstadt-Recife the Dutch applied very advanced norms of urban regularity, and in the eighteenth century there is no lack of cases where the absolute and monotonous perfection of the gridiron system was applied, such as Vila Bela de Santísima Trinidade, Vila Nova de Mazagão, Vila de Macapá, Vila de Pinheiro, Vila Vicosa en Porto Seguro, and in the Indian villages (*aldeias*) laid out by military engineers. The mining cities of Minas Gerais have a free design adapted to the movements of an irregular topography, and that freedom is very similar to that of the Mexican mining cities. Undeniably, a greater flow of urban spaces results, with visual surprises occurring during a walk through the streets. As in Mexico, the freedom of the layout of the urban mining centers was due to extremely rapid growth caused by the sudden influx of large groups of people who formed an unplanned community. At first, the abrupt topography was of little interest to those searching for gold and diamonds; the routine movements between the house, the warehouse, and the mine were what established the foundations of what later would be definitive streets. In Sabará, for example, the source of wealth was in the river; consequently, the city developed sequentially along its banks. The prescribed rules for imposing a certain order were applied to mining cities when their urban character was almost set. Nevertheless, it is still surprising that in the city of Mariana, founded in 1710, standards of orthogonal design were applied in 1740 when they wanted to improve the urban plan.

BAHÍA

With the founding of Bahía (1549) a new phase in the process of Portuguese colonization in Brazil began. After the failure of the system of territorial division of the captaincies aimed at effecting decentralized colonization, the founding of Bahía initiated a new policy that in fact concentrated everything in the newly founded city. In order to distribute control of the immense coast, Rio de Janeiro was established toward the south (1567) and São Luis do Maranhão toward the north (1615). These three centers were the ones that really initiated complete control of the territory.[19]

The initial plan for Bahía, circumscribed by a walled trapezoid with corner balusters, was the work of Luis Dias, who shared with Tomé de Sousa the position of *"maestre das obras de fortaleza e cidade do Salvador."* The first plans for the new settlement have been lost, but it is known that the original area was quite small and that the fortifications had to be expanded. On both sides of the *Terreiro de Jesus* the checkerboard design predominated, and if it was not more regular, notes Paulo F. Santos, this was perhaps because of the irregularity of the terrain.[20] In several Dutch and Portuguese plans from the beginning of the seventeenth century, the city reveals its definitive shape, divided into a *cidade alta* with its main squares, and a *cidade baixa* with all the port installations and commercial buildings. The plans for the upper city ran into a rather irregular topography, but despite this the effort to achieve regularity is apparent; however, when the progressive growth of the city could not limit itself to the plain that was the site for the nucleus of the foundation of city, all the principles of regularity were completely forgotten, and little by little the city invaded the surrounding hills and ravines. The old plan persisted within the context of the great contemporary city and acquired the value of a seminal element.

The city, throughout the passage of time and its own evolution, is something that persists despite its transformations and functions. The streets of the Pelourinho District, the ones that open into the Terreiro de Jesus or the Palace Square, may be the expression that states with greatest force and precision the complex collective organism that the city is because, at the base of this organism, the totality of streets and squares is identified with the original plan. The significance of these constants might be that of a past that continues to live, whether in the monuments or in the persistence of the plan. The growth of Bahía in recent years has demanded the sacrifice and the disappearance of urban ensembles as well as of significant landmarks like the Church of the Sé. The city tends more toward evolution than toward conservation and, in the process of evolution, the conservation of landmarks represents a stimulus to development itself. In spite of some losses, probably due to the fact that the function of the buildings had become isolated from reality or was anachronistic with regard to technical and social evolution, Bahía conserves most of its historic landmarks because they have been the primary elements of the city and have been invested with a more stable, permanent, and decisive character. Aside from their artistic value, one must take into account their presence and history and their quality as urban facts that have generated their own life. The context of these monuments, defined by the orchestral value of old Bahía's atmosphere, the narrow hilly streets, the palaces turned into boarding houses, the houses that are insignificant and at the same time indispensable for the value of the townscape, and the great vitality of the Bahian people, make of Bahía a complete, magical, and bewitching monument.

Although there are a few architectural examples dating from the final years of the sixteenth century—the Church of Nostra Senhora de Gracia

(Our Lady of Grace) in Olinda, for example—Brazilian colonial architecture of that century has practically no monuments that testify to a building activity that is in any way comparable to the works that Spain left in her American colonies. One need only remember the impressive quantity and quality of the Mexican convents to understand the different orientation and procedures of Spanish and Portuguese colonization. Brazilian colonial architecture belongs to the seventeenth and eighteenth centuries, and is manifested as an unchanged extension of the architectural sense of the mother country. The new combinations and reinterpretations of imported models, which in the Spanish American colonies frequently produced a differentiating specificity, are almost completely lacking in the Brazilian replicas of European models. The central European influences and the Italianisms that one notices in various Brazilian buildings are, after all, the same influences that characterize the architecture of Portugal.[21]

Bahía, which maintained its status as capital until 1763, contains some key monuments that allow us to identify transmitted models and, at the same time, to indicate the influence that those monuments had on other colonial structures. For example, the Church of the Jesuit College and the Convent of San Francisco with its magnificent cloister, introduce characteristics unique to Portuguese architectural typology. The preference for a single nave hall-church, the ceilings with wooden imitation vaults, the total absence of a dome, the presbytery or *capela-mor* that is very deep but of reduced dimensions compared to the width of the nave, the minor spatial importance of the crossing, the building bulk, the facades with designs derived from civic architecture and the absence of salomonic columns and *estípites* are only a few of the characteristics of the Luso-Brazilian churches that differ so radically from the Hispano-American ones. Moreover, it should be stated that the Church of the Jesuit College—today the Cathedral of Bahía—is Portuguese from both the conceptual and the material point of view. In fact, the stones of its exterior and interior walls, arches, portals, moldings, and many other elements, were shipped as ballast, ready to be assembled at the building site. This custom was repeated in hundreds of representative works in the Portuguese colony. It not only reveals the scarcity of skilled local labor, but also explains the greater dependence on the architectural forms and ideas of the mother country. It is not unusual to find cases of a monument built in separate pieces in Portugal and then shipped to Brazil for assembly. It is clear that this procedure excludes any possibility of occasional local contributions.

The Jesuit temple of Bahía derives from the Jesuit churches of Espíritu Santo in Évora and São Roque in Lisbon, built almost at the same time by Alfonso Alvares, beginning in 1567. There is greater similarity to the Church of Espíritu Santo in Évora, for in both the Bahian temple and its model the crossing is emphasized by arches that are larger than those of the side chapels; in São Roque in Lisbon, on the other hand, the arches of the chapels and those of the transept are of the same dimensions. The church at Évora, although adapted to the Jesuit program of achieving maximum space for the congregation and begun one year earlier than Vignola's temple in Rome, shows regional characteristics such as the lack of a dome, galleries or tribunes over the side chapels, and the narthex-vestibule of the entrance. In the city of Évora these same characteristics appear in the late Gothic Church of São Francisco (1460–1501) and there is no doubt, as Germain Bazin has been claiming since 1949, that Alfonso Alvares took them into account for the project of the Church of Espíritu Santo. The presence of Felipe Terzi in Lisbon did not change the local character of the temples that Alvares built for the Jesuits. Felipe Terzi repeated Vignola's plan in the Church of São Vicente do Fora, also in Lisbon, but concessions to local taste are evident in the composition of the facade.

The major difference between the Roman Jesuit prototype of Vignola and the Portuguese Jesuit churches lies in the interior space. The custom of emphasizing the similarity of Italian, Portuguese, Spanish, Central European, and American Jesuit floor plans often leads one to forget that what determines architectural values and what ultimately defines the interior spatial value produced by that building is what is built above these plans and what defines the interior spaces created by these elevations. For that reason the similarity of the floor plans may be of only relative importance when the spatial results are completely different. The Jesuit church of Espíritu Santo in Évora, like the one in Bahía, is covered by a false barrel vault that extends the whole length of the single nave from the entry to the presbytery or *capela-mor*. This solution produces a static space within rectangular limitations in which the crossing is spatially insignificant. In the Church of São Roque in Lisbon the lack of a dome in accentuated even more by the hall-like space. These churches have floor plans that clearly reveal adherence to and acceptance of the Jesuit program. However, despite the similarity, the resulting space is totally different when compared to Vignola's Church of Gesú in Rome, the mother church of the Jesuit Order. The Roman church, the model that exercised the greatest influence on the religious building of the order, has its point of greatest spatial impact in the crossing; the four arches interrupt the continuity of the vault to support the great dome in which the space is extended and heightened. The effect produced by the spatial interpenetration of the nave, the transept, and the dome is lacking in the Portuguese Jesuit churches because the hall-type solution of scant spatial interest predominates in them.

Another element that contributes to the accentuation of the hall effect of the Luso-Brazilian churches is the proportion of the *capela-mor* arch in relation to the width and height of the nave: it is a smaller arch in the wall of the chevet that gives access to a presbytery whose dimensions are also smaller. It is not comparable to the majestic high arch of the Roman churches that permits the uninterrupted continuity of visual and spatial sweep up the apse. In Bahía, one has the impression that there is "too much wall" at the opening of the *capela-mor*. This disposition, which undoubtedly reached Brazil with Francisco Dias, goes back to the late Gothic, and is evident as well in the church of São Francisco in Évora, already mentioned. One must remember that the similarity of spatial distribution in the Churches of São Francisco and Espíritu Santo has led to assumptions concerning the autocthonous Portuguese origin of the single nave church with lateral chapels that was later used exclusively by the Jesuit churches. Similar solutions are found in the Spanish Gothic, and it is almost certain that the lateral chapels of Gesú in Rome have medieval antecedents. If this disposition in Portugal anticipates Gesú in Rome it is of only relative importance because the marked dissimilarity of the spatial conception in the Italian and Portuguese Jesuit churches is what really differentiates them. Spain applied the pomp of Rome to her churches in the American colonies; Portugal, on the other hand, repeated her own local characteristics to the letter.

The facade of the Church of the Jesuit College in Bahía, completed around 1680, is more closely related to the Portuguese Jesuit temple of Santarem (1676) than to those of Évora and Lisbon. It is a smooth facade, of great sobriety in the two lower portions—a sobriety more palatial than churchlike, a compromise between civil and religious architecture crowned by a somewhat overadorned coping. In fact, there is not enough space for the volutes, and they are squeezed between the main facade and the small volumes of the towers. A less than elegant solution that, although related to the facade of Santarem, is very far from the Jesuit prototype that Giacomo della Porta gave to Vignola's Gesú in Rome.

The other key landmark in Bahía is the Convent of São Francisco. The facade of the church has more graceful proportions, and the vertical sense is accentuated by the contorted main facade rising between the two even higher towers. The placement of this facade has a well-defined urban spatial effect: at the same time that it sets the outer limit of Anchieta Square, giving visual emphasis to the religiosity of its volume, it also achieves integration with the Terreiro de Jesus in a happy urban solution of interrelated spaces. Although the construction of the convent began toward the end of the seventeenth century, almost all the work was completed in the first four decades of the eighteenth century. The point of greatest architectural value is concentrated in the cloister; it is small when compared to those of Lima and Mexico City, but it has great quality and elegance in the forms and proportions derived from the early Tuscan Renaissance, forms that are not strangers to Portugal and that can also be seen in the Franciscan convent of Guimarães (1600). The cloister of Bahía is superior to those of Olinda and Recife, built by the same order, and there is no comparison to those of other religious orders.

The interior of the Church of São Francisco is covered with profuse ornamentation that invades the walls of the transept, vaults, and chapels; it is the most baroque interior of the Bahían churches, and the criteria for the realization of that illusory, dazzling, unreal atmosphere are not very different from those that determined the Mexican altarpieces. Despite the formal and chromatic differences that exist between Hispanic and Portuguese altarpieces, the tendency toward the spectacular is evident; the excesses of the Mexian baroque are more impressive and more imposing in their dimensions, due in part to the spatial differences between the presbyteries and transepts of Spanish lineage and those of Portuguese origin.

The differences in decorative intensity are even more obvious in the facades; in Brazil decorative excesses like those in Hispano-America do not exist. What prevails is clear, symmetrical, and simple architectural design over smooth surfaces; the *horro-vacui* kind of decoration is not favored and for that reason the cubic volumetric mass, at times heavy and somewhat static, is even more apparent. As in the case of Portugal and Central Europe, there is a frequent contrast between exterior sobriety and the richness of interior decoration. Nevertheless, an exception is necessary to prove the rule, and this is the facade of the Third Order of São Francisco adjacent to the Franciscan convent. It is a "Mexican" facade that demands attention more because of its exotic flavor and incompatibility with the environment than for its originality. In Mexico it would pass almost unnoticed. According to the documents, it was completed in 1703, that is, five years before construction began on the neighboring church of the Franciscan convent. Despite the daring quality of this facade, the traditional Portuguese distributive scheme is not at all changed.

Bahía, also called the Catholic heart of Brazil, has approximately fifty churches. The popular count raises the number to 365; this liberality is similar to the famous and imaginary 365 churches of Cholula in Mexico.

From the seventeenth century until the middle of the nineteenth century the type of the Portuguese church was repeated with insistent monotony. There was variety in the design of some details, such as the movement of the facade or the form of the spires of the towers that changed from pyramidal to bulbous, but the traditional characteristics of the floor plans and the disposition of the facades did not depart from the patterns transmitted from the mother country. The architectural principles that appeared in Bahía in the middle of the seventeenth century were maintained throughout the eighteenth century and underwent no substantial alterations in the nineteenth.

The Bahían churches, for example, Carmen, Rosario, Pilar, Bonfim, Concepción, and many more, in addition to being invested with individual historical and architectural value, made a great contribution to the environmental and visual values of the urban context. The position of the churches in the rolling topography, the facades in the squares and the avenues (*largos*) and the towers rising above the rooftops seem to have more of a strategic-environmental function than a religious one. When one reaches the *Largo de Pelourinho*, coming down Alfredo Brito Street, the sequence of facades, towers, and roofs establishes a felicitous environmental integration full of movement and rich in visual surprises. The buildings of a certain architectural value mix and alternate with anonymous and modest structures to compose a harmonious townscape.

Among the many churches that stand out in the urban profile, in addition to the ones already mentioned, Santa Ana and Nostra Senhora de la Concepão de la Plaia are especially noteworthy, the first because it has a cruciform plan and dome, almost unique not only in Bahía but in all of Brazil, and the second for the daring diagonal placement of the towers. Built in the *cidade baixa* between 1739 and 1765, the church of Concepcão do la Plaia shows the influence of the official architecture that dominated Lisbon before the earthquake of 1755. It is another church prefabriacted in Portugal in stone and shipped to Brazil in separate numbered pieces. The Portuguese stonemason Eugenio da Mota was expressly contracted to put together the architectural puzzle, and he remained in Bahía until the work was completed.

The procedure of preparing the building pieces in the mother country was not limited to those elements that required the intervention of expert artisans, as was the case, for example, of the portico of the Church of Carmen in Rio de Janeiro, but also frequently included plain ashlar for raising the walls. This transmission of forms, more material than conceptual, can be explained by the lack of native skilled labor for this kind of work and the scarcity of Portuguese artisans in the colony. Also, the projects were often worked out in the mother country, and when they were laid out in Brazil they were also repetitions of traditional schemes; in this activity the military engineers had primacy. These related factors contributed to the establishment of a high degree of dependence of colonial Brazilian architecture on Portugal. A somewhat different situation developed in the gold-mining region of Minas Gerais in the second half of the eighteenth century. This was due to the isolation of the area, the distance to the coast, the impossibility of transporting heavy imported pieces, and, principally, the formation of a regional cultural environment in which mulatto artisans replaced the Portuguese and took active part in works of great sensibility.

However, I think it is appropriate to point out that the degree of architectural copying in the Hispano-American colonies was not analogous to that of the Luso-Brazilian colony. There is no doubt that American colonial architecture was either Portuguese or Spanish, an extension of the architectural sense of their respective mother countries, but homogeneity was more evident in the Luso-Brazilian works than in the Hispano-American ones. This is not to say that a colonial architecture was produced in Spanish America that was significantly different from that of the mother country, but rather that it did not reach the degree of homogeneity that existed between Brazilian and Portuguese architecture. The fact that Brazilian architecture had a more emphatic level of duplication than the Hispano-American assumes the existence of different systems in the imposition and application of the dominant culture, different procedures in the transmission of forms and concepts (Spain never sent a prefabricated church to its colonies) and differences between Portuguese and Spanish Catholicism. Portuguese Catholicism was more social than religious and, in any case, less fanatic or dramatic; the channels of transmission were different, as were its various contributions and the background of its practitioners. In short, although it is a question of marginal differences, the Hispano-American works achieved a degree of individuality in which new combinations had an important role, as opposed to Luso-Brazilian works that were reproductions of the forms of the mother country rather than new combinations.

NEITHER ABSOLUTE ORIGINALITY
NOR TOTAL REPRODUCTION

It is indisputable that the colonial architecture of Hispanic-America was building activity controlled by Spain. However, although her political, administrative, and religious control extended to all aspects of culture, it did not interfere with the artistic contributions of Flemish, German, French, and Italian Catholics who, in greater number than may be supposed, took part in architectural activity. The transmission of non-Spanish European architectural patterns was a differentiating factor that also explains the lack of direct relationship among various American monuments and their Spanish models. Also important was the influence of the treatises, principally Italian, that were frequently consulted by the Spaniards themselves. Kubler has pointed out the problems of European, non-Iberian contributions to Latin American colonial architecture, and has clearly demonstrated that increasingly broader knowledge of these sources throws into doubt the opinion that Latin American architecture was an extension of an Hispano-Portuguese architectural sense.

Besides pointing out that Spanish historians still consider American events as a provincial extension of Spanish history and, consequently, as more an extension of Spain than of Europe, Kubler indicates the methodological errors in the histories of Latin American colonial architecture "that are made and substantiated with no reference to Europe and frequently without even mentioning the connections to the architecture of the Peninsula."[22] A more profound study of non-Iberian influences and "an extensive discussion of these many sources emanating from Germany, France, and Italy would have created a conflict with the theory of the Hispanic invariables and self-sufficiency, and with the Hispanic interpretation of seventeenth-century Spanish architecture as a national style that owes nothing to sources outside the Peninsula."[23]

Another contributing factor to differentiation was the coexistence, in the same work, of forms from the past with forms that were more in touch with the current idiom—that is to say, the frequent strained marriage of formal expressions belonging to a remote historical past with others that were more contemporary and that reflected a different taste. For example, a church like the Cathedral of Puno is classified as Andean baroque, but only the modest ornamentation of the facade bears any relation to that style. All the rest— what is most important, such as volume, space, and structure—repeats experiences that go back to the Middle Ages.

Concerning the union of architectural characteristics from different periods in the same work, I suppose that the explanation lies in the fact that in the colonies one did not think about innovative statements; what prevailed was what the authoritarian principles of the system had shown to be useful and functional. For that reason the same plan, the same volume, and the same space were often repeated; the ornamentation, the most vulnerable and changeable part of the architectural mass, is what varied the most. Ornamentation does not affect the spatial tradition of the building even when it produces great variety in esthetic effects. Because of its superficial character, ornamentation is adapted to the surface of the building, and that allows it greater variation as well as more contemporary adaptation to current taste. Today many churches built on Medieval principles of construction are thought to be baroque only because the decoration of the facade or the plasterwork and altarpieces of the interior are baroque.

The variety of European contributions, the provincial character of colonial architectural expression, the conditions of dependence, the disparate cultural levels in the colony and the mother country, the influence of the environment (antiseismic solutions, for example), the use of different materials, and the employment of labor that was frequently unskilled were factors that helped determine the unique character of many colonial works. In order to avoid misunderstandings I want to make clear that my purpose is to point out what is unique to colonial architecture and not to state that this architecture is conceptually different. Colonial architecture is a repetitive activity, but the sum of the factors I have noted contribute to a uniqueness that cannot be ignored.

The architectural types that were transmitted to America introduced Spanish and European experiences, and although they were transformed and gave birth to variations in the New World, they reflect the kind of events that depended on centers of European cultural influence. Because of their condition as receivers, the American colonies tended to accept elements of different cultural origins and to mix forms from different sources and periods. It was not surprising, therefore, that colonial architecture, despite its being essentially a reproductive activity and an extension of the European sense of architecture, produced some differentiating traits. What we wish to establish is that the building tradition was transferred directly from the Old to the New World, but that the product of that transfer did not remain unchanged. The transformations did not produce an expression original enough to be called American, but neither can it be interpreted as an imitative activity that did not basically differ from European achievements. In this regard there exists two well-defined and contradictory positions among the historians who deal with this subject: on one side is the group which claims the American originality of colonial architecture, on the other are those who find no difference whatsoever between the European architectural image and its projection in America. To my mind, both positions are unacceptable. If colonial architecture did not constitute an American phenomenon, neither was it an imitative extension that maintained a formal and immutable similarity to European models. The similarity gave way to some variations on the dominant artistic models. Those variations were appropriate to provincial manifestations, but they achieved an individuality that justifies a more thoughtful analysis.

The transmission of Iberian architectural types to America is an indisputable fact that is manifest from the first building during the period of conquest at the beginning of the sixteenth century until the end of the colonial era. The Gothic, the Isabelline, the Renaissance Plateresque, and the Mudejar styles arrived with the Spanish conquerors; then, always with some delay, there followed the expressions that accompanied changes in taste during the three centuries of domination. There are innumerable examples that repeat Hispanic forms: they run the gamut from the already noted traditional building systems associated with architecture, to formal relationships, symbolic meaning, and ideological content of a monument that had acquired a special representational significance. To cite one case among many as an example, this was true of the Cathedral of Vallodolid. Its influence is evident in Mexico City, Puebla, Esquipulas (Guatemala), and Córdoba (Argentina), and despite the process of formal variants produced on American soil, the relationship to the Hispanic temple is easily identifiable. Other Spanish cathedrals like Jaén, Sevilla, Cádiz, as well as minor churches, had an influence on Latin American projects for religious buildings.

From the plan of a church to the details of Arabic ornament, one can point to the Hispanic origin of many architectural elements and, at the same time, find the continuity and persistence of artistic expressions derived from previous historical experiences and older formal traditions. So it is that the Mudejar, which ends in Spain with the Catholic monarchs, prolonged its existence in America into the nineteenth century. The carved ceilings of São Francisco and Santo Domingo in Quito, built at the end of the sixteenth century, do not suffer by comparison to those in the Alcazar of Sevilla. The ceilings of rafters and joints, corbels, tie beams, and decorative interlacing that echoes Mudejar carpentry in a great number of works throughout the seventeenth and eighteenth centuries have no chronological nexus with the life of the forms. In Venezuela all the churches built during the second half of the eighteenth century adopted the technique of Mudejar ceiling work, and, in 1830, after Independence, the same system was still employed. The anachronistic presence of Mudejar elements in America during the seventeenth and eighteenth centuries prolonged the life of ancient traditions and techniques that had been abandoned in Spain since the sixteenth century, and laid the groundwork for the problem of the coexistence in the same work of forms belonging to different periods. The frequent result was that the baroque facade of a church hid behind it a structure rising from a floor plan of Medieval conception covered with a Mudejar ceiling.

The coexistence of outdated forms with contemporary forms was customary in the American colonies. The absence of direct contact with the centers where creative cultural movements were generated prolonged the life of the traditional forms. If Spanish architecture of the seventeenth century was backward compared to other European countries, it is natural that the backwardness must have been even greater in the colonies and, consequently, the persistence of ancient formal traditions more pronounced. A concern for being up to date with stylistic idioms was more evident in representative works of major Latin American cities; in the building of minor centers that preoccupation had no way of manifesting itself and, therefore, obsolete forms and techniques were employed that kept traditional systems alive.

The transmission of forms belonging to the repertoire of non-Iberian European architecture has awakened little interest among scholars, although it is one of the most decisive contributions to the principal works of major centers, if not to popular manifestations. The indifference toward the study of non-Iberian European contributions is explained by the fact that since the awakening of interest in colonial architecture, its almost exclusive Hispanic affiliation has been insistently pointed out. The spread and repetition of that concept has given rise to a complacent acceptance based on superficial criticism, supported by scholars concerned with emphasizing the constant Hispanism of events. Spanish historiography, bent on viewing colonial architecture in Latin America as a provincial extension of Spain, is partisan when it makes use of comparisons that show the formal connections with Iberian antecedents because it does not broaden or deepen the research to indicate the origin of the model. Acceptance of the similiarity between an American work and one in Spain is not sufficient to confer Hispanic paternity on a specific form; the model may date from a more distant period or have its origins in a non-Iberian site. Gothic antecedents in Spain are cited for the Gothic examples in Latin America and, in the same way, Renaissance forms are interpreted as extensions of the Spanish Plateresque.

The transmission of non-Iberian contributions is more frequent and significant than is usually outlined by almost all of current historiography. Only a few scholars such as Palm, Kubler, and, recently, Santiago Sebastián, have made a more profound study of these relationships. Despite this indifference, one cannot ignore the fact that for three centuries, and by means of the most diverse routes, influences reached Latin America that did not come from the Iberian Peninsula and that contributed decisively to the establishment of the unique character of colonial architecture.

The influence of illustrations and treatises on architecture is evident in countless works. The engravings stimulated inspiration, the invention of variations, and, most important, were viewed with the certainty of their irreproachable validity. The design of a portico by Vignola or the influence of the forms of Palladio, Michelangelo, Alberti, Ricci, Delonne, Dietterlin, Bramante, Pozzo, and, above all, Serlio, appeared from Mexico to Argentina, sometimes in an uncertain and hesitant manner, sometimes with an imitatitve decisiveness that undeniably copied the model. The prestige that these models enjoyed extended the time that they were in vogue. Serlio was copied from the sixteenth century, as in Actopan, Tunja, and Quito, to the eighteenth century, as in Antigua and Guatemala, and almost at the end of the colonial period was an influence on Francisco Guerrero y Torres in the plan of the Pocito de Guadalupe.

At this point I should emphasize the fact that citing Iberian and non-Iberian transmissions separately is not based on a desire to classify contributions competitively in order to determine how much colonial architecture owes to Spain and how much to the rest of Europe. What I do maintain is that colonial architecture continually defined its character on the basis of the contributions of European architectural experience and, consequently, cannot be considered solely as a Spanish-American expression. If the difference between Iberian and non-Iberian contributions has been emphasized, this is basically due to the desire to point out both the methodological errors in Spanish historiography and the appropriateness of reconsidering the exaggerated proportions reached by the term *Hispano-American* when applied to examples of colonial architecture.

Nationalistic interpretations are equally unacceptable. I can accept nationalism when it is understood as the conjunction of national aspirations directed toward achieving development and national independence, but nationalism and criticism cannot be joined. "Nationalism deforms perspective and demands sacrifices of intelligence."[24] It is incompatible with objective judgments and produces partisan interpretations.

The defintion that Justino Fernández gives of Mexican art is of doubtful validity when he considers that "all the art that has been produced in our country from the pre-Columbian period until today is currently recognized as Mexican."[25] Although he points out that "the relationship between the art of New Spain and European art is undeniable," the definition tries to recognize as Mexican every artistic activity that has occurred within the territory that is today delineated by the borders of the political map of Mexico. Analyzing artistic manifestations produced within the geographical limits of each of the present-day Latin American republics in terms of nationality is the same as analyzing in terms of French, Spanish, or Lebanese those Roman structures built during the period of the Roman Empire in the territories that are today France, Spain, and Lebanon. An analysis of this kind would give importance to something that in no way determined the character of the works. The ruling esthetic norms definitively determine physiognomy, and these were the same for all of Spanish America: those of Europe.

In my opinion there is also a dangerous inconsistency in the interpretation given by Mexican artistic nationalism to colonial works. It is clearly absurd to try to Mexicanize the cultural expression of a period of domination prior to national independence because, like it or not, nationality is a historical category that emerged in the nineteenth century. Before that time all of Hispanic-America was an ideological unity because it was a Spanish colony; that unity, and not the undeniable differences among the component regions, was the greatest determining factor in its artistic manifestations.

To interpret as Mexican the colonial architecture of Mexico means assigning it the same character of autonomous expression that corresponds to pre-Columbian manifestations. And this truly is unjust because only the pre-Columbian period was really autonomous and independent.

The fact that the Mexican baroque is different from the European baroque does not have its causes in the creative impulses of the "Mexican spirit." These impulses "radiate out from a focal point that lies outside the field of artistic activity,"[26] and Mexican differences are the result of the same specificity that produces the reception and adaptation of transmitted European architectural standards in America.

Moreover, the Mexican baroque is not only "different from the European," but different as well from the South American. This is explained by the differing intensity of contacts, transmissions, and influences from different sources in the two parts of America. Although Mexico has more colonial religious buildings than all of South America, they do not exhibit the variety and quantity of Flemish and Italian influences found in South American architecture. In other words, the Mexican baroque has closer ties with Spanish forms and, for that very reason, a smaller number of examples derived from a more erudite repertoire. "The map of Hispanic art that is still to be drawn will show us the reappearance of those same factors that determine the aspect of the arts on the Iberian Peninsula."[27]

While Mexican criticism makes claims for the legitimacy of their baroque by considering it an almost autonomous antecedent in the evolution of Mexican art, Spanish criticism considers it as a subproduct of the Hispanic: "One more manifestation, albeit an important one, of the Spanish baroque," in the words of Angulo. It is obvious that both positions are untenable because the nationalistic interpretation does not take into account the spurious character of colonial artistic manifestations and, on the other hand, the Spanish interpretation, based on self-sufficient, ethnocentric hermeticism, apparently does not realize that artistic geography and political geography are different. The qualitative and quantitative variety of architectural expressions in Mexico is so enormous that it is difficult to concentrate on only one of them.

The pre-Columbian sites, the convents of the sixteenth century, the cathedrals, the baroque churches, and the works of Villagrán García, Ramírez Vásquez, Luis Barragán, and Félix Candela, are only some of the links in the long architectural chain that makes its unquestionable presence felt in Mexico—a presence that is not understood here as the persistent continuity of a supposed Mexican architectural sense or as the presence of a spirit that has been vibrating ever since the pre-Hispanic period. Rather, we consider it as the presence of man at different historical stages, as the presence of expressions produced in moments of autonomy, subjugation, and self-determination. Pre-Columbian architecture has nothing to do with colonial, and to search for a prolongation of its concepts and the survival of its spirit in the colonial period suggests ignorance of the fact that pre-Columbian expression came out of independent development and, for that very reason, has autonomous authenticity. The conquest interrupted the pre-Columbian architectural process and in its place imposed forms derived from Europe. From that moment on American architecture lost its autonomy and became a manifestation of dependence.

Moreover, the indigenous population, forced to internalize an alien vision of the world, suffered "the degradation of assuming as their own image what was only a reflection of the European world view that considered them racially inferior because they were black, Indian, or mestizo."[28] Today the trauma suffered by indigenous cultures does not allow us to formulate appreciations that attempt to explain the persistence of pre-Columbian creativity in colonial works. The fact that the pre-Hispanic artistic inheritance can be used as an instrument of national self-affirmation concludes with the reevaluation of an art that was never appreciated in the colonial period and that at most was seen as an exotic manifestation worthy of curiosity. Today there exists a definite consciousness of the values and creative potential of pre-Columbian art and architecture. To join such manifestations to colonial ones in order to justify the *Mexicanism* of both leads to confusions that interfere with our perception of the significant differences between two expressions produced at such different times.

The emotions felt when walking along the "Street of the Dead" in Teotihuacán, through the ceremonial square of Monte Albán or Chichén Itzá, are very different from those that colonial space evokes. The spatial disposition of sixteenth-century convent atriums, mistakenly related to pre-Columbian antecedents, does not produce the impression of majesty that emanates from the spaces of Teotihuacán, skillfully ordered to the rhythm of serenely horizontal geometric volumes and forms. The concepts are not only different, they are opposite, and it is a mistake to believe that only large dimensions have an emotional influence on our perceptions; the citadel in Teotihuacán and the nuns' house in Uxmal are invested with the same monumentality, and one does not need physical magnitude to recognize great architectural values and different spatial concepts.

Pre-Columbian architecture and the colonial architecture of the sixteenth century make up the two most important chapters of architectural history in the territory that today is Mexico. They are more important, in my opinion, than the ultra-baroque, overloaded with ornamentation, with a propensity for sensationalism, and almost always with great imbalance and disassociation between structure and embellishment. The convents of the sixteenth century have a volumetric force of a Medieval flavor that, although monotonous in typological repetition, gives evidence of structural sincerity that is imposed without artifice.

Notes

1. Mariano Picón Salas, *De la conquista a la Independencia,* Mexico City: Fondo de Cultura Económica, 1965, p. 106.

2. Darcy Ribeiro, *Las Américas y la civilización,* Buenos Aires: Centro Editor de América Latina, 1969, p. 74.

3. Fernando Chueca Goitia, "Invariantes en la arquitectura hispanoamericana," *Revista de Occidente,* no. 38, Madrid (May 1966).

4. Antonio Bonet Correa and Víctor Manuel Villegas, *El barroco en España y en México,* Guanajuato: Universidad de Guanajuato, 1967, p 61.

5. Justino Fernández, *El retablo de los reyes,* Mexico City: Instituto de Investigaciones Estéticas, UNAM, 1959, p. 263.

6. Fernando Chueca Goitia, "El método de los invariantes," *Boletín del CIHE,* no. 9, Caracas, Universidad Central de Venezuela (April 1968), p. 104.

7. George Kubler, "Ciudades y cultura en el período colonial de América Latina," *Boletín del CIHE,* no. 1, Caracas, Universidad Central de Venezuela (January 1964), p. 81.

8. Ibid.

9. Ibid.

10. George Foster, *Culture and Conquest,* Chicago, 1960.

11. Stanley and Barbara Stein, *La herencia colonial de América Latina,* Mexico City: Siglo XXI Editores, 1970, p. 25.

12. Marcos Kaplan, *Formación del Estado Nacional en América Latina,* Santiago de Chile: Editorial Universitaria, 1969, p. 78.

13. Stein, op. cit., p. 43.

14. Ibid., p. 26.

15. Ibid.

16. Ibid., p. 42.

17. Ibid., p. 27.

18. Ibid., p. 45.

19. Paulo F. Santos, *Formacão de cidades no Brasil Colonial,* V Coloquio Internacional de Estudos Luso-Brasileiros, Coimbra, 1958, p. 78.

20. Ibid., p. 82.

21. It should be noted here that the study of colonial architecture in Brazil has a well-documented and serious bibliography that fortunately is not marred by partisan judgments produced by nationalistic enthusiasms. The research of Lucio Costa, Paulo F. Santos, Augusto da Silva Telles, Rodrigo M. Franco de Andrade, the publications of Brazil's Office of the National Historical and Artistic Patrimony, the works of Robert Smith, Germain Bazin, J. B. Bury, Mario Buschiazzo, and others, constitute an indepensable source for further consultation.

22. George Kubler, "El problema de los aportes europeos no ibéricos en la arquitectura colonial latinoamericana," *Boletín del CIHE,* no. 9, Caracas, Universidad Central de Venezuela (April, 1968).

23. Ibid.

24. E. Rodríguez, "El nacionalismo," *Life,* vol. 26, no. 7 (September 1965).

25. Justino Fernández, *Arte mexicano de sus orígenes a nuestros días*, Mexico City: Editorial Porrúa, S.A., 1968, p. 1.

26. Erwin Walter Palm, "Perspectivas de una historia de la arquitectura colonial hispano-americana," *Boletizn del CIHE,* no. 9, Caracas, Universidad Central de Venezuela (April 1968), p. 34.

27. Ibid.

28. Ribeiro, *Las Américas y la civilización,* p. 103.

4 / External Influences and the Significance of Tradition

MAX CETTO

THE MEXICAN CONTRIBUTION TO COLONIAL ARCHITECTURE

Ten years after the conquest and destruction of Tenochtitlán by Cortes and his soldiers, the Indian Juan Diego, on his way to mass in the village of Tlatelolco, had a vision of the Virgin Mary who expressed her desire that a church be built in a nearby village—the same one, in fact, where the venerated Sanctuary of Guadalupe was later constructed some miles to the north of the new capital of Mexico. On the exact spot where the vision took place, however, the small chapel of El Pocito (the well) was built. Today this chapel is surrounded by the countless houses that shelter the ten million inhabitants of Mexico City; to the north the hill called Tepeyac protects it from the pollution of constantly expanding industrial areas.

This elegant chapel, whose construction did not begin until 1777—that is, 250 years after the legendary vision—is not only profoundly rooted in the religious life of the colony, but also possesses great significance in the history of New World architecture. It is undoubtedly the most notable case of external influence bridging a span of more than fifteen hundred years.

When the chapel was being built, men and women of both the lower and upper classes earned indulgences by manual labor. Among the artisans who contributed their work as an act of charity was the master Don Francisco Guerrero y Torres, who was born in the neighboring district and directed the construction work for fourteen years. He also designed the floor plan, which was published in the *Gaceta de México* (Mexican Gazette) in 1791. This plan is surely the most articulate and suggestive in all of Latin American colonial architecture.

As Diego Angula Iñiguez has shown, the architect took as his model the plan of a monument of classical antiquity, an anonymous temple whose ruins still existed on the outskirts of Rome at the beginning of the sixteenth century. Serlio reproduced it in the *Treatise on Architecture*—translated into Spanish in 1552—but because the remaining walls were not very high he could only attempt a reconstruction of the elevations and could not give an exact idea of its covering.

This is where Guerrero y Torres had to count on his own resources. Fortunately his imagination not only allowed him to resolve the design of the facades and the shaping of the roof, but also inspired him to create an interior organization that was far superior to the spatial monotony of almost all the Mexican churches of the period.

This small work of art is composed of a large oval chamber surrounded by four chapels, with another rotunda in front and a mixtilineal octagon in its rear portion. The whole is crowned by splendid domes covered on the outside with blue and white mosaic that extends to the nonfunctional parapet, which hides its connections to the lower walls of red volcanic *tezontle*. The harmony of the building is completed by fine carving around the doors and the star-shaped windows that constitutes, according to Mario J. Buschiazzo, "the most masterful and daring expression of American baroque."[1] I am happy to add that the twentieth century has contributed to the future preservation of this architectural treasure: owing to the unevenness of the subsoil surrounding the well, the chapel was leaning more than a meter and was in great danger of collapse. Modern engineering techniques have recently succeeded in shoring up the foundations and raising the chapel floor so that it is now level.

Retracing the route, today called Calzado de los Misterios (Road of the Mysteries), that Juan Diego took on his way to mass, we reach an urban complex composed of the ruins of a pyramid, the sixteenth-century Church of Santiago de Tlatelolco, and a group of tall buildings, among them the new Ministry of Foreign Relations. This complex is called the Plaza de las tres Culturas (Plaza of the Three Cultures) since the buildings represent the ancient Aztec era, the colonial centuries that followed, and the present international civilization that, especially after the events of recent years, should probably not be identified with culture.

If the small chapel of El Pocito is a notable example of external influence, the Plaza de las Tres Culturas, for better or worse, constitutes an eloquent parable of the meaning of tradition. The fact that the first subjects in our study are on Mexican soil does not mean that other countries, such as Guatemala, Colombia, Bolivia, or Peru, offer a less fruitful harvest of historical documentation. The ones we have chosen are exemplary for their far-reaching temporal significance within a circumscribed spatial dimension.

THE PERSISTENCE OF THE URBAN GRID PATTERN

At this juncture we would like to point out that the few pages at our disposal do not favor or even permit the development of this subject according to established inductive or deductive methods. Such methods would require compiling all the materials possible, or beginning by some other means to establish a foundation that is broad, strong, and solid enough to support the uncomfortable weight of the chronological, sociological, geographical, esthetic, and technological superstructure which, in turn, would need to be integrated and fused with all the architectural documentation in order to prove our theory. And the author, an architect whose brief experience of the reality of Latin America was acquired during a trip through most of its countries in 1968, would have to depend on the historians, who would be indispensable for such a task. But on reading the papers of the international seminar held in Caracas in 1967, "The Situation of the Historiography of Latin American Architecture," one discovers that practically all of the papers delivered on that occasion begin with a *captatio benevolentiae* that deplores the lack of materials and tools needed for accomplishing scholarly work.

Only a few art historians from the New and Old Worlds dared to make conclusive statements concerning the architectural relationships that exist among the Latin American countries themselves, among all those countries and the Iberian Peninsula, and, finally, the relationship of Spain and Portugal to the Islamic world and to the rest of Europe, not to mention the reverse influence on the Continent flowing back from America.

Brazil is generally afforded a special position, due as much to the absence of pre-Columbian architecture and to ethnic differences as to the fact that the first political and cultural influences emanated from Portugal and not from Spain. Most of the countries, sometimes compared to "an archipelago of cultures of similar origin and nevertheless isolated, closed off, almost incommunicado among themselves," have preserved many qualities in common during their four centuries of architectural history: their differences lie more in the quantity of outstanding monuments, and in the rate or rapidity of their development, than in their essence.

For all of these reasons, and in order to avoid tedious repetitions, we will not attempt to exhaust the topic here. Instead, we will confine ourselves to pointing out one or two of the most characteristic examples in order to establish their architectural relationship, even at the risk of being criticized for applying rather personal criteria or for a fortuitous selection of documentation that omits so many other examples.

The Archivo de las Indias (Archive of the Indies) in Seville preserves the plans of more than one hundred cities founded in the colonies during the first fifty years of the sixteenth century. At that time Europe already possessed extensive theoretical literature on urban planning, although there were few opportunities for applying these theories that had been formulated during almost two thousand years of urban tradition. In America the relationship between theory and practice was reversed, and the opportunities for putting theory into practice, unparalleled since colonization by the Roman Empire, surpassed by far any available knowledge, at least at the beginning. It is not surprising that the first cities founded by the colonizers on the Atlantic islands and in the Antilles were simple fortified ports of informal layout. An exception is the plan of Santo Domingo, dating from the very end of the sixteenth century, that copies the plan of Santa Fe de Granada where the military camp of the Catholic monarchs seems to have been transformed into stone.

Naturally Cortes, who was after all a soldier, applied the same principles to the founding of the first cities on the American continent. Rather than losing themselves in discussions of erudite theories, he and his soldiers had to solve real problems with their own hands in the building of Villa Rica de la Vera Cruz, as Bernal Díaz del Castillo relates:

> We set out the plans for a church, a market, the arsenals and everything neces-sary for a city and we built a fort. . . . Cortez himself was the first to begin the work, carrying earth and stones on his back and digging foundations; all his captains and soldiers followed his example; we labored unceasingly . . . some of us digging foundations and others raising walls, working in the quarries or making bricks and paving stones. . . . Others worked as carpenters and the blacksmiths made nails.[2]

The new urban plan in checkerboard form that soon became typical, with the church and the market at the perpendicular intersection of the two principal streets, constituted an improvement over the simple crossroads village derived from the *castrum romanum*. Barely three years later, in 1525, this solution was reaffirmed and exalted when the conquerors began the construction of the capital of the new provinces on the same island that the destroyed capital of Montezuma had occupied. This location, vehemently opposed by Cortes and his officers, was finally accepted for strategic and political reasons. As we know now, building the city on the lake was dis-astrous from an ecological point of view because of the marshy subsoil and the increasing difficulties of adequate drainage and a pure water supply.

Although the advantages of such a choice may seem doubtful today, Tenochtitlán/Mexico City continues to be the most notable fusion on the continent of external influence and local tradition since the day when Alonso García Bravo, the famous topographer who prepared the plans for Villa Rica de la Vera Cruz, began the layout for the new capital. The old city had been leveled, destroyed district by district as the bloody conquest made its daily advance. One could only make out the exact grid pattern of its principal avenues, the canals and the blocks of dwellings generously intertwined with plazas. García Bravo was clever enough to place the main square, together with the cathedral and Cortes's palace, in the former sacred area of the center, and to adapt the whole plan of the city to what was left of the native inheritance, surprisingly similar to the scheme of Cortes, a soldier who probably knew little or nothing of the development of European urbanism since the days of Hippodamus.

But in the imperial court of Charles V, where Cortes would proudly relate the progress of his urban building campaign, the powerful elite, both lay and religious, was indeed conscious of that inheritance. From the early days of the colony a constant stream of advice from the Peninsula supported the discipline of the gridiron plan with its central plaza. When, finally, the royal ordinances were compiled into the Laws of the Indies in 1573, they reflected few changes with regard to earlier recommendations, and had much more direct effects.

For more than twenty-five years historians have speculated and argued as to whether the general application of the checkerboard as a normative model for the New World is derived from the theoreticians of the Italian Renaissance, especially L. B. Alberti and the classical master Vitruvius, or if, on the contrary, it is based directly on the traditional plans of the Spanish Reconquest, preceded in turn by the orthogonal plans of medieval English, French, and German cities. Supported by the authority of Rome, the orthogonal concept was disseminated by the writings of St. Thomas Aquinas and was related therefore to Aristotle and his references to the Greek city planner Hippodamus, to whom the invention of the checkerboard plan is usually attributed.

The term *Hippodamic plan* is a very superficial description insofar as it can refer to cities located in the plain or in the mountains, and to solutions that range from the insipid monotony of Miletus, the native city of Hippodamus, to the admirably varied and terraced configuration of Priene, and even to that of Alexandria, the superb creation of Dinocrates, Alexander's city planner, a century later. Checkerboard solutions had existed two thousand years before that in villages that sheltered the builders of the pyramids in the Nile Valley and in similar settlements on the banks of the Indus and its tributaries.

My purpose in reviewing the wide proliferation of the orthogonal plan is not to establish its distant influence on Latin American town planning but, on the contrary, to formulate and at the same time respond to the question: why can't a particular human creation emerge independently in different parts of the world, and why must it be limited to forming part of a single tradition?

The experience of the Mexican capital furthered the checkerboard plan in other cities founded in the following decades in Mexico as well as other regions of Latin America. In some areas, especially in Peru, the conquerors encountered a highly developed urban civilization that had organized its settlements geometrically. In Cuzco, the Incan capital, the result was a close fusion of new buildings with those from the pre-Conquest period.

There are towns with irregular layouts owing to the abrupt topography that characterizes the sites of mining centers like Guanajuato and Taxco in Mexico or Ouro Preto in Brazil. Here, as in Salvador de Bahía, the first capital of Brazil, the topography also agreed with the innate preference of the Portuguese for irregularity—which may relate to the negligent attitude of the government toward city planning. But in other regions, even where precedents for it did not exist, the grid was applied regardless of climate, topography, or other ecological circumstances.

Many art historians celebrate the imposition of this system by the Spanish crown as an undeniable achievement of Western civilization. The experience of four centuries of urban development forces me to disagree with this assertion. The authoritarian rigidity of the checkerboard with the main square at the intersection of the *cardo y decumanus* or, in its absence, at the very center of the planned whole, the uniformity of the building blocks, and the width of the streets have, on more than one occasion, proven to be not only an impediment to urban economic expansion but of rather dubious visual quality as well.

Caracas, the capital of Venezuela, and her port, La Guaira, constitute two examples of these alternative possibilities. The first, rising between imposing mountain ranges, was designed in 1567 following a rigid model, while the flexible linear plan of La Guaira, founded thirty-five years later, was for some reason determined by the topography of the site and not by the Laws of the Indies.

In general, however, there was no immunity to the plague of the grid pattern: after overrunning the Spanish colonies it not only returned to Europe, where it proliferated under varying economic conditions for three or four centuries, but it also returned to the American continent, determining the configuration of most of its new cities as well as their surrounding country-side.

THE INFLUENCE OF CIAM AND THE GARDEN CITY

The tendencies of the twentieth century promulgated by the so-called region-alists, the apostles of the English garden city and of analogous reform movements in Central Europe, had scarcely any effect on the planning of Latin American cities.

Only in the late 1920s did the International Congress of Modern Archi-tecture (CIAM) gather together the loose ends of urban practice and theory; a new international exchange of ideas began to animate those who were pro-posing an adequate environment for man. The CIAM, made up of a select group of avant-garde architects, investigated the problem methodically, be-ginning with basic living units, then the rational means for their manufacture, and finally their organization into functional cities.

After five years of meticulous studies, of work sessions and congresses, the efforts of the CIAM culminated in the Athens Charter of 1933, a pro-grammatic statement that has had a decisive influence on the work of a whole generation of city planners. The tenets of the charter were based on analyses of urban life, scrupulously categorized according to its four functions: living, working, circulation, and recreation.

There is no doubt that the CIAM Mediterranean cruise that preceded the formulation of the charter was dominated by the theories that Le Corbusier had been developing in various writings for more than a decade. That was not all: to give reality to his theoretical manifestoes, Le Corbusier at the same time designed projects of a utopian character for several cities: Paris, Buenos Aires, Rio de Janeiro, and São Paulo, all precisely organized according to Cartesian coordinates, with tall buildings in the center where traffic arteries intersected at different levels. Le Corbusier wrote: "Man walks straight ahead because he has a purpose . . . the winding road is for the pack-donkey . . ." (*Urbanisme,* 1925). Flying over the Argentine pampa, he noted in astonishment: "At 1200 meters I have seen cities of the original colonization, rectilinear settlements or checkerboard designs" (*Précisions,* 1930).

Due to the political events that led to World War II, the Athens Charter was not known beyond the inner circle of CIAM until its publication in 1942 as the conclusion and appendix of a book entitled *Can Our Cities Survive?* At that time the weak points in the charter were already known. These stemmed principally from the aseptic isolation of the four functions of city life, but the worst flaw was the omission of plans for a civic center that would serve as the nucleus of the city's cultural identity. The civic center is a very significant concept in the fluctuating exchange of urban ideas across the centuries and between continents, and it is not at all surprising that the author of *Can Our Cities Survive?* the Spaniard J. L. Sert, used the words "a visible expression of the highest aspirations of man" to underline the importance of such a center.[3] At this point he introduced into the program of CIAM, of which he was a member, a concept that goes beyond utilitarian needs, and with the precise intention of reaffirming the continuity of this tradition Sert cited a passage from the royal ordinances for new cities, (Laws of the Indies), proclaimed by Philip II in 1573 that described the *plaza mayor,* the main square.

A few years after its publication the Athens Charter began to have an influence on Latin American town planning. In 1942 Sert himself, together with P. L. Wiener, undertook a project, which was never completed, for the Cidade dos Motores (Motor City) in Brazil.[4] The next application of the principles of the CIAM occurred in a housing project by C. F. Ferreira in the state of São Paulo, which demonstrated two very Corbusian characteristics: the elimination of the concept of the street as a space framed by the facades of the apartment buildings, and the use of by laws to raise the house off the ground so as not to interrupt the garden and recreation area. In the meantime similar projects were constructed in Brazil, Chile, and Colombia—some of these achieved individual architectural expression, for example, the curvilinear Pedregulho housing complex by Reidy in Rio de Janeiro, built from 1950 to 1952.

A good example of the rapid assimilation of external influences is the planning of Carlos Raul Villanueva in Venezuela. His first housing development, "El Silencio" in Caracas, was built in 1941; probably the first slum-clearance project sponsored by a Latin American government, its arcaded square, articulated by two fountains, was still reminiscent of Renaissance motifs. A second project built two years later in Maracaibo is one of the rare applications of the concept of the English garden city in Latin America: single-family units in short rows of three-stories surrounding a community center with its market, school, and church.

From 1955 to 1957 the Banco Obrero (Workingman's Bank), with a group of young architects under the direction of Villanueva, built three enormous groups of high-rise superblocks intended for 160,000 former farmworkers and shantytown inhabitants. These units show the undeniable influence of the CIAM charter, including the lack of interest in community centers, as did Le Corbusier's *unités d'habitation* well known at the time throughout South America.

Between 1950 and 1960 prismatic apartment towers like those in Caracas were being built everywhere. Their appearance varied only slightly, depending on improvements in technology, and in general they are grouped in monotonous rows of parallel units with no reference to the rural or urban landscape of which they form a part. At best, their placement and the distance between them are determined by optimum exposure to or protection from sun and wind.

During this period the greatest opportunity for a coherent application of the principles of modern city planning to the planning of a new city came from President Juscelino Kubitschek's decision to build the new capital of Brazil on the inland plateau one thousand kilometers from the coast. In a competition open only to Brazilian architects, an international jury awarded the prize to Lucio Costa, teacher and spiritual leader of the generation of architects who had worked with Le Corbusier on the Ministry of Public Education project in Rio.

Costa's project conformed exactly to CIAM's urban theories; they were still in vogue, and the new capital was going to be the best example of their shortcomings. But the airplane shape of the Brasília plan also contains elements more recent than those in the Athens charter: the principal traffic axis and an artery that borders the residential districts, as well as the streets that run parallel to it, are slightly curved to avoid the monotony of super-blocks. These streets cross in the physical center of the city, with the monumental axis of the fuselage, an avenue 360 meters wide flanked by uniform ministry buildings, opening into the Plaza of the Three Powers, the civic center surrounded by government buildings. The urban complex is surrounded on three sides by branches of an artificial lake.

The project has been criticized for its inhuman scale and its autocratic monumentality; several writers have related it to Imperial Rome or to the reign of Louis XIV, speculating on how similarly Hitler or Mussolini would have expressed their power in urban terms if they had had the opportunity to build a new capital. But there are other precedents for this style. One example is L'Enfant's plan for the city of Washington, which was celebrated, at least at the time, as a symbol of government of the people, by the people, and for the people.

It is curious that, to the best of our knowledge, no critic has yet related Brasília to a more recent urban creation that constitutes its immediate precedent, namely Le Corbusier's project for Chandigarh, the new capital of Punjab in India, which antedates Costa's plan by six years. The old master presented the same superblocks; he curved the principal avenues in the residential districts very slightly; he had them intersect at the center with a monumental perpendicular axis pointing toward the Capitol and the Assembly, the Secretariat, the Palace of Justice, and the Governor's palace (which has been replaced by a plan for the building of a museum). Completing the similarity to Brasília, it is all enclosed by two rivers.

We end the comparison here, for not having seen Chandigarh in the reality of its urban landscape, we find ourselves obliged to leave unanswered the question whether its scale is any more human. We would like to be able to affirm that the scale is balanced sufficiently to establish a reasonable relationship between the two horizontal dimensions and the third, that is, the vertical, a relationship that Brasília unfortunately lacks. We are almost certain that in Chandigarh the proportions of the buildings in relation to the plaza they delimit, and the disposition of smaller elements on the ground, are such that a person who dares to cross the square can overcome the threat of agoraphobia and perceive the ambience as a pleasant spatial experience.

INTERNAL REELABORATION OF EUROPEAN TYPOLOGIES

We have dealt extensively with the theme of city planning because it was within the urban environment that the heritage of European ideas and aspirations was transferred in a primitive and energetic manner to the new Latin American reality. Well-known art historians have described the development of architectural motifs and the stylistic changes they underwent when they were transplanted from the Old World to the New.

It would be fascinating to analyze the use of the salomonic column in the civic and religious architecture of the colonies, and to observe the appearance and development of the *estípite* (inverted pyramidal pedestals). But these are only decorative elements, and their importance in architectural terms—for example, in the organization of volumes and spaces—is very limited. If it is true that European influence was decisive in the formation of the urban image in Latin America, we can see at the same time that new building programs imposed by different conditions led to that influence being overcome or modified. With respect to specific buildings, at times the adoption of regional solutions led to a *sui generis* tradition.

Mario Buschiazzo defines this new and powerful factor as "the drama of the Indian in his transition from a life that is totally outside Western notions of enclosed space . . . his fear of interior space."[5] This state of mind that combines innate lack of interest in the interior with a clear preference for open spaces was taken into account by the Mexican missionaries; this is the reason for the enormous success of the open-air chapels of the sixteenth century. The chapel of the Indians, as the open-air chapel was called, was essentially an annex to a church or convent that allowed mass to be celebrated outdoors by an unlimited number of Indians. Whether or not one assumes some precedent in Europe, in New Spain the open-air chapel was used in some of the most functional and original works of religious architecture, for example, San Juan Teposcolula in the state of Oaxaca.

Subsequently, the preference for the exterior aspect of buildings became even more pronounced. Manuel Toussaint, the great admirer of the Mexican baroque, describes the result: "The great baroque and Churrigueresque churches . . . are essentially works of sculpture more than of architecture. The facade is like a retable emerging from the nave, rising up in front of the church, and turning into stone in order to withstand the elements. The towers as well as the dome are covered with sculpture, and often the entire building seems the work of a pastry chef, all meringue and colored paper."[6]

This passage suggests another Latin American tradition: the irresistible passion for covering the walls with ornament, paintings, mosaics, sculptures, wrought iron, or other intriguing textures. Fernando Chueca Goitia observes: "The wildest baroque ornamental fantasies were superimposed on the most austere, rigid forms . . . an inner contradiction that accounted for decoration taking over as it pleased without regard for architectural principles."[7] In this paragraph Chueca Goitia is referring principally to metropolitan Churrigueresque architecture, but his observation is equally valid with respect to baroque architecture in the Spanish colonies where, in many cases, and not only in the eighteenth century, the splendid ornamentation has hidden the fact that the spaces it encloses are, in architectural terms, primitive and insignificant. One need only think of the works of Borromini, Guarini, or Balthasar Neumann as examples of the sophisticated level of spatial creation that could be achieved with the concepts and resources of the period.

Although few in number, exceptions fortunately exist in the Spanish colonies—for instance, El Pocito, mentioned at the beginning of this chapter. In Brazil there are significantly more examples. Each manifestation, whether economic, cultural, or architectural, seemed less regimented and more open to private initiative in the part of America colonized by Portugal. The flight of the Indians to the interior of the territory and the subsequent importation of black slaves led to a very different ethnic composition that was further accentuated by the great influence of non-Iberian Europeans.

The curvilinear plans of the so-called *arquitectura mineira* (architecture of the Brazilian state of Minas Gerais) show no relationship to the regular plan of the Hispano-American church; rather they seem to have their origin in Italian, Bohemian, or Bavarian designs. The exterior of the Church of the Rosary (Rosario) in Ouro Prêto is of superb sculptural quality, and if the architect, Manuel Francisco Araujo, had known how to give a positive resolution to the ceiling he would have achieved a perfect interior space, comparable to Dominikus Zimmerman's Monastery of Wiess in Bavaria. The plans of the two churches are surprisingly similar. They are separated by a period of only forty years, and both represent the culminating point in the evolution and liberation of interior space.

FROM HISTORICAL STYLES TO THE MODERN MOVEMENT

A generation later, at the end of the eighteenth century, neoclassicism dominated the Western world. The triumph of this movement in America was based on the fact that its ideology was identified with the French Revolution and, as a consequence, it was welcomed in all the nations that had won their political independence from Europe. At that time Latin Americans considered their baroque buildings as nothing more than symbols of Spanish and Portuguese domination, and they directed their attention toward the forms of neoclassicism, thus substituting French influence for Iberian.

This process varied in character and intensity according to the level of development of direct contact. In some countries the growing immigration of Italians, French, English, Spanish, and Germans gave impetus to an extremely cosmopolitan period. As a result the center of Buenos Aires, for example, lacking colonial architecture, is very similar to Paris or London.

The arrival of art nouveau, another European import introduced during the first decades of the twentieth century, marks the end of this development. Gaudí, the great, solitary master of this style, had no notable influence on Latin American architects, with the exception of Juan O'Gorman, whose admirable house in Mexico was, unfortunately, recently destroyed. In the major cities few buildings that followed this style are left. It is typical of the cyclical change in taste that monuments of the period in which this style flourished, for example, the Hospital Español (Spanish Hospital) in Buenos Aires or the Palacio de Bellas Artes (Palace of Fine Arts) in Mexico City, are no longer considered in bad taste today as they were previously.

Those who were not very certain of their good taste or culture resorted to Andalusian colonial, to California Spanish, or to some other historic revival that emerged periodically as a reaction to, and parallel to, the waves of dependence on international movements. The high points of such tendencies can be noted during the decade following 1910, in the 1940s, and again in our time as folklore is being reevaluated under government sponsorship. As late as 1943 the new National Palace in Guatemala City was built in colonial style, as was the 1947 project for the building of the Society of Peruvian Architects in Lima.

Secondary waves arise in relation to the pre-Columbian cultures that are even further removed from contemporary problems. The result of these anachronistic designs is found in houses that do not correspond to our life-style or to our social conditions, in museums lacking adequate lighting, in hotels decorated in Mayan or Aztec style in glaring contrast to their modern and luxurious conveniences.

Denying the passage of time does not help to solve functional problems, to find an acceptable regional style, or to search successfully for authentic national expression. At the time of World War I some Latin American architects were already concerned with these problems, but their isolated voices found no echo. In the middle of the 1920s European functionalism appeared as a new source of inspiration, helping to free the younger generation of architects from the sterile formulas of their national academies or the Academy of Fine Arts in Paris.

The students of Villagrán in Mexico proclaimed the slogan of Le Corbusier—*La maison est une machine à habiter*— at almost the same time that Gregori Warchavchik published the *Manifesto of Functional Architecture* in São Paulo, Brazil, in which he affirms his adherence to that same principle. Appropriately enough, the first functional buildings were designed in Mexico and Brazil, but they were not generally accepted. In 1939 the pages of a single issue of an architecture magazine were enough to include all the works of modern progressive architecture built in Mexico up to that time.

In Brazil the break occurred in 1936, when Le Corbusier, on his second trip to Latin America, spent a month in Rio de Janeiro as consultant to the project for the Ministry of Education and Health under the direction of Lucio Costa and a group of his students, among them Oscar Niemeyer and Eduardo Reidy. In addition to his active collaboration in that project, Le Corbusier reached a wider public with a series of six lectures; his stay in Rio was of incalculable educational value and had a lasting influence beyond the borders of Brazil. The widespread influence of Le Corbusier became evident following World War II when construction increased sharply in most Latin American countries. A recounting of all the projects inspired by the work of the great master would fill a book; we will mention only some of the most outstanding examples.

In Brazil Reidy began the series with his undulating housing development of Pedregulho, inconceivable without Le Corbusier's precedent in Algiers. In Venezuela, as we mentioned earlier, Carlos Raúl Villanueva, whose architectural imagination and originality were reflected in his projects for Ciudad Universitaria (University City) in Caracas, could not resist the attraction of the *unité d'habitation* when he collaborated on the design of housing developments.

On the other hand, in Chile, several admirers of the French master had successfully adapted his concepts to the technical, topographical, and climatic conditions of their country, thus finding in a quiet and discreet way their own architectural expression. This was true not only of residential housing, for example, the excellent apartment units of Portales in Santiago, but of creations such as the church of the Benedictine monastery in the hills overlooking the capital. Even while some exterior aspects of this church are reminiscent of the La Tourette convent of Le Corbusier, its articulation of spaces and volumes is totally original.

The most outstanding work of modern architecture in Chile is the CEPAL[8] building in Vitacura. Its architect, Emilio Duhart, studied with Walter Gropius at Harvard, a fact that does not seem to have exerted a very marked influence on Duhart's thinking. Later he went to Paris to work with Le Corbusier at the time when the famous studio on Rue de Sèvres was developing the architectural designs for Chandigarh. There is no doubt that the brutalist treatment of the surface and some sculptural details of the CEPAL building show the influence of Le Corbusier, and that its dominant snail-shell spiral is very similar to the Chandigarh Assembly. At the same time, this particular form can be related to the spiral of Chichén Itzá or the cosmic shapes of Machu Picchu. If one adds to this the undeniable confrontation between the introverted reserve of the building and the rigid profiles of the Andes, it is evident that the CEPAL headquarters in Santiago constitutes a noteworthy dialogue between current international influence and the timeless invariables of the continent.

There is no formula for such integration that can be applied in the same way to other countries and conditions. The major Brazilian architect Oscar Niemeyer, for example, believed that he should effect a clear separation between his style and the influence of Le Corbusier which, after the latter's collaboration on the Ministry of Education building, became overwhelming. With some minor exceptions, such as the Chapel of Fátima in Brasília, Niemeyer achieved this separation, beginning with his declaration that he was the legitimate heir of the eighteenth-century masters of the Brazilian baroque. Rational investigation and the pure lines of International Functionalism were replaced by sensuous curves and exuberant forms. In some cases, by means of horizontal perforation, Niemeyer does compete with the fluidity of interior spaces that was the most significant achievement of the *barroco mineiro*. His special talent and style attracted the next generation of architects and the general public beyond Brazilian borders.

The tendency to favor structural quality and indeterminate contours did not depend exclusively on the Brazilian prototype, but in a less spectacular way it also had its roots outside Latin America in the careers of masters such as Frank Lloyd Wright and Alvar Aalto. The Rio de la Plata region owes most to the North American genius. Wright's influence is found in various houses in Punta del Este and other resorts, and in the interior of the headquarters of the Banco de Londres y América del Sud (Bank of London and South America) in Buenos Aires. Other examples also recall Wright and Aalto, but they are widely dispersed and therefore do not seem as influential as they should have been—the program of the Peruvian group *Agrupación Espacio* (Space Group), the dining rooms of the Park and Davis plant by H. Klumb in Puerto Rico, or the project by Rogelio Salmona for the Society of Colombian Architects. Salmona studied with Le Corbusier and yet, in spite of this, he reveals the indisputable influence of Scandinavian architecture in his housing developments in Bogotá.

The genius of Aalto seems to have influenced C. R. Villanueva when he designed the marvelous Aula Magna and the stadiums of University City in Caracas. It is also apparent in the imaginative details of the brickwork of buildings by Eladio Dieste in the suburbs of Montevideo.

On a continent that values feeling above rational clarity, the strict line and the right angles of the so-called International Style, represented by Walter Gropius and the Bauhaus, could never have had a profound influence. Whatever influence functionalism does have stems principally from the formal variety developed by Mies van der Rohe during his stay in the United States and commercialized by the firm of Skidmore, Owings, and Merrill. The Brazilian version of this school has its center in São Paulo, where architects like Eduardo Kneese de Mello, Henrique Mindlin, Vilanova Artigas, and others constitute a "paulista" (of São Paulo) group, close to the international movement, in contrast to the "carioca" (of Rio de Janeiro) architects led by Oscar Niemeyer. Of course, there are regional characteristics even within this rigid style—for example, in Buenos Aires where, apart from proverbial Argentine sobriety, one can still feel the impact of the lectures and classes given by the distinguished Italians Bruno Zevi and Pier Luigi Narvi during the 1950s.

IN SEARCH OF ONE'S OWN TRADITION

Such differences are of secondary importance and do not obscure the fact that, as has happened in the rest of the Western world, every Latin American country, depending on the state of its technology, should now have its own Skidmore, Ownings, and Merrill, with curtain walls and all the other neo-academic formulas. Moreover, the smaller these countries are, the more they seem subject to eclectic tendencies based on the work of all the renowned architects taken together—the famous Latin Americans, more contemporary architects such as Eero Saarinen and Louis Kahn, and others whom we cannot mention for lack of space. This kind of eclecticism may be considered a tool and, therefore, rather useful at first as a form of apprenticeship. But it should be overcome in time, giving way to direct understanding of the realities of environment, city, and nation.

Under present circumstances cases like these occur frequently: the government buildings in one of the state capitals in Mexico look like half-size copies of those on the Plaza of the Three Powers in Brasília; Niemeyer's apartment house in Berlin is identical to a block of ministry offices in Brazil; a school of architecture in São Paulo uses the same construction and is covered with the same form as the mausoleum of the Cementerio Norte (North Cemetery) in Montevideo.

Countries like Colombia, Peru, Guatemala, Mexico, and others with an architectural tradition almost two thousand years old deserve to have their cities protected against the indiscriminate, worldwide uniformity of architectural concepts and their visual expression. In these countries pre-Hispanic inspiration was not completely extinguished during the three centuries of colonial art; by means of fusion and penetration it has survived to such an extent that this common fund of tradition can enrich the architectural vocabulary of our own time.

Without applying any ornamental detail from Uxmal to his model, Pedro Ramírez Vázquez, the architect of the new Museo de Antropología (Museum of Anthropology) in Mexico City, has succeeded in interpreting the language of Mayan architecture simply through the proportions of the interior patio in the museum.

The predilection for vivid colors and surfaces of varying textures, the monumental scale of the exterior spaces, and even other characteristics that are less attractive, make Ciudad Universitaria (University City) in Mexico the example of an architectural style that could not have been conceived in any other historical or geographical circumstances. The two most famous buildings of the University, the Olympic stadium with the sculptured murals of Diego Rivera and the library by Juan O'Gorman, where the book-stacks building is completely covered by polychromatic stone mosaic, are eloquent testimonies to the continuity of a tradition that goes back to pre-Columbian times.

Will this kind of architectural concern still be valid for the next generation? We should be aware that within the next thirty years the conditions of life throughout the world, especially in the so-called Third World, of which Latin America forms a considerable part, will have changed profoundly.

Prefabrication and the standardization of the building process will have to be developed to their fullest in order to satisfy the needs of the growing masses of the future society and to raise their standard of living to an acceptable level. This development can quickly convert architecture into a subordinate branch of a giant industrial enterprise. We should recognize that questions such as foreign cultural influence and the importance of tradition in architecture will probably be of small interest to those who have to confront problems of shelter and survival for vast numbers of human beings by the beginning of the next century.

Notes

1.   Mario J. Buschiazzo, *Historia de la arquietectura colonial en Iberoamérica*. Buenos Aires: Emece, 1961, p. 68.

2.   Bernal Díaz del Castillo, *Historia verdadera de la conquista de la Nueva España*. México: Ediciones Mexicanas, 1950, p. 92.

3.   José Luis Sert, *Can Our Cities Survive?* Cambridge: Harvard University Press, 1942, p. 230.

4.   Ibid., p. 232.

5.   Mario Buschiazzo, *op. cit.,* p. 50.

6.   Manuel Toussaint, *Arte colonial en México*. México: Imprenta Universitaria, 1948, p. 357.

7.   Fernando Chueca Goitia, "Desgracia y triunfo del barroco," in *Boletín del Centro de Investigaciones Históricas y Estéticas*. Caracas, Universidad Central de Venezuela, no. 8, October, 1967, p. 117.

8.   Editor's Note: CEPAL is the "Comisión Económica Para América Latina" of the United Nations, known in English as ECLA-Economic Commission for Latin America.

5 / The Current Crisis in Latin American Architecture

RAMÓN VARGAS SALGUERO AND
RAFAEL LÓPEZ RANGEL

THE QUESTIONING OF TRADITIONAL VALUES

Fernando Salinas, in his book *Revolutionary Architecture of the Third World*—which with the works of Roberto Segre marks the beginning of a new presentation of the architectural problems of our underdeveloped countries—points out the following characteristics of the architecture in dependent countries: 1) the contrast between the luxurious buildings for the minority and the poverty of the majority, 2) the steadily increasing housing shortage, 3) the difference between rural and urban standards of living, 4) land speculation, 5) the minimal contribution of the state to the solution of the housing problem, 6) the cooperation of crafts and advanced technology in resolving isolated problems, 7) the concentration of building investment in the large cities, 8) the use of imported materials as a consequence of industrial underdevelopment, 9) the anarchy of types and dimensions of building materials, 10) the loss of architects' efforts and talents to the isolated problems of the ruling class, 11) the small number of technicians, 12) the subordination of esthetic solutions to the limitations of an uneven technology.[1] In order to continue to develop this important line of reasoning—the only one, in our opinion, that offers an objective point of view—it becomes necessary to reevaluate the notions concerning the development of modern architecture that are current in our countries—notions characterized by their partial and purely technical focus. In other words, it is necessary that the emergence of architectural modernity in Latin America be analyzed by means of an integrated study that views architecture as *part of the historical process* in our dependent countries. This, in outline form and with the limitations that a study like this imposes on us, is what we will try to accomplish here.

The Latin American functionalist movement came to the fore during the late 1930s and early 1940s, when Latin America was becoming integrated in a more dynamic way into world capitalism, characterized at that time, as we have already sketched elsewhere, by the appearance of Germany and the United States as imperial powers and their projection toward "the colonial world," replacing Great Britain in our area. From that moment on the configuration of Latin American countries began to acquire the definitive characteristics of modernity which incorporated them, although in an under-developed way, into the world of what was called in the West mass societies or consumer societies.

A closer look reveals that the new architecture in Latin America also emerged (as was the case in Europe) under the banner of the antiacademic struggle. On our continent this was directed against the official art of the independent republics during the nineteenth century and the first decades of the twentieth, characterized by the imposition of neoclassicism and the subsequent participation in the romantic movement; throughout the world a climate of historicism and, eventually, modernism was created in response to the problems of capitalist industrial production and its invasion of creative processes.

HISTORICAL ANTECEDENTS OF THE INDEPENDENCE PERIOD

In a contradictory way backward nations have the privilege of observing their own future in the more developed ones. They can (and in some few cases it has in fact happened) pass more quickly over the historical distance that separates the arrow from the rifle, simple cooperation from capitalist co-operation. It is not surprising that the institutionalization of the bourgeois regime in Europe, effected by the French Revolution, has had such a notable influence on the development of all our countries, which have tried to implant constitutions and similar legal and ideological precepts in an effort to achieve the level of development reached by those countries. The separation of Church and State, the disentailment and mercantilization of large land-holdings and their subdivision into small properties that would encourage the independent farmer, the abolition of slavery, the promulgation of the rights of man, and the unrestricted respect for the "sacred rights" of private property (in the words of Juárez) are only a few of the many relations of production that our nations adopted with a view to bridging the gap between economic imperialism and the native bourgeoisie in the process of maturation. These were ideas taken from the English and French Revolutions and implanted in America at the time when Spain was falling under the heel of the French hussars, a situation which the incipient Latin American bourgeoisie took advantage of to free themselves from the mother country. There is a historical coincidence in the appearance of Morelos, Hidalgo, Bolivar, O'Higgins, and Sucre, and a very understandable similarity in their Latin American ideals. The nineteenth century was beginning.

If in the colonial period the pentaphonic and monodic music of the indigenous peoples had been combined with European polyphony, theo-logical metaphysics with a belief in magic, Christian liturgy with ancient rituals, and vaulted convents and cathedrals with huts of palm leaf and mud, in the period of independence the influence of France, the revolutionary center of the world, began to flourish next to all these Hispano-Indian elements. Harmony was replaced by polyphony, religious music by waltzes, polkas and mazurkas; journalists and political writers assumed the stature of Jacobin tribunes, and baroque altars and facades were replaced by neoclassic porticos. At this time of social convulsion a nationalist tone of popular cast began to make timid, occasional appearances, giving shade and color to our literature, music, painting, and architecture. There was no audience for concerts, but we had concert artists; the people were illiterate, but blood-and-thunder novels were published in installments; we had not mastered stone-cutting or the calculus of the medieval guilds, but we built domes . . . of mud, and with earthen arches.

Historically we did not have at our disposal the scientific theory needed to understand that development comes substantially from raising the average productivity of labor and the level of the productive forces, and that in general terms laws and precepts cannot go beyond the level reached by the productivity of labor. Norms and constitutions appropriate to higher stages of culture were being imposed on countries where the majority of the population lived in primitive conditions within the structure of an Asiatic mode of production. When this occurred, ordinary reality undertook to mutilate and weaken the laws that they imagined could go beyond customary rights and privileges. The soaring flights of architecture were weighed down by rudimentary technique. It is symptomatic, for example, that with very few exceptions no Gothic arches were built.

Despite the fact that historical materialism had not yet been elaborated, one of the dialectical laws that this science later established was applied empirically. We mean the law that although the juridical, political, and ideological superstructure does depend, in the final analysis, on the level of development of the productive forces, these forces being the principal pole of the contradiction (between themselves and the relations of production), it can happen in some cases that relations of production become momentarily more advanced than the level of labor productivity and may then exert influence on that level and cause it to rise more quickly than could result from the natural rhythm of the means of production and the skills of the laborer. Mao Zedong said:

> It is true that productive forces, economic practice, and the economic base generally play the principal and decisive roles; whoever denies this is not a materialist. But it must also be admitted that, under certain conditions, production relationships, theory and the superstructure play the principal and decisive role. When the development of productive forces becomes impossible without a change in the relations of production, this change plays the principal and decisive role . . . [in this way] we avoid mechanistic materialism and we firmly defend dialectical materialism.[2]

This possibility has been converted into a constant in dependent nations, whose history reveals in its most general outlines the repeated efforts of the native bourgeoisie to catalyze the processes of development by applying the latest fashion in matters of organization, technology, and philosophical-economic doctrines in a desperate, historically frustrated effort to oppose the necessary consequences of world capitalist organization.

An indirect effect of the French Revolution was the political independence of almost all the countries in Latin America. This independence, however, opened the doors to another kind of imperialism characterized not only by the plundering of natural resources but by the exportation of capital. This did not make imperialism more benevolent; on the contrary, it was much more devious and bloody. At the time of independence the few capitalist enclaves that existed in America, basically localized in the extractive industries producing for foreign commerce, realized that the very laws they had imposed could not achieve their goal if productivity were not accelerated. As we have indicated elsewhere, this was sought through agricultural development and the strengthening of the small farmer who, by making the immense, idle feudal estates productive, was supposed to create thereby a national market. Simultaneously, the Indian communities which until this time had owned the lands they worked communally, were dispossessed in order to create a free labor force, comparable to the European, that could serve as a reserve army for industry and agriculture. They began to establish the first banks and to encourage manufactures and the few existing industries. But until this time the native bourgeoisie did not have at its disposal the necessary capital to advance toward a more or less classic capitalist process. Artificially created, it reached adolescence without having behind it a level of artisanry, manufacturing, and the accumulation of capital that would have permitted it to take the historic leap. For this reason it had to accept, and in many cases welcome, the entrance of foreign capital that had, on the one hand, the economic and technical means for developing or implanting new industries and that, on the other, gave impetus to class distinctions, the division of labor, and the mercantilization of all products; all of this was accomplished through enterprises in which the organic composition of capital was very low. The imported technology and the means of production in general were not anything like those that imperialism worked with in its own countries. However, the rate of profit had to be the same, and this could be achieved only by increased exploitation of labor, the reduction in the cost of the labor force to a point far below its value, and the extension of surplus labor time to unimaginable levels.

LATIN AMERICAN ACADEMICISM IN THE NINETEENTH CENTURY

In effect, the Latin American countries, freed politically from the Spanish and Portuguese crowns in a global movement that constituted the breaking of the Iberian colonial pact, entered their new stage at the time of the full decadence of the baroque and the rise of neoclassicism, favored in Europe by the triumphant bourgeoisie and some enlightened monarchies. The new ruling classes in Latin America were tied to the new hegemonic centers and shared the idea that the development of our countries was possible only if based on the export of raw materials and some food products, and the import of nondurable consumer goods produced by European industry; *when they opened the doors to the capital of the Old World they also took the forms of European culture as their model.* As we have noted previously, however, this was not simply an arbitrary and irrational imposition of values. In fact, in the case of architecture, *neoclassicism would become the civic expression of those power elites who by means of the rationalist-mechanistic ideology of classical European canons were manifesting their conception of the economic and cultural destiny of our societies.*

The baroque, which in the final years of the viceregency had entered into its mortal agony by virtue of the artistic standards of the Bourbons, undoubtedly represented the style of the "colonial period," that is, of Peninsular oppression and domination from which the new ruling class felt itself to be the liberator; at the same time, the art of the Counter-Reformation expressed the kind of relationship between Church and State that was breaking down in the nineteenth century with the proclamation of bourgeois liberties and the installation of secular societies. For that reason, during those years of liberation and construction of new societies, to suggest the adoption of the baroque would have meant an unacceptable return to the past (none of which contradicts the fact that later a national inspiration for our architecture would be sought in the forms of the viceregency). The magnificent pre-Columbian art was generally unknown and underrated by the educated classes of the nineteenth century, and for that reason it could not be considered—at least on the level of "high" esthetic proposals—as an answer to the new formal problems presented by republican civic buildings.[3] Neoclassicism was, moreover, clearly the form of architectural language that expressed the secularization of culture, universities, and education in general that was being initiated in the New World.

This process of secularization was a form of Europeanism, since Latin America had no comparable tradition. As a consequence, in the field of education, for example, "advanced" European pedagogues were invited to America: Joseph Lancaster was brought to Caracas in 1824 by Bolívar; the Scot James Thompson was invited to Argentina by Rivadavia in 1826–1827, and remained in Chile, Peru, and Colombia until 1831 teaching the Lancasterian method.[4] In the field of architecture, a legion of French and Italian architects was brought to America to develop "the great forms of universal architectural art" in the major cities that were the new centers where political decisions were made, or in key sites for the economic enclaves. In all these centers the breakdown of colonial urban structures was already in progress, beginning that hundred-year road toward the attainment of their modern physiognomy.

It is evident that within this context we cannot study in any depth the problem of the countries in question, or approach the particular problems of the twenty-one Latin American nations. For purposes of methodology we will take a sampling of the most representative countries without in any way implying an underestimation of the others. Quite the contrary, we believe that an approach to the total problems in all our countries is a task that should immediately precede this one. However, considering that *along general lines* we are united by a single historical process, we believe that our treatment of the question can have some validity. There are, at the moment, cases that are special not so much because they differ from the totality, but because they are in a state that others have not yet reached: we refer in particular to Cuba (the Chilean experience has, for the time being, been frustrated) where almost fifteen years of socialist civic building necessarily implies specific analyses, which have already been initiated in the works of Segre and Salinas.

In Brazil, an exceptional case in which intensive civic building was carried out during the period of transition from the Regency to Independence (1808–1821), in contrast to other Latin American countries where the period of anarchy impeded this, Juan VI called the French architect Le Breton to head a sizable group of sculptors, painters, and architects (among whom Grandjean de Montigny was outstanding) in order to complete the "enormous task of *civilizing* creole taste."[5] Later Louis Leger Vauthier built the Theater of Santa Isabel in Recife, the Theater of Belén in Pará, and the Theater of São Luis in Maranhão. Similarly, in Mexico, in 1843, the Academy of Fine Arts, part of the viceregal tradition, was reorganized with the intention of "henceforth providing European teachers, chosen from among the best."[6] Thus, in 1856, the Italian architect Javier Cavallari arrived in Mexico and gave new direction to the teaching of architecture in accordance with the European experience, although Mexico already had an important neoclassical tradition at that time in the work of the Spaniard Manuel Tolsá, builder of the Palacio de Minería (Palace of Mining), Damián Ortiz de Castro, and Francisco Eduardo Tresguerras, designers of the towers of the Metropolitan Cathedral and of the Church of Carmen in Celaya respectively. In any event, the modalities imposed on the academy were a definitive indication of the architectural Europeanism of Mexico.

In Chile, the French architect Brunet de Baines, commissioned by the government, established the first school of architecture in the country, and the Italian architect Joaquín Toesca built what may have been the most important work of that period, the Palacio de la Moneda (Palace of the Treasury), in the center of Santiago; the building was destroyed in 1973 by the military junta. The capital itself reformed its urban plan in accordance with French taste through the work of the "Chilean Haussmann" the mayor Benjamín Vicuña Mackenna. In Argentina neoclassicism gained prominence throughout the whole of the nineteenth century and the beginning of the twentieth, thus following the tradition of the final years of the eighteenth century in the work of the Jesuit Blanqui. Toward the end of the nineteenth century Buenos Aires experienced an apogee of civic building that lasted for several decades and that gave to the city its definitive physiognomy; its greatest stewards were, perhaps, Julio Dormal, architect of the Colón Theater (1908), and Alejandro Christophernsen, architect of the San Martín Palace.

In this way the republican neoclassicial stamp was being imprinted on the former baroque physiognomy of Latin American cities (and occasionally on the pre-Columbian as well, as in the extreme case of Cuzco, Peru), and although the fundamental structure of the colonial checkerboard layout was maintained in almost all of them, the new Haussmanian criterion was superimposed on it, most clearly in the areas of growth (the Paseo de la Reforma in Mexico City, the Alameda in Santiago de Chile, the opening of wide avenues as the result of the demolition of colonial walls in Lima). Buildings of monumental character were erected even in the central areas of the cities; their pompous classicism expressed the ideology of an oligarchy that was trying by all means possible to maintain a precarious internal peace, and that through *positivism* was concerned with presenting an image of prosperity and culture in a world where the masses had been made marginal by the privilege of the ruling class. In this way architecture and city planning played their ideological-political role in our countries, representing the equilibrium that the oligarchs were trying to maintain during the so-called period of independence.

The demographic process also expressed these changes. As a part of the economic vitalization produced by the new form of integration of Latin American countries into world capitalism, a new population structure was produced that began the process, although naturally on an incipient scale, that in the twentieth century would result in the "macrocephalic urbanization" that has lasted until our day.[7] This phenomenon became apparent at the end of the colonial period. Rio de Janeiro, with fewer than 50,000 inhabitants before 1808, grew to 135,000 inhabitants when it became the seat of the Portuguese court in 1823. Buenos Aires, with approximately 25,000 inhabitants in 1778, reached 40,000 in 1801, and 55,000 in 1810. Caracas, with 18,600 in 1772, grew to almost 50,000 by 1812. By the end of the nineteenth century Latin American population was increasing even faster, growing from 33 million in 1850 to 63 million in 1900; the process of urbanization was accelerating at the same time. São Paulo, which had little more than 30,000 inhabitants in 1872, had grown to almost 65,000 by 1890, approximately 240,000 by 1900, and by 1920 it had, incredibly, reached more than a half million. Buenos Aires grew from 187,000 inhabitants in 1869 to 675,000 in 1895 to a million and a half in 1914.

TWENTIETH CENTURY: CONSOLIDATION OF DEPENDENCE

It was the dawn of the twentieth century; it was the *Belle Epoque,* and it had to be suitable commemorated: they built great theaters, seats of government, legislative palaces, and great residences. Stupefied by the feast, brimming over with optimism, their own chatter kept them from hearing the call with which the proletariat of the world, with the Russian Revolution of 1917, was bringing to a historical close the ephemeral period of capitalism. But this historical process was dialectical, not mechanical. The sumptuousness and extravagance with which all their works were realized and the importing of European architects were out of step with their own esthetic ideology and technical possibilities—and thus the appearance of a motley and anarchical conglomeration of forms in which Greek facades were mixed indiscriminately with Islamic vaults, in which the freely undulating lines of art nouveau were reproduced in wood and mortar, and in which the forms of an ideal past that was alien to them were repeated over and over again. The dialectic that exists between technology and the ideological content that tries to express itself by means of that technology inevitably stopped them. As long as they continued to build with traditional materials and the techniques that corresponded to them, all they could do was fall, very much against their will, into the repetition of forms that had been tried many centuries before. Pomp and the search for sumptuousness had to be expressed in forms that had been minted in the past.[8]

Reinforced concrete was already known in Europe and steel had made its appearance in architecture, but the logical forms that correspond to them, technically or ideologically, had not yet been found. Let us bear in mind the contradictory effect, best appreciated in art nouveau, between the materials used and the adopted form. In this sense, in order for the architecture of a developed and imperialistic bourgeoisie to mature, there would have to be a stage of experimentation and progressive control of technology. This is the role that corresponded historically to the Bauhaus. On the other hand, capitalist development itself required rationalization in all orders of production, a fact which only reaffirmed the anarchy of the system as a whole. It became increasingly obvious that the new architectural genres, the new necessities imposed on daily life, and the new technical resources produced by the gigantic advance of productive forces were totally incompatible with the borrowed forms that architecture had taken over in its period of gestation. Little by little the criticisms of earlier stylistic characteristics became more bitter and fundamental, opening the way for a rationalization of architectural design that would agree with the means which now could be mastered.

Economic anarchy had a part to play in all of this. The crises that for capitalism are the gauge for measuring how well or badly its interests are progressing, forced them to see, with the crash of 1929, that economic liberalism could only survive at the risk of devouring itself. The need for rationalization of processes became so pressing that even the most reactionary sectors of society willingly accepted the appearance of interventionist governments that would regulate all producers. In Latin America it was the moment when there was repeated insistence on establishing economic planning for the economy (the six-year plan of Lázaro Lárdenas in Mexico, 1934); it was the opportunity for Marmaduke Grove to decree the Socialist Republic in Chile (1932), and it was the time when the nationalist process in Brazil began.

This moment coincided with the popularization of new European rationalist tendencies, with the transplanting of functionalism from the industrial countries to the backward tropics of America. Functionalism, in addition to its profound linguistic content to which we will refer later, represented the capitalist rationalization of architecture based on extraordinary technical advances. Class power was expressed in special forms derived from the domination of steel, concrete, and, in general, the industrialization of all building materials. These forms, much simpler than those which historically preceded them, allowed efficient construction, the democratization of the sense of life, the flow of interior space and flexibility in use; they stimulated the architects who saw in them the instrument, the springboard that would permit them once more to leap over their backward condition. Once again, now in the area of architecture, they were trying to bridge the gap that separates the arrow from the rifle. Functionalism was the stylistic mirror in which the bourgeoisie came to feel itself expressed; it permitted them a much greater volume of production than previously, and it was adaptable to the new, simplified life-styles that the world system was giving impetus to. However, functionalism had to undergo a series of adaptations to the terrain so that it could adjust to the level of local technology. And just as many centuries before they had tried to copy forms with inadequate building systems, in the same way now the functionalism of steel, concrete, and industrial materials had to produce an "underdeveloped" functionalism in Latin America, a clear expression of the modalities that superstructural manifestations must undergo when faced with limitations imposed on them by the concrete level of the productive forces.

Functionalism, which in Europe was mainly directed to the solution of the needs of the middle and wealthy classes, acquired in our case an indisputable social tone. The ideas of low-cost housing units and of housing developments for the working class were among the topics that evoked most interest from 1930 on. Since the movement evolved under the worldwide influence of the Soviet revolution and the fight against fascism in Spain and Germany, and since it seemed evident that the working class had moved to the forefront, there was no lack of petty bourgeois "leftist" elements who, repudiating everything that seemed to recall that which was "reactionary, bourgeois and individualistic," proposed a "socialist" and intentionally "antiesthetic" functionalism. American functionalism differed from its predecessor in these two fundamental traits: the low level of its technology and pretentions which were not only social, but "socialist."

THE MEANING AND PARTICULARITY OF FUNCTIONALISM

As we have shown, at the end of the nineteenth century and during the first decades of the twentieth, neoclassicism in architecture came to an end in almost all the countries of the area with manifestations of European architectural romanticism: so-called historicism, especially in derivative revivals, art nouveau, and various forms of modernism which in reality gave the cities a physiognomy that was close to chaotic (obviously, among the revivals, were references to the colonial baroque which still survived in residential buildings in various cities, and to pre-Columbian forms). The dissolution of neoclassicism was precipitated as much by the appearance of buildings that were engineering accomplishments as by the proliferation of commercial construction that was favored by the process of urbanization and the capitalist system in the midst of its development—works that were marginal in terms of the "great" esthetic concepts of educated men.

If it is true that the beginnings of the functionalist movement emerged from proposals by the intellectual elite of the artistic avant-garde which was more or less tied to European movements, the fact is that *the new architecture was called upon to be the expression of a society characterized by the eruption of the masses in all orders of social life and the appearance of "populist" politics among the new elite of dependent capitalist power,* events that formed part of the new integration into the world system, to which we have made reference, and that were characterized fundamentally by the move of our countries from an exporting economy toward the creation, as Ruy Mauro Marini has pointed out, of "an authentic national capitalist economy," insofar as it was taking shape as a condition with the rise of an "industrial economy"; in our countries this occurred under the sign of dependence.[9] Therefore our contemporary movement was born under a double sign of crisis: the conflictive problems of rationalist architecture throughout the capitalist world that were particularlized and made more pressing because they were adapted to a system of dependent capitalism.

Certainly the antiacademic struggle directed against stylism, ornamentation, figurative rhetoric, monumentalism, the work of art, the unique object, and so on, that was also the purpose of the Central European avant-garde—culminating in the Bauhaus, the school of Le Corbusier, and, with significant differences, Soviet constructivism—had a contintent-wide character in Latin America although at first there was no organic connection among the different groups struggling for change. But there was an important circumstance: *in order for architecture in our countries to develop it was necessary for the state to take over the movement,* and this was something that was happening gradually. As Arnaldo Córdova points out with reference to Mexico: ". . . the truth is that, as in all underdeveloped countries, the state at a certain point became the principal, if not the only promoter of social development due, above all, to the enormous dispersion of productive factors and the weakness of modern economic relationships."[10] This fact points out the connection between the destiny of the new Latin American architecture and the destiny of our states and all their political and ideological inconstancies. Furthermore, it gives to the conceptual foundations of our theoreticians the *social* imprint that is, generally, characteristic of them. Naturally, the influence of so-called private enterprise was not lacking but, with very few exceptions, it was not the most significant factor.

Thus, at the very start of our contemporary architecture, different groups and personalities emerged as its pioneers: in Brazil, the country that undoubtedly produced the most vigorous movement and figures that have been of the first rank even on an international scale—Oscar Niemeyer, for example—"Art Week" was organized in São Paolo in 1925; one of its results would be Gregori Warchavchik's *Manifesto of Functional Architecture,* with its clear Corbusian line. This, together with the first residential buildings by Warchavchik himself, marked the initial episode in contemporary Brazilian architecture. The activity of the avante-garde continued, and in 1936, on the eve of Getúlio Vargas's *Estado Novo* (Vargas's new regime, seen by many as corporativist), the Brazilian government decided to develop the new architecture. It is well known that Le Corbusier—who had visited Brazil in 1929—was invited to participate in the project for the Ministry of Education and Health that would be completed by a team of vanguardist architects: Carlos Leáo, Jorge Moreira, Alfonso Eduardo Reidy, Oscar Niemeyer, and Ernani Vasconcellos. This building, in which the influence of the French master was obvious, and which was modified by elements that pointed to the development of an individual, local language, represented the starting point of an intense civic activity in which the impulse of the power elite was decisive. This building activity by the Brazilian state had its spectacular and unique culmination—although with dismal results— in the construction of Brasília.

The "idyllic" relationship between avant-garde architects and the state was not, as one could easily infer, a simple act of esthetic or intellectual sympathy. The new Brazilian architecture emerged as a necessary fact for the industrial and commercial bourgeoisie and its representatives in power. And at the same time, in the reconciliation of the classes, it became the expression of that power whose social concessions to the workers were made within the framework of control by the *Estado Novo.* This explains the social character of the most significant works. The bourgeois ideology of power, with its idealistic and reformist freight, also gave content to Corbusian esthetic theories with their nationalist modalities—a peculiar form of architectural populism in the largest country in Latin America.

The rise of the reformist movement in Mexican architecture showed great similarities to the case of Brazil, but here architectural populism in its early stages met a fate contrary to the Brazilian. If in the country of Warchavchik and Niemeyer its preoccupation with esthetics and creative fantasy would culminate in the almost sculptural refinements of Brasília, the statements and concepts of the Mexican avant-gardists would lead, in their desire "not to get involved with beauty" (Juan O'Gorman) and in their devotion to the "service of the people" (Juan Legorreta), to an almost devastating poverty. Of course, this was the result of their peculiar relationship to the state that was determined by how it used architecture to carry out policy.

The Mexican state of the 1930s, as we know, was the result of an armed peasant revolt that, under the direction of urban middle sectors (bourgeois strata), established a system that cleared the way for that integration into the world capitalist system that we have already referred to several times. The participation of the rural masses and of small syndicalist groups in the revolution made it imperative for those in power to reconcile the social classes with socialist proclamations in which responsiveness to popular demands—which never went beyond a carefully measured-out distribution of land and certain limited concessions to the urban workers—was held up as the supreme reason for being of the "revolution that became a government." Implantation of the right to private property for all Mexicans followed the abolition of Porfirian privilege (1877–1910), and this first stage of the post-revolutionary state unfolded in a climate of redemptivist nationalism. Public works, necessary for the capitalist development of the country, were handled with a keen political sense for the manipulation of the masses and social reforms in such a way that in a society divided into classes and dominated by the bourgeoisie, a true mystique of the people, the Indian, and even the proletariat was created.

Architecture played an important role in this process, so much so that as early as 1933 the avant-gardists, a few years after their first statements, were absorbed by the state; they shaped their concepts and their subsequent civic application around the mystique that would cause them to change the anti-academic and anti-Porfirian struggle into an attack against *esthetics* for being antisocial. Thus Juan O'Gorman, Juan Legorreta, Álvaro Aburto, and others, developed programs for government construction (schools, "minimal housing units" for workers) with an architectural ideology based on a great structural simplicity carried to its extreme, making a show of their scorn for the work of art. And if at this stage the influence of Le Corbusier was obvious (his "Towards a New Architecture" was published in its entirety in one of the first specialized periodicals of the time, *Edificación*), the influence of Hannes Meyer, although with a special interpretation accommodated to this ideology, was no less important, and even a decade later he collaborated with the Mexican architectural movement. However, the development of the economy, the ideology and politics of the state would lead the architects to their reconciliation with esthetics. In an irrationalist and phenomenological context that was naturally pleasing to certain sectors of the ruling class, the task of establishing the theoretical base for the new position fell to José Villagrán García. In the 1950s the movement led to a search for Mexicanism inspired in the pre-Columbian past, an attitude that was especially manifest in the monumental University City in Mexico City. In this way, in full expansionist euphoria, a second variant of Mexican architectural populism was established in which the governing bourgeoisie tried to leave the imprint of its ultimately useless enthusiasm for setting the grandeur of the country on the unsteady base of capitalist social disequilibrium and economic dependence.

When Carlos Raúl Villanueva established himself in Venezuela toward the end of the 1930s, having completed his studies at the Ecole des Beaux Arts in Paris, oil had already replaced coffee as the principal export product, and its exploitation by transnational companies was already moving ahead at full speed. The history of the country of Bolívar was being arranged around the interests of the petroleum enclaves, and the battle among different regional oligarchies culminated in the installation of a real military regime (*maximato*).[11] The regime had made the first agreement with the petroleum companies to provide the state with income that revitalized the traditional economy and, consequently, accelerated capitalist relations and stimulated the development of the urban sectors, the formation of the middle class, and, naturally, of the working class. The capital of the republic, with all the problems of underdeveloped cities, was in the midst of its great expansion. This historical situation favored the work of the pioneers of architecture and urbanism. Within the politics of a regime that by 1941 was already opening up toward the middle classes and making labor concessions, without abandoning its dictatorial tradition, Villaneuva, the central figure of the movement, succeeded in realizing important public buildings; the School of Architecture of the Central University of Venezuela itself was established at this time. In a recent paper presented to the sixth Latin American Conference of Schools and Faculties of Architecture, Miguel Casas Armengol of the University of Zulia stated in this regard:

> Architecture and architectural education in Venezuela received an initial impetus from diverse public works that demonstrated the possibilities and usefulness of the profession . . . several housing developments throughout the country were promoted by the Banco Obrero (1937), by the Master Plan for Caracas in 1939, and the El Silencio apartment blocks in Caracas in 1941. . . . Consequently, architecture in Venezuela began principally because of public demand from the governmental sector. . . .[12]

In this way Venezuelan architectural populism was developed in response to enormous, pressing problems and mass demand, especially by the middle class, for their resolution. Venezuelan architecture in its peak period was, to a large extent, and expression of this correlation among the forces of different social classes, in which the thrust of the middle class in occasional alliance with the workers was evident in governmental decisions whose fundamental motive was capitalist control of the taxes and payments of foreign oil companies. These resources in the hands of the state also favored civic estheticism that, without matching Brasília, reached the limits of sumptuousness, especially in the construction of University City in Caracas, where the concept of a synthesis of art in which important international artists participated (Vasarely, Calder, Arp, and others), gave it, despite regionalizing elements such as openwork parasols, a stylistically cosmopolitan character that seemed paradoxical vis-à-vis the general problems of the country.

Argentina represented a special case in which the state, in the first stage of the contemporary architectural movement, did not assume the role of supporting the avant-garde. The result, as Francisco Bullrich pointed out, was that the pioneers (León Durge, Prebisch, Vilar, and many others), feeling the vacuum of state indifference, entered a period of crisis: "And if in Argentina modernism had been developed with apparent vigor between 1931 and 1939, the fact is that by 1940 many of those who had adhered, even if only superficially, to this new attitude quietly began to defect."[13]

In fact, in those first decades of the century during the transition from an agro-exporting economy to an industrial economy based on substitution of imports (this occurred in all the countries of the area), a dictatorial government like Argentina's, fearing the political ascendancy of the urban masses that was tied, in a certain sense, to the radical movement of the first two decades, followed the old European architectural tradition that had so glorified the capital and the other major cities. However, the very dyanmic that operated in Latin America, and that in Argentina took shape with industrialization, of necessity demanded civic expression; this was realized under the protection of a small and obviously weak private sector, while the class in power remained indifferent to new issues. In fact, it was not long before the new populist tone of the state, openly expressed under Perón, took over the new architecture and used it in the formation of the modern image that its cities have today and, similarly, in the manipulation of ever-increasing mass demands.

This fundamental fact was at the base of Argentinian architecture, which also developed in a play of tensions among the esthetic tradition, the private character of a large number of important buildings (for example, the headquarters of the Banco de Londres y América del Sud in Buenos Aires, the work of Santiago Sánchez Elía, Federico Peralta Ramos, Alfredo Agostini, and Clorindo Testa), the monumental projects (for example, the numerous buildings of Mail and Telecommunications, some schools of University City in Caracas, and many others), and the demand for social solutions that only the state could provide.

THE FALLACIES OF DEVELOPMENT

World War II, unleashed by imperialism, its aftermath expressed in the rise of new socialist countries, and the bloodshed of the Korean War (to cite only the most important historical events), loosened the ties of dependence, offered the countries of Latin America better prices for their agricultural products and cattle, and opened the possibility for increasing the establishment of precisely those consumer goods whose products they had been deprived of because of the war. In this way, to the benefit of native producers, they took over a market that had belonged to foreign capital. This circumstance, combined with the fear of finding themselves dragged down by the crises in the central countries and the always latent hope of becoming self-sufficient, gave rise to developmentalist theories according to which the future was at hand and success depended only on governments' greater or lesser astuteness in taking advantage of opportunities.

If architecture in all class societies has been devoted, in general terms, to the solution of the needs of the economically privileged classes, the rapid pauperization of the working classes combined with their gradually rising consciousness has ripened the crisis of the system as a whole as well as in its civic manifestations. This crisis, with its social and ideological symptoms, is expressed *quantitatively* by the inability to provide adequate shelter for the majority of the population in our countries, by the lack of hospitals, schools, and recreational centers, as well as by the excessive urbanization of our countries and the ensuing urban anarchy. This is the best evidence available for demonstrating the crisis in the system and in the architecture that operates within it. Salvador Allende said:

> In Latin America the brutal difference between a minority in control of power and wealth and the great masses on the fringes of culture, health, shelter, food, recreation and leisure cannot continue to exist. We have said it many times, and we only need to quote the statistics: in Latin America there are more than twenty million human beings who are barely acquainted with money as a medium of exchange. In Latin America there are 140 million semiliterates and illiterates. In Latin America there is a shortage of nineteen million housing units. Fifty-three percent of Latin Americans are undernourished. In Latin American there are seventeen million unemployed and more than sixty million people who work only part time. Therefore, the capitalist regime has demonstrated its inefficiency, and the exploitation of man by man, characteristic of this situation, has resulted in crisis.[14]

CONCLUSION. THE ROAD TO CRISIS

Throughout this essay a central thesis has been maintained: the crisis in Latin American architecture is operating in three fundamental directions: 1) because it belongs to an international movement of rationalism that is today in a process of decomposition by virtue of its operation within the capitalist system; 2) because it belongs to the dependent capitalism of our under-developed area; 3) the essential result is that the density of Latin American architecture is intimately tied to the historical destiny of the classes in power.

These facts point out its destiny. The failure of developmentalist policies that during the 1950s seemed to offer a view of capitalist development in continual ascent, ruined the hopes and plans of the oligarchies for cultivating prosperous nations. Continuing inflation, the superexploitation of labor (Marini) and the tendency toward that "resurrection of the model of the old exporting economy" (also pointed out by Marini in the work we have cited) which are the expressions of dependency with regard to hegemonic centers (basically the United States) have precipitated in our countries a crisis whose end cannot be seen with the present structural framework. The states are bringing to a point of crisis not only their economic decisions but also their cultural ones. Architecture moves between the two in a headlong rush that has produced a continent-wide movement of schools or architecture to find explanations and objective solutions; in reality our problems are common ones, our history is a common one. Fernando Salinas's points are still valid, although the notion of state intervention in the solution of housing problems should perhaps be modified. The fact is that in a certain sense the state contributes very little to the problem. But in our countries the connection between architecture and the state makes it the only force that has confronted so-called social architecture in a meaningful way. The problem has its roots in the fact that this kind of architecture functions within the populist politics of manipulation of the masses—so accurately described by Arnaldo Córdova in the case of Mexico[15]—that its designs serve the interests of the classes in power, and therefore the solution in depth of popular needs remains in the background.

Notes

1. Fernando Salinas, *La arquitectura revolucionaria del Tercer Mundo.* Havana: Centro de Información Científica y Técnica. Tecnología, Serie 4, 1970.

2. Authors quote from the Spanish edition of *On Contradiction:* Mao Tse Tung, *Sobre la contradicción, Selected Works of Mao Tse-tung,* Peking: Ediciones en lenguas extranjeras, vol. 1, 1968, p. 359.

3. This did not prevent them from using pre-Hispanic formal elements in some works (such as the Porfirian monument to Cuauhtémoc in the Paseo de la Reforma in Mexico City) during the romantic period of revivals, especially in those countries, like Mexico and Peru, that had advanced cultures during the pre-Columbian period.

4. P. Henríquez Ureña, *Historia de la cultura en la América Hispánica,* 3rd ed. Mexico–Buenos Aires: Fondo de Cultura Económica, 1959, p. 75.

5. L. Castedo, *Historia del arte y de la arquitectura latinoamericana.* Santiago de Chile, Buenos Aires, Mexico City, Quito, Bogotá, Madrid, Barcelona: Editorial Pomaire, 1970, p. 217.

6. J. Fernández, *El arte moderno en México.* Mexico City: Antigua Librería Robredo, José Porrúa e Hijos, 1937, pp. 81–110.

7. The median world urbanization rate, excluding Latin America, was 27.8 percent in 1950, while in our area it was 32.9 percent with a tendency to increase. In the same way Latin America is characterized by the domination of the major population centers (almost always the capitals of the countries) over the other cities in the nation.

8. Authors quote from a Spanish edition of *History of the Russian Revolution:* Leon Trotsky, *Historia de la Revolución rusa,* vol. 1. Buenos Aires: Editorial Tilcara, p. 24.

9. R. M. Marini, *Dialéctica de la dependencia.* Mexico City: Serie Popular Era, 1973.

10. A. Córdova, *La formación del poder político en México,* 2nd ed. Mexico City: Serie Popular Era, p. 9.

11. H. Cardoso and E. Faletto, *Dependencia y desarrollo en América Latina.* Mexico City: Siglo XXI, 1969, p. 89.

12. A. M. Casas, "Un estudio exploratorio de la interacción de la educación superior, recursos humanos y desarrollo nacional en Venezuela." Mimeographed, Maracaibo, 1972.

13. F. Bullrich, *Arquitectura latinoamericana.* Buenos Aires: Editorial Sudamericana, 1969, p. 46.

14. Salvador Allende and Fidel Castro, "Allende y Castro dialogan sobre América Latina." Mexico City, *El Día,* October 6, 1973.

15. A. Córdova, *La ideología de la Revolución Mexicana.* Mexico City: Editorial Era, 1973.

6 / Industrial Design: An Ambiguous Reality

GUI BONSIEPE

DESIGN, SELF-DETERMINATION, SOCIAL CHANGE

There are extensive connections between architecture and industrial design, between designing buildings and designing products. This fact should cause no surprise since an intrinsic mutual affinity exists between these two areas. Both fall into the same anthropological category of design, and both are manifested in the creation of the tangible, concrete physical structures that surround us. The environment is one of several areas in which architects and industrial designers intervene to create a reality that exemplifies collective self-realization in a society.

It has been repeated many times that the Latin American subcontinent (with a few heroic exceptions) forms a dilacerated reality, a reality that is not its own, one that has been imposed, borrowed, imported, remote-controlled, and heterodetermined by foreign interests. The condition of living in non-identity, outside of oneself, separated from one's own identity, object rather than subject of one's own history, characterizes alienation as one of the forms of dependence.[1]

Design offers a means, albeit modest, of liberation from dependence insofar as one begins to design one's own reality instead of continuing to live immersed in an alien reality projected from outside. If one proposes to design products, such as utensils, appliances, production goods, equipment for collective use, it is appropriate to ask with what focus one is designing, because a universally valid and acceptable definition does not exist for any socio-political system.

We can reject in advance design that is pompous and born of the willful and missionary fervor of the individual who thinks of himself as nothing less than the savior of the world. Even more important, we must reject the false hope—the result of overestimation of one's own capabilities—that by means of product design one can make a decisive change in the social structure. Design is a corollary to, but not the protagonist of, social change. But this does not mean that the task of design can be postponed to the distant future when society, which now barely allows the majority of the population to survive, has been transformed.

THE CULTURALIST VARIANT IN INDUSTRIAL DESIGN

Industrial design appears in Latin America in two variants: the cultural and the promotional. In the European interpretation, culturalist tendencies predominate; these assign to the industrial designer the role of "humanizer of technology." Behind this interpretation is the fairly widespread tendency to demonize technology and blame it—and not the social organization within which it is practiced—for being the central threat and evil for mankind. The culturalist approach, packaged in high-flown phrases and full of good perfectionist intentions, is related to the "good design" movement that tries to educate the ordinary consumer through products chosen for their real or supposed qualities of design. Aside from its elitist character and the emphasis placed on the external aspects of industrial products, good design degenerates surreptitiously, despite the intentions of its proponents, into another vehicle for promoting sales. From this sociopsychological point of view it becomes basically a procedure for canonizing the taste of a sector of the middle class that assumes the role of opinion maker. Preferences and consumer habits are molded by means of a small group of people who function as arbiters of product esthetics, filtering out what is visually attractive or desirable from what does not correspond to the laws of the group. A very vague conception of quality is adhered to, and too much importance is placed on the formal characteristics of the product. In the end, visual necessities triumph over vital necessities. Good design obeys the desire, European in origin, to reconcile profits and culture.

THE PROMOTIONALIST VARIANT IN INDUSTRIAL DESIGN

Those culturalist concerns are of no special importance in the North American approach. Industrial design unhesitatingly submits to commercial interests: to increase earnings through rapidly paced formal innovation. The term *styling* is generally used to describe this variant of industrial design; its indisputable example is the automobile, especially the Detroitosaurus. Styling signifies design that suggests a new, improved product—an impression created by changes in the skin—while the structure of the product remains the same. Styling, then, is the continuation of the old in new clothing. If the principal function assigned to the industrial designer is to accelerate the circulation of merchandise through the mechanism of psychological obsolescence, one can well understand his subordination to marketing as well as to advertising.

The contradictions of industrial design break out in virulent form in styling, where we witness the conflict between the interests of use-value and change-value. The use-value of a product is tied to the satisfaction of the user's needs, while change-value, on the other hand, is the focus of the seller's interest. To these two concepts of classical political economy a third has been added—the promise of use-value. This is the essence of styling. It atrophies formal or esthetic innovation.

In this regard a critic of contemporary society writes: "From the moment change-value is imposed as the motivation for producing goods a split occurs: as a concession use-value is produced, but with the help of specific techniques and efforts the appearance of use-value, the esthetic promise of use-value, is also created."[2]

The emancipation of esthetics culminates in styling as a specialized design activity in the preparation of an attractive appearance for industrial products. Industrial design in its esthetic dimension is not immune to styling and the necessarily frenetic efforts to promote the merchandise carnival with renovated fireworks. The esthetics are intrinsically ambiguous since appearance can also encourage illusion and deceit and provide, therefore, a tool for manipulation.[3]

Harsh and justified criticisms have been made of industrial design when it is conceived of in terms of styling and helps to create false needs. However, it would be too simplistic, and basically an act of betrayal, to reduce industrial design to styling and to deny that despite the limitations imposed by a specific socioeconomic organization, industrial design can help to solve problems that affect the majority of the population. Some of industrial design's general options have been described by a designer in the following way: "We can assume the role of artist, find clients and exhibit our formalist triumphs in the Museum of Modern Art; we can sell ourselves and make the cash registers ring at Macy's; or we can solve problems."[4]

But the problems in the dependent nations are so different from those that burden the developed nations, and the economic, technological, and cultural restrictions are so distinct, that we should question the validity both of existing definitions and of the experience of central, industrialized countries.

AN ATTEMPT AT CLARIFICATION

Before analyzing the profound differences between industrial design in the central nations and in the hinterland, we should attempt to clarify the concept of industrial design since a good amount of confusion surrounds the issue.[5]

By industrial design we understand a professional activity in the broad field of technological innovation. As a discipline that takes part in the development of products, it is concerned with questions of use, function, production, market, profits, and the esthetic quality of industrial products.

The questions of use refer to the direct interaction between user and product, and are determined by considerations such as convenience, practicality, safety, versatility, maintenance, and repair. Ergonomic factors are also included.

The questions of function refer to the physical-technical principles of design, and are determined by considerations such as technical feasibility, reliability, and power transmission.

The questions of production refer to the means and methods of manufacturing a design. Factors that influence this are available machinery, the level of skilled labor, feasible tolerances, standardization, and assembly.

The questions of market refer to the potential demand on the part of individual or institutional buyers. Important considerations are needs and preferences, priorities, pricing, channels of distribution, and product diversification.

The questions of profit refer to the excess created by a productive activity, whose appropriation, depending on the type of economy, will be either private or collective. Profit can be expressed in monetary terms or in terms of general social relevance. In the latter case it cannot be quantified by accounting methods.

To end this summary classification there is the question of esthetic quality—in other words, the formal characteristics of a product. Here the decisive factors are coherence, treatment of detail, color, texture, graphics, three-dimensional configuration, and detailing.

We can summarize the essentials of industrial design in the following way:

The industrial designer is concerned especially, although not exclusively, with the improvement of the use-qualities of industrial products. From the point of view of design, a product is first of all an object that provides a service and therefore satisfies the needs of a user.

The industrial designer is concerned with defining the formal qualities, that is, creating the physiognomy of products and systems of products that form a part of the artificial human environment.

Industrial design is an innovative activity within the general framework of technological innovation.

In the mind of the public, industrial design is strongly identified with consumer goods. It should be pointed out, however, that the industrial designer is also active in the area of capital goods, products for collective use (for example, hospital equipment) and packaging for consumer and industrial use. Certainly not all industrial products benefit from the skill of the industrial designer—only those interface products with which the user comes into direct contact through manipulation or perception. For that reason the products of the mechanical engineer and of the industrial designer do not coincide completely. The design of a ball bearing is not an industrial design problem. As with architecture, the transitions between mechanical and industrial design are not clearly defined, and territorial fears arise easily as a defense against an imagined intruder.

But these unjustified fears are also symptomatic of an obsolete, monodisciplinary work style. The design of products, especially when they are highly complex, is the result of teamwork—not only the straightforward design disciplines, such as industrial design and mechanical engineering, are involved, but also nondesign disciplines such as marketing, economics, industrial engineering, and social psychology, which influence the final design of the product.

From this we can deduce what industrial design is not, or should not be. It is not an artistic polish on a "crude" design. It is not plastic surgery. It is not the wrapping of supposedly ugly products in new, attractive, and imaginative forms. Certainly industrial design can be practiced in this way, but it has tragic consequences for dependent countries in the squandering of scarce economic resources and its alienating effects. Moreover, the distinction between the "gut" designer and the "epidermal" designer is a false one, since there is no clear line of separation between the inside and the outside of a product. Structure and form should represent a coherent whole and not a conglomeration of often incompatible parts.

The question of whether or not industrial design can be considered as art has been either resolved or superseded; it is as irrelevant today as the sophisticated debates in the Middle Ages concerning the gender of angels. On the other hand, the question was an important chapter in the history of industrial design during the period of the protodesigners, when an attempt was made to integrate the artist into industrial production from which he had been completely excluded. It would be a mistake to think of this integration as an effort to apply form to the object or to introduce beauty into a product. Rather, industrial art, a synonym for industrial design in the early 1920s in the Soviet Union, seemed to go beyond prerevolutionary art. The introduction of art into industry was not viewed as a means of saving art, or as an estheticization of the product, but as an improvement in production itself. With exemplary clarity one of the representatives of LEF wrote: "Social and technical functionalism is the only law, the only criterion for measuring artistic activity, that is, for inventing forms."[6] Almost half a century later one can look with sympathy at this passionate integration of the artist into the production of material culture; but in the interim the inadequacies of the interpretation according to which industrial design is an extension of art, with other means and in another medium, has been clearly demonstrated.

INDUSTRIAL DESIGN AND TECHNOLOGICAL POLICY

Industrial design depends on the existence of two technologies: a production technology, more precisely a manufacturing industry, and a distribution technology. Without this base, industrial design is relegated to a mere superstructural game.

The formulation and implementation of an autonomous technological policy—including industrial design—is threatened by the tendency of the multinational or supranational corporations to move toward a new international division of work: the moving of certain production processes to the periphery and the concentration of research and development—that is, technological innovation—in the central nations. In this way the less industrialized nations can hope for the desired wave of industrialization, but one that is limited for the most part to the production of consumer goods with a relatively low degree of elaboration, or to industries that require a good amount of labor but not a high and costly level of education, or, finally, to "dirty" industries (mining, iron and steel, chemical) to avoid further pollution of the central countries and thus bypass payment of the costs of governmental measures to protect the environment and to halt the alarming process of erosion of the biosphere that has become so apparent in recent years.

With few exceptions Latin American countries will continue functioning as an overseas proletariat for the economies of the central nations,[7] of course, dressed in new clothing that is more "modern" and "dynamic." The forms of unequal exchange will become sharper, and the price of this reflected industrialization will be very high for the dependent nations: not only the predictable depletion of their natural resources, so systematically inventoried in the cadastres made with the help of satellites, but even more important, the negative effects of industrial production—garbage dumps, erosion, pollution, reduction of the underground water table, salinization and desalinization of the soil, accumulation of wastes and toxic residues.

Faced with this possible—and probable—future, statements to the effect that less industrialized countries are privileged in that they can learn from the errors of the central nations have a hint of either hypocrisy or naïveté. It is true that one can learn from the mistakes of others, but there are serious doubts whether dependent countries will really be able to apply this knowledge in the process of their own industrialization.

We have pointed out the general schema of "reflected" industrialization in which the development of a reproductive rather than an innovative technological capacity is encouraged in the peripheral nations. Apparently the capacity to reproduce designs from the central nations, especially durable consumer goods, indicates a higher level of technology, but this does not overcome technological and cultural dependence. If a country possesses a technological stock for producing goods, no matter how complex, but continues to reproduce the models of the central nations, it increases its cultural dependence and solidifies its position as a subsidiary nation.

The development of original designs lies within the general framework of the policy of substitution of imports that was initiated and made official in Latin America during the 1950s. According to the observations of specialists, this policy generally has not brought about the desired economic results. It has especially favored products manufactured by light industry to the disadvantage of capital goods since both domestic and foreign investors prefer investments in sectors that do not imply a long-term commitment and that allow an easier estimate of demand.

With regard to design, we can distinguish two variants in the policy of substitution of imports: repetition of foreign designs and substitution for them of designs developed in the country itself. In accordance with this policy, designs for the most part refer to home appliances (refrigerators, stoves, water heaters, irons, blenders, television sets), that is, to products of a low- or mid-range complexity whose technology is well known. There is no special know-how involved in a refrigerator or plastic chair that would justify the payment of patent rights. Nevertheless, there are Latin American countries that continue to pay for this kind of fiction. When there is no know-how that can be patented, foreign enterprises shrewdly have recourse to a substitute that can be monopolized: the trademark. As an image, the trademark represents an elusive, illusory concept, a substitute for the real knowledge that would be worth paying for (even if one considers the traffic in knowledge in the form of patents as obsolete, as a legal and not a technological concept).

The basically simple mechanism of the trademark can be illustrated with an example taken from the bottling of soft drinks, which is controlled by international consortia. The technological secrets of these drinks ("black," orange, and "multicolored") can be reduced to sweetened, colored water that is given a specific taste. The basic chemical substances used to manifacture these drinks are common knowledge and present no major technical difficulties. To differentiate what is identical, the firms use packaging: the bottle, its shape, texture, and graphics. Through the specific design of the bottle, protected as a model and established as a "trademark" product, the colored waters are diversified and the underdeveloped consumers are permitted to imbibe an international drink. By their shells ye shall know them.

The right to use a specific formula for the drink is linked to the obligation to put the liquid into bottles of a specific design (the identification card of a specific trademark). But the story does not end here. Let us suppose that, as frequently occurs, there are domestic companies that manufacture bottles. In this case the production of millions and millions of trademark bottles begins; the investment is made with the internal resources of the country. After achieving the circulation of enormous quantities of bottles, the foreign consortium has a powerful weapon for economic blackmail. It raises the price of the formula and the country has no alternative but to accept the new price in order not to lose its own domestically financed investment in trademark bottles.

THE TRANSFER OF DESIGN

The example of bottle design for soft drinks illustrates one of the ways in which the transfer of designs is achieved.[8] But there are other strategies that are also operative. Aside from the reproductive transfer of design—with or without the payment of patent rights—we can also identify the strategy of adaptive transfer. Two kinds can be distinguished:

Technological Adaptation of Design

In this case the foreign design is adapted to the technological possibilities of the country, which generally requires a redesign, taking into account technological-industrial resources and parameters, such as available machinery and materials, quality of manufacture, the work force, and volume of production.

The objective is to reproduce a foreign use-value in accordance with internal resources. This work sometimes implies the introduction of decisive modifications in the original design. The difficulties of redesign should not be underestimated; the amount of innovative work needed may be considerable.

Functional Adaptation of Design

In this case the foreign design is adapted to the specific requirements and needs of the adapting country's context. Upon submitting the foreign design to rigorous analysis, it becomes necessary to formulate new specifications that will correspond to that context. This approach implies a great number of modifications, some of them fundamental, and can even lead to the development of a new product.

It is important to note that in both cases the foreign design serves as the point of departure and not, as in the case of copies, as the end product.

Finally, we must mention the design transfer of software, especially of knowledge with regard to design methodology. We should, however, maintain a healthy caution so that the methodological experience of the central nations is not taken as unshakable truth, especially now that the "methodological furor" of the 1960s has passed and there is widespread disillusionment concerning the instrumental value of design methodology, at least in its present form.

THE TEACHING OF INDUSTRIAL DESIGN

As for the education of industrial designers, Latin America offers a panorama as varied as those countries in which industrial design is now recognized as a profession. Frequently it vegetates in the faculties of architecture, functioning as an escape valve for the pressure created by overpopulation of professionals in the field of architecture. The affinity between these two kinds of design has already been pointed out and, consequently, the convenience of coordinating the education of architects and industrial designers, but this affinity should not serve as an argument for interpreting training in architecture as a preliminary to entering the field of industrial design; it is not a continuation of architecture on another level, but an autonomous field that requires corresponding technical preparation.

Elsewhere we find industrial design associated with the teaching of visual communication in a department with the generic name Department of Design. During their five or six years of study, students take a sequence of courses that includes graphic design, packaging design, and product design. However, the advantages of a broad view of special areas of design do not compensate for the risks of ending up with a versatile improviser who suffers from the so-called Leonardo da Vinci syndrome. In the case of greater maturity and specialization, students enter either graphic design or industrial design after a common preparatory foundation year.

The wandering of industrial designers through faculties, schools and departments of architecture, applied arts, fine arts, and even engineering, indicates their status as members of an errant discipline. At the same time, institutional insecurity in the teaching of industrial design emphasizes one of its characteristic qualities: neither art nor science nor technology, although related to all three, industrial design does not find its proper place in the traditional academic divisions of the university. In its search for a home it is exposed to the hazards of local conditions, and any effort at a solution that attempts to place industrial design within this traditional framework is only a palliative, an illusion.

Faced with these limitations in the search for a proper and independent home, one might choose a road outside the university. Since we are dealing with a relatively new area which favors an open and experimental attitude that is difficult to achieve in a rigid and obsolete structure like the Latin American university (in this respect no different from the European or North American), the possibility of creating an autonomous school of design suggests liberation from the weight of academic institutionalism. The promise of this approach is demonstrated in two examples that have in the past, and still have today, a certain influence on the teaching of design (architecture, industrial design, and visual communications). We refer to the Bauhaus in the 1920s and the ULM school (ULM is a professional magazine published by HfG, the Hochschule für Gestalt ung school of design, in Ulm, the Federal Republic of Germany) in the 1950s and sixties. Their innovative contributions to the content and method of teaching design were possible cause of their independent character as institutions outside the university framework. But this model of the isolated institution also shows the weaknesses and lack of permanence in the extrauniversity route: the danger of asphyxiation from lack of direct and permanent interaction with other disciplines. This lack of interaction cannot be overcome by means of occasional courses that summarize various topics related to problems of design. Instead of achieving effective integration between the sciences and design, there is only a varnish that covers the insufficiencies of design without eliminating them. However, as a provisional solution, this isolation may be the most viable course of action. While in the majority of Latin American universities the education of industrial designers takes place within the context of one of the four variants mentioned previously, in 1970 in Cuba an independent school of design was created that is connected to centers of production.

As a didactic schema, the basic course of one or two years' duration, also called the foundation course, which originated at the Bauhaus, has been widely accepted. As the name indicates, the objective of this course is to offer to the student a foundation for later specialization. This basic course is universal in the teaching of design, although the inherent danger in the concept of the basic course was pointed out years ago: the tendency to cut off from later courses and to consider it as a closed and self-sufficient entity, and the tendency to widen the breach between "free" or "nonapplied" exercises and projects that are linked to the concept of function.[9] The didactic objective of the basic course can be summarized as sensitizing perceptive and design skill, and offsetting and correcting visual illiteracy—the dominant characteristic of middle and preuniversity education. The basic course rests on the hypothesis that during the initial phase of a project, work should be limited to a set of problems from which certain variables—function, methods of manufacture, costs—have been deliberately excluded; the real presence of these variables in industry increases the complexity of the problem to be solved to an unacceptable degree. The lack of accumulated experience with regard to the number and type of realistic exercises in the basic course turns it into a favorite field for didactic experimentation, especially when work does not require technological knowledge about manufacturing processes and the characteristics of materials.

Here we have touched on an extremely weak point in the current teaching of design: the scarcity of instructors with sufficient practical design experience. A demographic explosion of departments of design in the universities, similar to what has occurred in other parts of the world, is predictable. The dubious attractiveness and the glow of modernity which apparently surround the concept of industrial design have encouraged a phenomenon that has metaphorically been called *parachutism*. This phenomenon is very frequent and not at all surprising in the initial phase of an activity. However, excessive enthusiasm for the education of industrial designers should not make us forget one fact: the proliferating institutions for the teaching of design are subject to the difficulty and, at times, even the impossibility of practicing industrial design outside the university. As new courses of study are created, new jobs are also created. In this way the university offers to some of its graduates a means of survival, thus fulfilling one of its unofficial functions that reflects the contradictions of its environment: to absorb disguised unemployment.

The education of instructors with experience in the subject matter that they are going to teach can be realized in institutions that are attached to the university. This is the case, for example, in the Universidad Nacional del Litoral (Institute of Industrial Design) of the University of the Littoral in Rosario, Argentina, founded in the year 1960.

Among other matters discussed at various meetings at the regional as well as the national level (1968 and 1972 in Buenos Aires, 1970 in Valparaiso, 1972 in Mexico City), the question has been dealt with in regard to the teaching of industrial design, the appropriateness and inappropriateness of creating regional schools of design, and the need to coordinate these efforts. As one of the initiatives a plan was formulated for organizing a systematic exchange of experiences. But to date this plan is still in the project phase.

THE INSTITUTIONALIZATION OF INDUSTRIAL DESIGN

With relation to industry, industrial design is floating in a precarious situation. The manufacturing companies that have recourse to an industrial designer or that maintain units for product development are exceptions. The reason is obvious: it seems easier and cheaper to copy a foreign design than to invest in one's own design elaborated with one's own resources. Moreover, product development presupposes performance with a broader time horizon— that is, thinking in terms of eighteen to thirty-six months. As long as the idea prevails that the industrial designer is a kind of brilliant juggler in the handling of forms and elegant drawings, this activity will be excluded from the possibility of serious participation in the formation of material culture.

To correct this image is one of the functions of the design centers whose guiding pattern was created in London under the direction of the Council on Industrial Design, involved in the pursuit of a very specific end: to increase the competitive potential of English products in international markets. There are three instruments for competing in export markets: price, technological novelty, and design. For this reason industrial design attracts the interest of institutions dedicated to the promotion of exports. When industrial design is considered as one factor among others in the promotion of exports, its visual aspects enjoy preferential treatment because they are more easily accessible. In order to judge the real use-value of a product, the candidate must be subjected to comparative tests performed in laboratories equipped with the appropriate instruments. Moreover, the concept of use-value does not only include technical-physical aspects, but also their three-dimensional expression and their semiotic qualities. At the same time, what should also be included in the evaluation of use-value is concrete historical conditioning: on the one hand, the needs that form the dialectical counterpart of use-value, and on the other hand, the resources available for satisfying those needs. In this context the criteria for evaluation are derived—and not from a Platonic kingdom of universal values. It can be stated without exaggeration that a coherent methodology for the evaluation of designs does not exist and, therefore, present procedures for assigning the classification of good design to a product are on shaky ground; they are essentially limited to judgments based on personal taste.

A glance at the number of products exhibited at design shows proves the predominantly exclusive character of the works intended, in the main, for the social stratum with greatest buying power. The niceties of design serve primarily for the decoration of the individual microenvironment: chairs, sofas, lamps, rugs, porcelain, crystal. Chrome and leather, the preferred materials, are the star attractions in the semantics of wealth.

In 1964 the first design center in Latin America was inaugurated in Buenos Aires, dedicated to the promotion and diffusion of industrial design through the organization of contexts, thematic expositions, permanent or rotating shows of selected products, and seminars. At the same time professional groups were created in Argentina, Brazil, and Mexico, but despite these various efforts the level of institutionalization of industrial design in the three countries with the greatest technological development is very low. The reasons are obvious: in profit economies the initiative for generating original designs is random, depending on the investment activity of business enterprises. In planned economies, on the other hand, technological innovation can depend on general plans for industrialization and be realized, with a broad perspective, in state enterprises. This is the case in two small Latin American countries—Cuba and Chile—that have opted for an organization of their economies according to egalitarian principles.[10]

In Cuba the works effected up to the present time refer especially to individual and collective equipment (schools) based on detailed ergonomic studies, and to packaging designs. In Chile the designs developed by the Committee for Technological Research (INTEC/CORFO) include popular consumer goods, electronic products, food packaging, and agricultural machinery.

DIFFERENCES OF FOCUS BETWEEN CENTRAL NATIONS AND PERIPHERAL NATIONS

The development of products in less industrialized nations differs essentially from design in the central nations. The differences in technological levels are striking; in the central nations there is sophisticated technology with a great variety of materials, manufacturing processes, and specialized labor, and a rapid pace of technological innovation. Contrasting with the wealth of means, a large part of the industrial designer's skill is wasted in frenetic formal innovation, making him an accomplice to the deterioration of the environment, the squandering of resources, and alienation in the form of hyper-consumerism. This role has been denounced, even by representatives of the profession, to such a degree that a climate of discouragement and rejection of design projects has been created, especially among the younger generation. But the most important difference lies in the proportion between means and need. In the peripheral countries the volume of need is astronomically greater than the capacity of the productive forces and the volume of economic resources, while in the central countries the capacity of the productive forces and the volume of economic resources stifles needs, at least those that can be satisfied with products for individual consumers. The underdevelopment of the central nations with respect to the public sector and the satisfaction of collective needs was exposed years ago, although the channels of information, which are controlled by the central nations, tend to filter out those negative images that damage the highly publicized happy dream of one-dimensional man swimming in a sea of oversupply.

It is precisely this proliferation of products that should be questioned—an indispensable first step in establishing and creating an alternative design. The supply of consumer products in the central nations is created subliminally by a principle of microsocial organization: the division of society into purchasing families composed of individual consumers of individual products. If, however, we place a need (for example, food storage) on a gradated spectrum between two poles, one individual and the other collective, and we relate it to the limited resources available we can estimate alternatives: how many people can count on the satisfaction of the need on an individual, small group, larger group, or collective level. For there is no natural need in man to preserve food in individual refrigerators, no more than there is a need to move about in a steel box on four wheels that weighs a ton. Those needs and their perpetuation correspond, rather, to the growth needs of the steel, tire, and fuel industries.

Clearly, this approach loses its utopian character when it is part of a policy of redistribution of wealth that includes marginal and underprivileged sectors of society, particularly the rural population. For industrial design concerned with the comforts of the industrial city, this implies a Copernican return to the country. Moreover, for as long as hunger is not an apocalyptic spectre but a reality for millions of human beings, and a threat for many millions more, design skill finds a challenge of the first order in the design of products, installations, and systems for the production, preservation, and distribution of food.

Aside from design work in its restricted sense, the designer can contribute to the rationalization of product choices, to the development of a less anarchical and irrational products policy, to the standardization of components in order to increase productivity. In the case of a nation that must import finished products, the designer can participate in the evaluation of available supply options, contributing information as a basis for decision making by the institutions charged with importing.

These are some of the central tasks—certainly prosaic and not conducive to fame and fortune, but no less urgent for that reason—that the designer must face when making his concrete contribution so that the future of the periphery will be a real alternative and not a poor replica of a model taken from a world with no exit.

Notes

1. We use the term *dependence,* conscious of its negative connotations, in a strict descriptive sense to indicate an asymmetrical power relationship that generally implies for the dependent party a limitation on alternative decisions. The different manifestations of dependence should also be qualified. Technological dependence denotes inequality with respect to technological resources and, above all, the lack of internal capacity for, or of conditions favorable to generating one's own technology. Cultural dependence is characterized by non-critical internalization of the values of the central nations, contempt for one's own creative potential and overvaluation of everything that comes from the center, which is thought of as the basis for one's orientation. The variant of dependence is especially insidious because it is difficult to detect and counteract. We also qualify the above by observing that several Latin American countries are definitely on the way to overcoming dependence.

It should be pointed out that dependence does not necessarily imply exploitation, although one often accompanies the other: "Dependence is expressed in two ways: heterodetermination and exploitation. Exploitation (in a restricted sense) is manifest in all the forms of unequal exchange in which, either openly or covertly, there is a transfer of values from the exploited to the exploiter.... While exploitation presupposes the transfer of values, that is, appropriation as well as expropriation, dependence brings with it the loss of alternative behaviors without affording the dominant party a direct advantage." F. Schlupp, S. Nour, G. Junne, "Zur Theorie und Ideologie internationaler Interdependez" (unpublished manuscript).

2. W. F. Haug, "Die Rolle des Ästhetischen bei der Scheinlösung von Grundwidersprüchen der kapitalistischen Gesellschaft," in *Das Argument* 64 (1971): 196.

3. W. F. Haug, "Zur Kritik der Warenästhetik," in *Warenästhetik, Sexualität und Herrschaft.* Frankfurt: Editorial Fischer, 1972, p. 11. "By manipulation we understand non-terroristic control of thought and behavior by linguistic and esthetic means."

4. J. Doblin in *Design Quarterly,* 88, 1973.

5. To this end we have used a report by the Commission on Developing Countries of the ICSID (International Council of Societies of Industrial Design), 1973.

6. B. Arvatov, *Arte y producción,* Alberto Corazón, editor, Madrid, 1973, p. 78.

7. D. Ribeiro, *La Universidad nueva,* Buenos Aires; Editorial Ciencia Nueva, 1973, p. 15.

8. As has been correctly pointed out, it would be more appropriate to speak of "commerce

in technology" instead of "transfer of technology," since technology is one kind of merchandise among many (M. S. Wionczek, report at the international seminar "Application and Adaptation of Foreign Technology in Latin America," organized by ILDIS/CONICYT, Santiago de Chile, May 28–June 1, 1973). However, there are channels for the transfer of technology that are not covered by the concept of commerce. We refer to the copying or near-copying of designs from the central nations and the subtle cultural influences that penetrate dependent nations.

9. "The first year should be considered part of the total education of the industrial designer, and not separated artificially as a 'basic year.' It should have a character as logical and controlled as the rest of the courses." *The Education of Industrial Designers,* a report published by UNESCO/ICSID, 1965, p. 9.

10. This text was completed shortly before the military intervention against the popular government in Chile, September 11, 1973. The observations concerning Chilean industrial design are limited to the three years of the government of Salvador Allende Gossens.

7 / Technology

EMILIO ESCOBAR LORET DE MOLA

If architecture is the result of an interplay of components that are increasingly complex in their synthesis insofar as they increase in number as their intrinsic complexity grows, technology, the faithful and inseparable companion to architecture, is sometimes ignored, at times underestimated, and almost always disparaged as a factor that determines and facilitates architectural design. It is precisely the technological areas that have undergone the greatest qualitative and quantitative changes in the last three decades.

We must qualify this by stating that when we speak of technology in relation to architecture, we are referring not only to construction techniques but to the field in its broader aspects, from the control of the physics of construction, to the mechanical equipment of the building, to mathematical methods of matrices and systems, including the use of computers in the design, programming, and execution of the work. The fact is that these new tools in architecture allow for unthought-of possibilities in the solution of pressing social problems. We state this conditionally, since no one is unaware of the socioeconomic circumstances that must prevail in order to effect, at the necessary rate, the steps that architecture must take in the creation of the physical environment or framework of a society.

The role of technology in architecture depends on the sum of objective technical factors as well as on the attitude of the designer and even of the user, and this subjective element is of capital importance in the resulting focus. All of these factors are valid material for a study of the past, the present, or, what is more important, for an evaluation of the future possibilities of our continent.

THE PRE-COLUMBIAN PERIOD

In Latin America, once the Asiatic nomads who populated it during successive waves of immigration over several millennia were established on the land, and after the gradual settlements and the move from hunting societies to socioeconomic structures based on agriculture, the development of successive cultures began over most of the inhabitable area of the continent. It should be pointed out that when the Spanish and Portuguese conquerors arrived there were still nomadic peoples, principally in North America and in the southern cone of South America. Their way of life meant that they had little technical knowledge, including that of architecture, although there were some interesting solutions, such as collapsible tents that, without being architectural works per se, satisfied the parameters determined by that economic system.

On the other hand, the land-based cultures showed no homogeneity whatsoever in their level of development; on the contrary, cultures varied to an extraordinary degree, ranging from the primitive agricultural tribes of the Caribbean, Venezuela (their huts and shacks are still the dwellings of various groups of Venezuelan Indians), and the Antilles (their huts still house present-day farmers) to the advanced systems of human organization of the Incas, the Aztecs, and the Mayans in which high levels of technology were reached in construction in general and in architecture in particular.

Although this chapter is basically devoted to the field of technology, we must refer to factors that have a determining influence on it, that is, the physical environment, both climate and available materials, that allows architectural work. In the same way we must mention the production relationships that undoubtedly generate needs in the conformation of the physical setting of the society and therefore determine the development of technology. This becomes evident when one considers agricultural and hunting cultures like the Taína in Cuba and Santo Domingo, with a benign subtropical climate, fertile soil, and seas rich in fish, and with a social structure of primitive communism whose transformation of the environment to make it suitable for human life was necessary only in a reduced way—characteristics that were reflected in a simple architecture of tree trunks, boards, fibers, and palm leaves—and contrasts it with the elaborate culture of the Aztecs, with its slave economy, located on the temperate Anáhuac plateau, subject to a climate that, although moderate, demanded a deeper conditioning of the environment, with a highly complex social structure in which sui generis building themes like temples, pyramids, and palaces found ample room for development, and in which a beautiful and easily worked volcanic stone both permitted and demanded the development of building techniques adequate to established needs.

Because they are the protohistory of our contemporary technology, we refer to the dominant building systems of that time; leaving Antillean architecture, we can approach the continent at its northern tip and find, with few variations, similar solutions in the tropical and subtropical territories.

One finds a very different situation in the west central section of South America. The flourishing of cultures like the Muchik and Nazca, Chavin, Tiahuanaco, and, finally, that political-cultural synthesis that was the Incan Empire, leaves no room for doubt, even after the most summary examination of its architectural ruins, that the building techniques, planning, work, transportation, and mounting and fitting of stone were of a high level.

These were societies based on an agricultural economy, with a collectivist structure as far as production was concerned; their life, beginning with work, was shaped theocratically and directed by a governing aristocratic caste claiming divine origin. This generated rich architectural themes: palaces, fortresses, convents for the priestly caste or *Akllawasis, pirwas* or storehouses, *tambos* or inns offered the opportunity for and required the development of an architecture that did not reach Mayan, Teotihuacan, or Aztec levels of ornamentation although it more than surpassed them in technical-constructive areas. Walls of sun-or fire-baked adobe for minor buildings, and in major works of dovetailed stone (the fortresses of Ollantaytambo, Machu Picchu, and Sacsahuamán, the palace of Chanchán), stone combined with brick (the sanctuary of Huiracocha) formed the foundations and supported the roof of cut wooden beams and roof tiles of clay or stone.

The water supply was achieved by means of conduits and storage tanks integrated into the construction. Natural lighting and ventilation were usually effected by trapezoidal openings. The absence of mortar in the placing of stones in walls and terraces should be noted. It is interesting that the weight of some of the masonry was sometimes as much as thirty tons, which indicates solutions to problems of transport and mounting greater than those achieved by the Egyptians in the building of the pyramids, for it must be remembered that the topography, as in the case of Machu Picchu in Cuzco, increased difficulties enormously. The Incas controlled a large portion of South America—the present territories of Peru, Ecuador, and Bolivia, as well as parts of Chile, Columbia, and Argentina—that still preserves traces of a civilization in possession of a technology which, although undiversified for lack of draft animals and the wheel, was advanced enough to achieve works of great monumentality and scope.

The pre-Hispanic architecture of America lacked the arch and the vault, a technological limitation of great importance in their development, and one that gives an approximate measure of the level reached by Toltec, Mayan, Teotihuacan, and Aztec architecture; in their periods of greatest splendor they, especially the Mayan, were highly developed agro-urban societies with an architecture that in its general formal expression and execution was greater than the Incan, even though the latter solved more complex construction problems. The characteristically rich treatment of parameters, terraces, and other elements of the buildings by the Mayas demanded highly developed facing techniques. First there was stucco, used in bas-reliefs of relative simplicity, for example, the large masks on the pyramids of Uaxactun or in Palenque where the reliefs show an undeniable control of technique. Later, carved limestone was used for pilasters, columns, and frets, and even later, in the Mayan-Mexican period at Chichen Itzá, we can appreciate, in beautiful examples of the characteristic plumed serpents, the evolution of an artistry that enriched architecture at the cost of impoverishing sculpture, which slowly became a mere complement to architecture. These walls, made of stone and profusely decorated, were usually built on a slant, without windows, and covered by roofs of beams and lime. In some cases their forms refer to the botanical antecedents of the architecture. The building complexes, disposed on terraced platforms, demonstrate their achievements in earth movement and adaptation to the topography, and the pyramids reflect their ability to construct and face elevated volumes erected to resolve religious architectural themes.

The Aztecs, the dominant empire at the time of the arrival of the Spaniards, had achieved a highly developed social organization although its structure was based on slavery and acute class differences. The capital, Tenochtitlán, the present-day Mexico City, was set in a lagoon and, like Venice, was crossed by canals. The Aztecs reached great achievements in urban drainage and canals, and the construction of buildings in this muddy environment demanded enormous control of building techniques, especially the laying of foundations. In the buildings themselves, in the palaces and temples, they displayed a great capacity for structural and decorative execution using blocks of stones in the walls proper, held together with a mortar of lime and sand, and faced with carved *tezontle* stone or integral bas-reliefs. They possessed hieroglyphic writing, and this naturally contributed to technological development, since although it is clear that building and other techniques were not viewed scientifically, knowledge of them was partially set down in writing, and transmission was not exclusively verbal or practical.

Their basic building material was lava or pumice stone, which in this region is a deep siena red and very practical for building since it possesses the required resistance and durability and is lightweight. Baked clay tiles were used extensively in roofing, although in many cases they had recourse to the solution of covered flat timbers and faced stones forming terraces and gardens.

The common people lived in huts made of adobe or reeds and mud with tile roofs, and these *macehuales*, as well as the nobles, or *pillis,* did without windows in their dwellings.

In regard to technology we can summarize this period in the history of Latin America by stating that there was unequal cultural development throughout the area; clearly, the high points of civilization were located in the Andes, the Anáhuac plateau, and the territory of present-day Guatemala and Yucatán. Their high level of development is unquestionable; they possessed a relatively primitive architectural technology, but if development had not been cut off by the conquests, they would have continued their upward progress, a fact proven by the evidence of continuing progress currently in our possession.

THE COLONIAL PERIOD

The profound impact of European control on the native cultures almost caused them to disappear. In architecture and its technology it effected a transposition of stages and levels that corresponded logically to political and economic changes and new social structures. Now dependent on a distant metropolis, the organization of territories in areas that at first produced gold and silver and then other minerals or agricultural products was solidified in philosophy with the replacement of polytheistic religions by Catholicism, in politics, with the replacement of native governments by viceregencies and general-captaincies, in social structure, with the replacement of existing superstructures by a colonial class structure. In short, there were foreign rulers and a native population that was subjected to forced labor. A consequence of these profound changes was the fact that architectural themes corresponded to new state schemata—to churches, fortresses, palaces, and administrative buildings that were literally raised on buildings that had once sheltered the dispossessed American races.

Since labor was native, the materials were what was found at hand, and in some cases, for example Puebla and Cuzco, where the pre-Columbian walls served as foundation or base for the new buildings, a certain crossbreeding was necessary between European technology—more advanced, possessing the arch and the vault, knowledgable in principles of statics, using more developed tools for measurement and execution, such as the pulley and the tackle—and native technology—knowing the materials, the climate, and the geological characteristics of the country and transferring its skill in the carving and working of stone and wood to new orders and exotic styles. In this way an architecture emerged in Latin America that was different from the native original and was never the same as its European counterpart. Sometimes more schematic, other times with an extraordinary richness and elaboration, it was marked with an unmistakable American stamp. It is true that although at first this came about through an inability to achieve Spanish and Portuguese models, later, when the masons and foremen were American-born, they knowingly cultivated a formal expression to their own taste— sometimes rich, sometimes modest, but derived to a large extent from modalities of technology developed during the colonial period. Examples are the house of Christopher Columbus in Santo Domingo, the palace of Cortes in Cuernavaca, the cathedrals of Mexico City and Cuzco. At first timidly and then with non-European exuberance, the product of the marriage of the vault and the bas-relief, the arch and the hieroglyph, the classic order and *tezontle* stone proliferated in cities like Bahía, Lima, Quito, and Mexico City.

Our regions developed unequally: Mexico and Peru, the viceregencies, attracted the carriers of technical knowledge to a greater degree than other areas that had few or no precious metals. Other determining factors were geographical location, the health of the climate, and the docility of the population. Thus Havana owes its development early in the colonial period to the fact that it was an obligatory stop for the Indies fleet, a meeting place for ships from Terra Firma and Mexico. There, coralline or sedimentary stone with their hollow characteristics both limited and facilitated the realization of a baroque scheme that is immediately apparent in the Cathedral of Havana;

on the other hand, the wealth of the forests and the control of the techniques of naval construction permitted the execution of extraordinary carved ceilings, principally in churches and palaces. The presence of Spanish masters and architects on their way to the continent, waiting sometimes for six or eight months for the arrival of the fleet, had a decisive influence on the technology of construction in Cuba. The technique of baked clay tiles and slabs used extensively in vaults, arches, and stairways is due to the presence of Catalonian masters who at first were only passing through the country.

THE ERA OF INDEPENDENCE

Along with political liberty the wars of independence at the beginning of the nineteenth century gave a great impetus to architecture which was supposed to satisfy the needs of the new order in the new republics. Buenos Aires, which in the colonial period had been a humble port with little commerce, witnessed the building of numerous edifices that bore the imprint not only of the fashionable styles—first baroque and then neoclassical—but also of influences that were not always Spanish or native-born. Along with Buenos Aires, Santiago, Caracas, and Bogotá grew architecturally, and in Lima and Mexico City, next to the palaces of the viceregency, government houses, churches, and residences were built that pointed to a more developed mode of construction. Political and economic instability marked the first decades of the young republics, and the penetration of European and North American interests were concentrated in the sumptuously built capitals that characterized the period. French, English, and Italian architects influenced the visual appearance of these interests. The expositions of Paris and London, and their American counterparts, decisively influenced the architecture of our continent.

Iron began to be used as a building material. Vaults reinforced with iron began to form part of the buildings that comprised the dominant eclecticism. The Palacio de Bellas Artes (Palace of Fine Arts) in Mexico City, an example of this tendency, testifies to an epoch in which Western building techniques were beginning to be employed in Latin America without any modification whatsoever. Ashlar masonry was abandoned although it was still used as a facing, and for this numerous other techniques were also applied: stucco, bitumen, and overlay face the architecture of the late nineteenth century; beneath them steel and concrete begin their still-hidden work. Wood fell into disuse, and as a result the ability to carve and dovetail ceilings was lost, although it was still present as an interior decorative element in hand-crafted and other treated surfaces.

Brick was industrialized, as were tile and other ceramic elements, and at the end of the century cement replaced lime in the composition of mortar for setting stone and surfacing. In the same way, it was employed in foundations and structural elements of concrete, although reinforced concrete, lagging behind with regard to Europe, was applied only later in Latin America. In time it would find a very favorable environment for mass utilization in our countries.

THE PRESENT SITUATION

High and Popular Architecture

At this point we should note a characteristic Latin American phenomenon: the superimposition of technology as far as construction is concerned. This superimposition consists of the coexistence of very dissimilar levels in the execution of architectural works. Beginning in the colonial period, there is a marked difference between official architecture and that of the well-to-do classes on the one hand, and most of the urban and rural population on the other. Although the former are more or less up-to-date in terms of advanced technology, the latter is a kind of sample display of primitive technologies whose cultural and economic roots are clearly visible. Huts of adobe plastered with mud and reeds, and shacks of boards and palm leaves testify to the Quechua, Mayan, Amazon, or Taíno background of their inhabitants. This architectural dualism, rooted in the colonial period and extending to our day, between a high and a popular architecture, is the basis for a romantic folklore of so-called spontaneous architecture. Although this type of building can be analyzed, measured, characterized, and, most important, explained, it is witness to a lack of integration of the society into one single class or into a whole; there is a dichotomy that extends north from the Rio Bravo in Patagonia and determines society's solution in two counterpoised and antagonistic approaches: advanced technology and careful finishing on the one hand, primitive means and a low level of workmanship on the other.

During other periods the science of construction consisted basically of some elementary knowledge of materials, their resistance, properties, and form, that was sometimes jealously guarded by the guilds of architects but which in the final analysis was easily used once they were understood by technicians or artists. This situation has changed radically in recent decades. It is an objective fact that contemporary society with its architectural technology is not using it to the degree necessary for the solution of its most pressing social problems. What is disturbing is that society is fully capable of doing so. The explanation clearly lies less in the complexity of the technology than in the difficulty of obtaining the necessary economic conditions without a total restructuring of society.

The Function of Technology

On the highest levels, what does modern construction technology consist of, and what does it allow us to achieve once the necessary economic base is assured?

In the first place it permits an inventory of the needs of society and a proposal for a developmental master plan. This plan, in its architectural aspects, permits the establishment of an order of priorities with respect to the execution of works and these, in turn, can in every case be realized according to more rational building systems. An important factor, of course, is the detailed planning of the building industry, taking into account its sphere of influence and its relationship to sources of raw materials. The design of objects can be subjected, as are urban plans and the master plan itself, to modern systems analysis and to computers, thus obtaining optimum practical solutions. The programming of work can be realized in the same way, and both can be achieved in a minimum of time, the architect working together with the programmer, the technician of mechanical equipment with the computer operator. The use of mechanical construction equipment, like graders, backhoes, and cranes, speeds up the execution of the work.

All of these factors, along with the adoption of a broad standard of industrialization of construction within the concept of open prefabrication, would assure more ambitious plans for development to the required level and would increase the quality and variety of solutions.

A variety of sciences and disciplines would contribute to obtaining better results: the physics of construction with its careful analysis of climatic conditioning of habitable spaces, the study of man as a social being and his behavior within a physical context, the investigation of form, a determining factor in architectural expression, are expanding fields that are of increasing importance to architecture, that is, to the human environment, for from sign and object to environment there exists an easily perceptible aleatory unity with regard to the human being that differs only in degree. This view is not a flight of fancy; it is the objective statement of contemporary possibilities that are unfolding in many underdeveloped countries to the degree that these nations demand it. Latin America, with the exception of Cuba, is still not on that road. The technology of Latin American architecture continues to present the usual dichotomous picture, although the difference between the two architectures to which we referred earlier is now even greater.

The "population explosion" can be translated to mean a greater need for massive solutions in the fields of housing, education, and health. The economic restructuring that would facilitate the necessary industrialization of construction is glaringly absent and, held back by economic difficulties, some of our countries are timidly undertaking plans for housing or educational institutions that, though they may bring some relief, will not in the long run solve the problem. In quantitative terms the larger need is not satisfied and it is clear that the particular need is only partially resolved, with incomplete technical solutions executed with perishable materials, and basic requirements such as the incorporation of sanitary facilities into the dwelling left unsatisfied.

We can observe that the technological development of our countries is realized at the same rate as their economic development. In large segments of the population craftsmanship is still maintained, dependent on regional materials and limited economic possibilities. Thus, the technique of adobe walls with roofs of beams and tiles or straw is still current in much of Latin America, and is the almost obligatory shelter in extensive areas along the Pacific coast and in Mexico. Stone sometimes replaces adobe in the contemporary buildings of our cities. Simple mud over reeds is also used. The hut of wood or palm back with a roof of leaves or straw is very common, sheltering the peasant or aborigine in the Amazon and subtropical zones of the continent as well as in the Antilles. Another form of construction widely used in the outskirts of our cities, from Santo Domingo to Brasília, employs all kinds of metal, wood, and cardboard scraps in the building of the infamous shantytowns that house the enormous marginal population of Latin American urban centers. The use of baked brick and concrete block, varying widely in quality, is widespread and can be observed in modest suburban constructions as well as luxurious residences. This material is often completed by reinforced concrete used in slabs or isolated supports. There are comparable variations in the quality of labor.

Reinforced concrete is the basic element in conventional construction in our countries, and in recent years its finishing technique has reached a high degree of perfection, for it is used increasingly without facing, exposed with different textures, and taking maximum advantage of the formal possibilities in structural elements and roofs. An example of the first is the Banco de Londres (Bank of London and South America) in Buenos Aires, where it has been employed with great formal success in both the exterior and the interior of the building. An example of the second are the magnificent works of Félix Candela in Mexico, where with the varied use of undulating surfaces he has resolved department stores, markets, and churches with great expressive force and economy of material.

Within conventional systems we should also mention the exceptional work of the Uruguayan Eladio Dieste, who, taking baked clay either in bricks or tiles as his basic material and basing structural solutions on appropriate calculations, has developed an optimum technique for this material.

Steel, generally an imported material in Latin America, is used principally in industrial structures like warehouses and only exceptionally in some buildings of lesser dimension. Mexico and Chile, in their school construction programs, have adopted solutions based on this material. The former has even employed it in constructions like the Instituto Politécnico Nacional (National Polytechnic Institute), and currently has extended that system to buildings for middle and primary education. In these cases it is a question of using industrial techniques in the construction, with steel ribs, slabs, columns, and panels from the factory mounted on the work itself.

As for the more advanced construction techniques used in Latin America, we will mention first the highly technical conventional systems of construction, which, without constituting a real industrialization of architecture, incorporate techniques of poured concrete, cast concrete, and the use of construction equipment in such a way that they take on characteristics totally different from traditional construction in situ. The system of the lift slab is one of the most characteristic, and consists of pouring or molding slabs in series around previously erected columns that are usually prefabricated; later the slabs are raised by hydraulic lifts and fixed on the columns to their final position where they are generally fixed by welding. In Cuba this has been used repeatedly, first in meat-packing houses and later in the Facultad de Tecnología (Technology Faculty) at the José A. Echevarría University of Havana for the teaching and administrative areas with an approximate extension of forty thousand square meters.

Another noteworthy system is that of movable molds, in which the walls are poured using coffers that are raised by lifts. The slabs, already prefabricated, can be placed after the fact or produced by movable coffers and placed while the structure is being erected. The first experimental building of this kind, seventeen stories high, has been built in Havana. In previous years this system was employed frequently in the construction of silos and water tanks in several Latin American countries.

Today some efforts are being directed toward the development of the technology of prefabrication or industrialization of construction in Latin America. Efforts have been made either by the state or private investment in several countries with varying success. In Chile different variants of light prefabrication in one-story homes are being used in slum clearance. Some examples are the Prensomat system of walls and partitions of corrugated aluminum, faced on both sides with impregnated "cholguan", the whole five centimeters thick. The ceiling consists of wooden ribs covered by sheets of asbestos cement. This system uses thermal insulation of polyfoam in sheets of ten-millimeter thickness. Another system is called Betonit: walls constructed of two prefabricated slabs of poured concrete that are joined to concrete piers and beams in planned patterns using wood and corrugated slabs for the roof. School construction in Chile has used prefabrication systems consisting of concrete pillars between which are placed .08-millimeter-thick slabs composed of a core of insulation between two layers of concrete. The ceiling is built of structural layers of a slate or asbestos mixture over a central girder of steel. These initiatives received a strong impulse during the government of the Unidad Popular (Popular Unity, 1971–73) when attempts were made to resolve on a massive scale the inherited shortages in housing and services.

In Guatemala a prefabricated system of prestressed slabs and girders has been used in school construction. Ecuador has a partial system of prefabrication, also used for schools, that consist of the use of industrial metallic structure and fenestration complemented by traditional building elements.

In the large cities of Latin America one can see some examples of buildings with curtain walls, in which almost all the exterior stripping and interior paneling is metal or plastic, although the structure is of traditional form. In some cases prefabricated concrete elements are found in the facades of these buildings.

In one form or another, various types of construction have been undertaken by prefabrication. The present economic structure and underdevelopment of our countries make it difficult, if not impossible, to develop prefabrication to the necessary degree. The preliminary bases required to make it possible would involve integral economic organization and total physical planning of the territory.

The Industrialization of Architecture in Cuba

After the revolution, Cuba decided to follow the path of industrialization of construction and to develop as far as possible the technology in this field. Beginning in 1959 with on-site prefabrication in housing for the agricultural sector, it subsequently directed its efforts to the industrial development of building components in industrial plants. Several building systems based on complete prefabrication have been developed, principally for housing, industrial, and agricultural projects. Among the first is the great panel four that consists of walls and floor slabs of reinforced concrete made in open-air shops. With this system various urban units have been built throughout the island, with seventeen plants already installed. Another example is the great panel system, produced in a closed and highly mechanized plant, with steam-hardened vertical and horizontal foundry; this plant, which produces seventeen hundred dwellings annually, is in Santiago de Cuba, where it is dedicated to building the José Martí District. This housing project, adapted to Cuban climate and customs, was designed and developed internally. In experimental form some buildings have been erected according to the IMS system, using Cuba designs; the system consists of prefabricated columns and floor slabs which are post-tensioned in the construction.

These systems are currently being applied according to the criterion of closed prefabrication, although the general tendency is now to aim at open prefabrication, that is, the possibility of interchanging elements from different projects and from different systems. In the housing sector they are also using traditional systems of portable brick walls and mortar blocks with floor slabs for in situ or on-site prefabrication executed by minibrigades of workers from all the labor centers of the country, although the tendency is to pass on to more industrialized systems.

At present practically all industrial and farming construction is executed employing columns, beams, panels, floor slabs, and even foundations produced in factories. Asbestos-cement has a good amount of application in the roofing of these buildings, in the form of corrugated slabs or flat tiles. In slabs and partitions they are also using Siporex porous concrete, manufactured in a plant that produces materials principally for the western part of the island. A uniform modular system has been established for all architectural projects except those intended for tourism; this regulates the dimensions of the elements and assures a better utilization of application possibilities. In the search for optimum solutions, a state agency with jurisdiction over standardization is also functioning, which determines, through dialogue with the rest of the organizations involved in each project, all matters that refer to setting the design norms. By standardizing the elements, coherence is given to the economy in the area of construction.

In various architectural themes prefabricated elements are also being used in Cuba. Rural as well as urban schools are being built according to these systems. The basic rural secondary schools are totally prefabricated in reinforced concrete, with prefabricated columns and girders, and floor and roof slabs of prestressed double T, as well as parapet panels on the outside. Recently their structure served to develop the dormitory program at the Escuela de Ciencias Médicas (School of Medical Sciences) where exterior and interior floor-to-ceiling panels were incorporated with carpentry and built-in fixtures.

The Sector de la Construcción (state agencies for construction) as well as the University of Havana are carrying on research in the field of construction technology and architectural design. The university, as part of its educational program, uses students from the School of Architecture for research and development, beginning in their second year. Special attention is being given to the physics of construction, that is, to ventilation, lighting, and conditioning of spaces, as well as to the incorporation of systems engineering as tools for the work of the architect. Digital computers are finally being used in the design process.

Having surveyed briefly the technology of architecture throughout Latin American time and space, we have seen how the two extremes of knowledge in this field have been found side by side. There is experimentation with the new polymers applied to construction, or with panels made of plywood and steel, and at the same time shanty towns (*cantegriles*) and adobe huts are still being built, expressing in this way the fact that our America in its architecture, as in its many other contrasts, is one.

The statistics of our social needs indicate that only with a sensible policy of industrialization and technological development of the basic themes of construction, housing, agriculture, and industry can those problems be resolved, for although the traditional methods suffice for modest projects or for those of reduced proportions, this is not the case when the volume of work that needs to be accomplished requires overwhelming amounts of labor, transportation, and time.

Although typical spontaneous architecture should be preserved as a value of our culture, a developed society cannot be structured with underdeveloped physical means, for we have seen over and over again the immediate correspondence between the true economic and social development of a community and the technological level of its architecture, a correspondence that does not obey formalist intentions, but is rather a reflection of the economic, political, and social situation.

8 / Communication and Social Participation

ROBĘRTO SEGRE

INTRODUCTION

Methodology and Criticism

The historiography of the architecture of Latin America has not gone beyond traditional schemata that are coincidental with a critical, essentially esthetic evaluation of significant works in formal terms.[1] The persistence and primacy of esthetic values comes from the schematization of the evolutionary process in art whose transformations are thought to be determined by their own dynamic, expressed by the successive stylistic changes that, projected into our own time, integrate the achievements of the modern movement.

Although contemporary architecture is counterposed to the traditional principles of classicism, it still has not abandoned certain statements from the rejected historical-architectural inheritance, for example, the persistence of a formal and spatial autonomy in individual works that are conceived of as monuments[2] representing the high cultural tradition and identified with the signs that have been assimilated by an elite that seeks to maintain the pure figurative values that characterize an architectural code whose constituent elements no longer correspond to the radical investment of content that has occurred in our century. Accepting the premise that monuments are witness to our historical inheritance, it is not a question of assuming an iconoclastic attitude or of renouncing the past but, on the contrary, of reevaluating that inheritance by placing it in a wider context, a total environment that in its entirety can reflect and represent significance that is assimilated not only by an elite that produces and consumes masterpieces, but by society as a whole (that is, social praxis) on its various levels: social, political, economic, ideological, and cultural.[3]

In certain periods of history monumental works achieved a significance that was based on a value system that could be read by different social groups. The buildings identified with socially transcendent functions brought together constituent elements of a communally valid code. This was due to the very close bonds that existed among social classes: the direct feeling of the ruled for the ruling class, expressed in the functions, meanings, and attributes implied in cultural codifications; corresponding to evident social oppression was the equally clear purpose of the symbolic attributes that were valued by the ruling elite and that were intended to affect society as a whole.

In contemporary society this universality has disappeared due to the greater complexity of social relationships and the accelerated process of destruction and renewal of forms. The persistence of urban popular culture, with its rural inheritance, has been replaced by the dynamism of mass culture[4] that takes over the values emanating from high culture and questions their indisputable hegemony. In order to maintain their validity and autonomy, the ruling class manipulates the level of culture that is expressed through "everydayness"[5] as a projection of the values emanating from the industrial consumer society: according to Reyner Banham and Robert Venturi this is commercialized *kitsch* disguised as the new popular culture; it corresponds to the psychological and consumeristic manipulation of the masses and transforms culture into another of the factors used to serve the economic interests of the monopolistic bourgeoisie. The latter defends its culture, identified with so-called pure figurative expressions—the monuments whose communicative transcendence reaches a small group within the society as a whole.[6]

This process has impinged decisively on current architectural criticism, on the recuperative efforts aimed at establishing a new scale of values based on a hierarchization that includes meanings that are marginal to the social comprehensibility of architecture. The valuing of monuments is in conflict with the concept of architecture as mass media;[7] the autonomous stylistic pronouncements of the architecture of *exclusion*[8] is opposed to the assimilation of products of the mass culture—the architecture of *inclusion* the persistence of individual works confronts the integrative patterns of architecture-as-system.[9]

Such formulations correspond for the most part to the future hypotheses of the function of architecture in industrially developed nations. Does this mean that their content is antithetical to propositions that are valid in the underdeveloped world? Do they perhaps imply concepts that cannot be assimilated by the Third World? We believe that, if local conditions are taken into account, the theses we have stated are not invalid when used in the analysis of Latin American architecture. On the contrary, their stronger connection to a complex social reality, and their focus on architectural codification based on strict description of communicative terminology and their reception at various cultural levels, permit a more objective analysis of Latin American architectural reality than that offered to date by critical historiography[10]—an understanding achieved by means of an interdisciplinary focus in which esthetic values would assume their proper value. It is evident, however, that the realization of these ideas—architecture-as-system for example—would require structural conditions that are present only in socialist Cuba and, in embryonic form, in Chile and Peru; they are not generalized throughout Latin America. These conditions lay the foundations for the homogeneity of the social collective—the essence of an architecture conceived in terms of a unitary pattern, the spatial delineation of a coherent social life.

Architecture and Language

The linguistic focus of architecture is not a recent phenomenon. Classical treatises, from Vitruvius' to Guadet's, represent an effort to codify a vocabulary, to systematize the formal components related to functional typologies by identifying social architectural themes. What is recent, however, is the analysis of architecture based on the transposition of a methodology used by contemporary linguistics, particularly by semiotics or the theory of signs,[11] an effort to provide a scientific basis for a theory that agonized in an anchylose state within the canons imposed by the classical tradition. At the same time, the development of structural anthropology permitted the establishment of a stricter relationship among cultural phenomena and the societies that generated them. When these elements were integrated, a new stage was opened in theoretical research into architecture, characterized by the scientific rigor of semiotic analysis, and clarifying the implicit meanings in architectural signs, beginning with the functional denotations generated by social life, and indicating the connections among the signs belonging to different linguistic systems.

What is the origin of the transformation that has occurred in the methods of critical analysis of contemporary architecture? (1) The basing of design on a scientific methodology using computers instead of a traditional bookish Beaux Arts approach, to resolve complex functional and design problems[12]; (2) the appearance of communiction theory in visual codes; (3) the clear contradiction between the hypothetical value of high traditional architecture and its slight meaning for and assimilation into the heart of society, as well as the increasing importance of a spontaneous architecture not controlled by architects as to formal intention; this "formless" architecture establishes a universe of alien and contradictory signs and symbols with regard to those included in the canons of architectural culture;[13] (4) the complexity in function of contemporary society and the dimensions of urban centers require the systematization of architectural signs—either symbolic or functional—in order to fulfill their purpose as the formal and spatial mediators between individual and society, currently submerged in a referential chaos.

Although semiotic analysis of architecture has detected the increasingly complex factors operative in the description of linguistic signs, the greatest emphasis of research has been on the semantic and syntatic dimensions— that is, on the study of the meaning of signs and symbols, beginning with their denotations—and on the study of the relationships among the formal components of a given vocabulary. If we limit ourselves to these points of view, we are again confronted by the predominance of architectural form and its esthetic evaluation, both estranged from the particular society that determines them. But if what interests us is the communicative value of architecture in relation to its receivers, it should be integrated into the higher system of social programming that includes: (1) the modes of production;

(2) ideology; (3) communication programs. Every sign system includes programs of behavior that are defined socially and culturally, but is, at the same time, linked to productive processes. Individuals perform work in the sense that "they produce a sign energy" whose ultimate object, the products, are meant to have a meaning and value: that is to say, communication is a part of the process of social reproduction.[14]

If architecture satisfies the essential needs of man, and constitutes the enclosure for all his basic social and individual activities, its study in depth constitutes the indispensable foundation for understanding the social assimilation of architectural signs and communicative receptivity and communal participation in the elaboration and realization of codes, not only conceived of in terms of cultural values, but also in their technical, functional, and economic implications. The contradictions among standards of living within the city and between city and country, the differences in services, environment, cultural values, and ideological content, either conscious or heterodirected, constitute the component factors of cultural programming, knowledge of which is indispensable for assimilating the diversity of meanings reached by architectural expressions as component parts of social programming, complex and contradictory, that characterize Latin American society—the product of rigid class divisions and economic dependence on the imperialistic centers of monopolistic capital.

All formal and spatial significance or symbolization arises from a hierarchy of functions: an ideological content, an instrumentalization of technology based on certain economic relations, the existence of a class strategy, or economic-cultural propositions conditioned by the interests of a certain social group: architecture-as-product is the result of the operation of these factors, situated at a specific level of social praxis.[15] These circumscribe dialectically the communicative content that a specific work possesses, a content assimilated by the society as a whole—the efforts at universality of language used in buildings by the state in its function as mediator within the community, or by a small nucleus of the community. Receptivity to the messages is based on the existence of a socially accepted code. Architecture implies a codification of formal and spatial elements, which at the same time includes the values placed on the cultural functions and representations of different social groups; these elements constitute the visible framework of the urban context. In a society there are, in architectural terms, different codes according to different social strata; forms and meanings can clash or be assimilated through the reciprocal influences of the models developed within each group.

An understanding of architectural development in Latin America requires the clarification of these factors to determine the importance of each to the diffferent levels of architectural practice, which is strongly influenced by internal social and cultural contradictions as well as the cultural experience of the developed world. The multiformity of the picture makes it difficult to characterize a national architecture or continental characteristics. In a certain sense the meaningful coherence of a Latin American architecture, if such should exist, would be produced by a horizontal strata reflecting the social, economic, ideological, and cultural identities that represent the different levels of Latin American social praxis,[16] the overcoming of contradictions and the attainment of a total culture that would give birth to homogenously meaningful architectural signs for the entire continental community.

Communication and Participation

Before beginning the concrete analysis of communication and social participation in Latin America, let us define the interrelationship that exists between both sociocultural phenomena. Let us assume that architectural communication begins with three essential roles—social, functional, and symbolic—which acquire a unitary meaning on the basis of the homogeneity of the social group; this implies both an acceptance of the functional roles operative in the community, and a culture that permits an understanding of the sign system.[17] Coherence among the different levels of architectual communiction is at a maximum when the social collective reaches a high degree of participation in all the decisions that arise within social life. However, there is a participatory variation that lies between the polar extremes of the creative-productive process realized collectively, and a variously directed architecture imposed by a group or an elite upon society as a whole.

Beginning with the industrial revolution, the methods of production and the nature of social relationships tended to lessen social participation in architecture until it was reduced, in the case of the habitat, to the characterization of minimal living space, especially in groups of limited resources. Opposed to elite culture there was mass culture, stimulated by mass means of communication, which by reaching many strata of the population, suggested that a new social participation was operative. However, the interests of the economic groups that manipulated these means of communication denied all possibility of creative social participation; they established the false myths and the false liberties that generated the alienation of contemporary man and his sense of distance from the surrounding environment.

It is evident that participation on a productive and decision-making level could be recovered in a homogeneous society that had no antagonistic internal contradictions. This principle is the basis of future hypotheses proposed in the industrialized countries, beginning with the principle of the forced obsolescence of urban structures and the possibility for all inhabitants to transform the interior (individual) and exterior (social) environment, including the habitat, structures of services, and so forth.[18] Is it possible to assimilate these ideas in Latin America? We will analyze how social participation is an important factor in the proposals for solutions that go beyond the precarious condition of underdevelopment, but that at present do not transcend productive participation, and never reach the higher stage of decision-making in which control would be in the hands of the social collective.[19]

ARCHITECTURE AND COMMUNICATION

Historical Analysis

Given the limits of this essay, we cannot explore in detail the significance of communication and participation in the history of Latin American architecture, but we can outline some aspects based on the factors we have just indicated.

Primitive societies are characterized by their integrative culture, which implies a high degree of social participation in productive processes and in the understanding of established symbols. This was the predominant condition in the communities of pre-Columbian America, where the architectural-urban environment, although materially, functionally, and symbolically hierarchical, reflecting social groups or castes, established an understandable referential framework for the entire community. Even when the pictorial or sculptural figuration of the Mayan or Aztec peoples was more easily assimilated by the military or priestly castes, the commemorative spaces defined by monumental architecture were used collectively in religious festivals. The enhancement of the man-made environment, from city to decorative object, was defined by the diversity of technico-economic levels and not by different formal or esthetic intentions. This coherence of purpose, in fact, reflects the cultural unity that allowed works of art from the high intellectual tradition to be placed on the same figurative plane as popular figures or ceramic objects.

The sudden appearance of the Spanish colonizer on the American continent destroyed the autonomy and esthetic coherence of pre-Columbian civilizations. The architecture of European origin established new formal canons with new symbols from the Hispanic culture that had been imposed on the conquered territory.

From the point of view of communication, colonial architecture can be subcategorized into: (1) The direct repetition of European codes brought by the colonizer, applied at various levels—the design experience and technology that allowed the construction of the first cathedrals in Santo Domingo, Mexico City, Puebla, and so on; the abstract ideal, apparent in the urban gridiron plan, that spread throughout the continent; the practical and cultural experience of the colonizers applied directly by them to the construction of cities and buildings, and also manifested on a more spontaneous and popular level. (2) Adaptation to local materials, techniques, or ecological conditions, still preserving the external codification that determined those forms that can be characterized as regional; according to Gasparini it is this that lends provincial character to colonial architecture.[20] (3) The communicative, ideological intention motivated by the need to convert local populations to the beliefs and values of Hispanic culture, synthesized in architectural crossbreeding or *mestizaje*.[21] (4) The reelaboration of external elements into the new synthesis, maintained at a popular level, which characterized rural or "spontaneous" architecture.

Despite the disparity among these tendencies we believe that during the colonial period Latin American architecture achieved a continental homogeneity that permits us to speak, geographically at least, of an environmental design. The ruling elite organized its sign system in the urban centers, from where the assimilated codes radiated out into the rural environment. These symbolic elements revealed their political, economic, and religious power by means of forms and spaces that could be identified and distinguished within the urban structure, whose layout was constituted by the habitat. There was a functional and formal equilibrium in the city, where social groups were assimilated within the orientation imposed by the hierarchy of values (formal, functional, and ideological) of the ruling class. As opposed to the monumental and symbolic particularity of the churches, palaces, and public buildings, there was the architectural standard established by functional persistence (the habitat as familiar introversion), technical recurrence (walls of rubble masonry, roofs of wood and tiles, lime stucco) and the popular stylistic interpretation of the basic functional elements of the architecture. A homogeneous code was established on a continental scale through the repetition of urban centers with common traits: the layout of the streets, the organization of open spaces—public plazas—the continuous walls in corridor streets with few openings to the outside, the coloristic values. These factors synthesized the urban unity of colonial architecture, a unity that was also projected onto rural buildings, on the elaborate level of the haciendas as well as on the vernacular level, in buildings that, without environmental limitations, achieved a creative, spontaneous configuration that was motivated by collective participation in the shaping process; the buildings of the Bolivian high plateau are a clear example of this.

Liberation from colonial dependence and the formation of the Latin American nations resulted in the loss of the homogeneous code elaborated internally by the local culture. Hispanic models were replaced by those from industrialized nations—England, France, and later on the United States—as colonial dependence was replaced by neocolonialism. The local bourgeoisie supported commercial and industrial development that was subject to the interests of European nations, and promoted the consolidation of urban centers that were now clearly differentiated from the rural areas. Heavy

European immigration at the end of the nineteenth century, as well as the progressive specialization and diversification of productive activities, brought about a more complex social stratification, destroying the equilibrium that had previously been maintained. The urban environment was transformed; it assimilated the new scale of values, imposed by themes and their formal and symbolic representation, that was identified with the individuality of eclectic buildings within the urban context. An exception was the development of Havana, where neoclassicism prolonged a visual coherence by means of a code that was assimilated at different social levels, and that characterized differentiated architectural roles, from the palaces of the center, designed by architects in an erudite language, to the doorways of vernacular dwellings all along the Calzadas Reales.[22]

The eclectic architecture of Latin America expressed cultural dependence on models developed by the European bourgeoisie and imposed by foreign designers without any assimilation of local traditions, and whose visual code, employed in the construction of public buildings, corresponded to an identification of the state with the ruling class. When applied to bourgeois mansions it indicated the semantic obsolescence of the colonial repertoire, its deterioration, not only by the gradual contaminations of class—the occupation of the colonial core by the poor—but also by the emphasis on the urban over and above the real culture, considered a subculture in terms of the system of values coming from Europe. On the other hand, by individualizing the bourgeois habitat, this architecture externalized the personal wealth of the continent when it distinguished great mansions within the urban layout.

At the end of the nineteenth century the capital cities of Latin America already possessed different levels of spatial characterization: the center, monumentalized by the presence of public buildings, the new districts of the wealthy bougeoisie, the homogeneous and continuing areas of the petit bourgeoisie. These were characterized by the transportation of the eclectic language used by the builders or by the stylistic particularization that identified their existence as a social group. The presence in Latin America of art nouveau was the final attempt to ornament in a unified way the life-style of the middle class. The emergence of the proletariat and the uncontrolled presence of utilitarian buildings—ports, warehouses, industries—implied the formal deterioration of urban outskirts and of part of the colonial core, thus ending the new configurative cycle in urban functions.

The substitution of exchange-values for use-values[23] in urban reality corresponded to the disappearance of the former unitary code. The architectural configuration of the city—and its functional-symbolic-communicative structure—was fragmented, sending a plurality of messages corresponding to the different social groups, although each group did not elaborate elements of the code, for these were heterodirected by the bourgeoisie in its class strategy to condition the life-style of the rest of society. This was realized at different levels of architectonic reality: promotion and control by the state (architectonic activity), professionals and private enterprise (architectonic practice), and the spontaneous forces that emerged in the development of social praxis (architectural practice) integrating architecture with daily life.[24]

After analyzing the significance of rationalism we will study in detail the roles these levels played in the development of contemporary Latin American architecture.

The architects of the 1920s reacted against eclecticism and the deterioration of the urban structure, assimilating avant-garde European theories that coincided with the political and cultural ferment in several countries on the American continent. If the cities of Latin America had lost the peculiar traits of colonial culture, and had become "modern" cities, why then not accept the revolutionary proposals originating in the industrialized world, and assimilate them within the local context as an expression of renovation and modernity on both the political and figurative plane?[25]

The failure of rationalism, in Europe and in America, as a revolutionary architectural movement has been demonstrated by contemporary critics.[26] Despite its few achievements, however, its proponents tried to establish an urban-architectonic order without the class connotations implicit in earlier works. Operating within the structures of the state, using works of social content, designers tried to recover a language that, in its strict representation of function, would in the very act of fulfilling function be comprehensible to the whole community. These efforts were absorbed by some progressive sectors of the various national petit bourgeoisie who, as participants in political power, desired to improve the living conditions of the poor and, in this way, weaken the sharp social contradictions that existed in the urban centers.[27] There was an effort to shape an architecture that, at least ideally, would be erected in different sectors of the city, would not be identified with a privileged "site," and would be the symbolic expression of social coherence. It was a mistake of utopianism to suppose that by means of a few community services they could regenerate a situation born of the hopeless abyss imposed by social and economic contradictions whose accelerated dynamic—unchanged by radical transformations—constituted the real configurative motivation of the urban environment. The hospital of Clínicas de Montevideo, the Solaire housing superblock in Buenos Aires, the Hospital del Niño in Mexico City, and the El Silencio housing development in Caracas bear witness to the unrealized desire of designers to recover formal coherence with the environment by hypothesizing an unrealized new society. Having distorted the ideological foundations of this effort, its inheritance was reduced to the commercialization of "pure" forms that became an excuse for modernity—the monotony of architecture as a change-value. Let us see how this direction characterizes the contemporary architectural-urban configuration, and what the significance is of the messages transmitted at different social levels.

Characterization of the Habitat

In the design of the urban environment the habitat plays a predominant role; its particular characterization expresses the life-styles of the society. The attempt to recover the coherence of the colonial habitat through rationalism was in opposition to the dynamic established by the following factors: the uncontrolled growth of the capital cities, the pressure of external and internal immigration, the dense concentration of commercial and industrial activities, the infinite extension of the urban checkerboard, and the constant increase in land values. Let us see how three levels of architectural reality—government initiative, economic motivation, and spontaneous action—defined the habitat.

The state assumed the double function of mediator and promoter in the development of the habitat. The enactment of urban standards and zoning regulations in and of itself established a formal prefiguration. The norms were broad enough to avoid conflict with private interests, thereby facilitating the territorial distribution of the different social groups. In other words, in areas with luxury residences space utilization was established according to open and horizontal development, differing from the regulations that allowed the compact verticality of the center, or the undistinguished city spread of the periphery. However, the differentiated types of architecture were not clearly established by the regulations, whose strict application generated contradictions within the built environment; a typical example is the appearance of residential towers in suburban garden districts.[28] Moreover, with the exception of street plans, the regulations did not organize the territory functionally by indicating a balanced relationship between habitat and services: for example, the limitless extension of bedroom communities.

Governmental action produces different configurations of habitat, transmitting specific ideological symbolic contents. The first level of action corresponds to the immediate solution of health problems caused by extreme conditions in the slums. The architectural solution that is applied is based on a simple material improvement of the dwelling unit; in other words, the provisional character of these endeavors means that there are no new ideas from the point of view of the design of the units of the urban whole: the *operación techo* (operation roof) housing project in Santiago de Chile is an example of this orientation. Greater elaboration, based on ideological and political motivations—that is, the externalization of the state as benefactor or the realization of the petit-bourgeois values contained in the "dream house"[29]—is manifested in the nuclei of dwellings designed according to foreign models, for example, the typical dwellings of the English garden-city. The cottage and chalet are the symbolic signs of the mythification of the habitat and of private property, whose transcendent exemplariness is projected onto the community. It is demagoguery, effected by various regimes in Latin America—the first presidency of Peron in Argentina or the dictatorship of Batista in Cuba—whose works, supposedly identified with a national project of populist origin, mask the needs and aspirations of the proletariat with the ideals of the petit bourgeoisie. The third kind of state initiative inserts models of contemporary habitat into the urban plan based, either conceptually or formally, on significant achievement of the developed world, pointing out concrete guidelines for the housing problem and generating a new urban structure opposed to the obsolete values and the predominant class interests in the city. The successful initiatives have, in most cases, coincided with a higher level of design, a positive factor that has its opposing negative polarity, that is, their slight transcendence within the social context resulting from the isolated and fragmentary character of the whole project. Although some of the best examples—the Portales district in Chile, President Alemán in Mexico City, Pedregulho in Brazil, the 23 de Enero housing project in Venezuela, the Unidad Vecinal La Habana del Este in Cuba— were planned by the most outstanding designers in each country, a critical analysis of the results indicates two basic negative aspects: high cost, a factor that contradicted the original intention of the buildings (meant for the proletariat, some of the projects were occupied by the middle class), and a scheme for the habitat that is antithetical to the life-styles and cultural traditions of the inhabitants. In other words, rather than socially inspired architectural actions, the buildings are imposed on society in what is called authoritarian urban planning.[30]

The building of superblocks is an idealized vision, a hypothesis for urban structure suggested by younger architects. It is clear that this idea contains two conceptual errors: the first is attributing excessive importance to esthetic values—a purist coherence of design—to the point of formal abstraction; this characterizes the habitat of Brasília, and eliminates every possibility for personal expression on the part of the inhabitants. The second error is to suppose that the mere construction of dwellings can restore the urban social fabric. The forms of living change, but the infrastructural conditions (lack of services) or the economic and social contradictions (unemployment or underemployment) remain constant. We do not agree, however, with those who reject these experiments as coercive in contrast to the allegedly positive qualities of the spontaneous habitat; the experiments indicate real progress, from the ideological and conceptual point of view, in the development of urban social life, even within the idealistic and esthetic limits that characterize some of these examples.

If we apply the second level of *architectural reality*—architectonic practice—to the habitat, we are confronted by the limits to action established by the economic-professional structures operative in bourgeois society. What emerges is architecture-as-product, characterized by its response to two fundamental polar opposites: esthetics and amorphism on the one hand, and the processes of implosion and explosion of the habitat on the other, a dynamic shaped by the sign system whose code comes from the cultural and economic conditioning established by the bourgeoisie.

The environmental deterioration of urban centers, their functional and esthetic chaos, the impossibility of exercising a regenerative total control have encouraged an opposing beautification of the enclosures of private life;[31] it is the "poeticization" of inhabiting, the dwelling conceived of as evasion or "escape". The architect assumes a fundamental role as the creator of the esthetic sacralizing the function "inhabiting" by means of external and internal formal attributes that are manifested in individual and collective dwellings. The stylistic character and the degree of formal coherence vary according to cultural and economic levels, from the sober assimilation of the poetic by the masters of the modern movement to the architectural caricatures generated by kitsch taste.[32] It is an architecture defined in large measure by an enlightened constituency that holds on to the significance of use-value, establishing the high standard of formal autonomy apparent in certain central areas or suburban residences. Moreover, it constitutes an escape valve, the coalescence of a free creativity that permits architects to express their talent without the inhibitions of strict material limitations: in Latin America the individual dwelling still maintains a fundamental significance that characterizes the directions taken by "high" architecture.

Much of the bourgeois habitat, however, corresponds to the tone set by the mechanisms of speculation—that is, architecture conceived of as exchange-value. This is amorphism or, as De Fusco defines it, "function without form" that anonymously covers urban districts with smooth continuous facades— the sad semantic remains of rationalist purism—that enclose the rectangular streets. If one accepts the legitimacy of the external configuration—an economic legitimacy in which one agrees to renounce the esthetic—a compensatory equilibrium is established in the sphere of what is arbitrary,[33] that is, in the interior space of the dwelling unit, the field of action for the inhabitant's free, unencumbered "participation."

These aspects of esthetic evaluation can be applied to two opposite movements in the forms of habitation: explosion and implosion. During this century the city has developed in a continuing centrifugal movement out from the center toward the fringes, a dynamic that is identified with the persistence of the private house, the principle of life in the outskirts that is based on the autonomy of the family and introversion within society as a whole. If from the ideological point of view this attitude corresponds to the principle of class purity—bourgeoisie "ghettoization" in reverse—at the same time estrangement from the symbolic monumental center means the loss of improved services and the experience of urban life. In reaction to this process of explosion there is the contrary movement of implosion, a phenomenon characteristic of Latin American cities in recent decades, represented by the construction of luxury high-rise apartment houses in the areas closest to the city. These residential towers take on the role of autonomous islands within the urban fabric, maintaining a social and functional purity that is encouraged, in some cases, by the inclusion of certain collective services. In this way the habitat is integrated into the consuming and decision-making center, compacting the urban hierarchy of power groups.

There is an action assimilated within a broad, differentiated social context that corresponds to architectural practice, a kind of spontaneous building that incorporates different attitudes ranging from the voluntarist (design) to the participatory (construction). Most of the urban territory in Latin America is occupied by this architecture, identified socially with the petit bourgeoisie, the proletariat, and marginal groups, whose segregation from the center and the better urban areas is furthered by economic-speculative mechanisms. The three social levels define three responses to the mode of inhabiting; these gradually lose their sense of the esthetic whose attributes are established by ideological and stylistic contamination from the models of the "high" culture—the classical ornamentation on the facades—or from petit bourgeois kitsch. Visual elements that express the assimilation of contemporary architectural codification, they are formal elements that are added to the functional typological structure in which schematas from the colonial tradition—row houses with interior patios, for example—still persist. Thus, occupation of the land becomes increasingly less dense as the city dissipates into the rural surroundings because of shifting borders caused by marginal districts whose configuration comes from the transition from dominant culture into subculture, and in which architecture is as precarious as the physical surroundings.

The Presence of Centrality

The history of urban centers reveals the significant dualism that characterizes them in the coexistence of symbolic representation and social participation; architecture's duty is to give value to the place as it expresses the functional, ideological, and symbolic content accepted by the community. On one hand, the buildings-as-symbol—church, town hall, palace—are identified with the ruling power structures; on the other hand, the spaces balance their symbolic-formal presence by inviting participation, that is, the communal use of the center. This equilibrium, preserved throughout history, was broken in the nineteenth century when the bourgeoisie erected new symbols—eclectic monuments representative of state functions—and subjected public spaces to a sense of control imposed by these monuments, the center achieving a hypothetical total symbolization of the community that was now identified with the state.

The change from a rural-craft society to an urban-industrial society was accompanied by an intense development of economic activities concentrated in the capital city, which became the center of both political and economic decision-making. Investment capital, banking, the headquarters of industrial and commercial control all required their symbolic-functional structures that surpassed and marginalized the symbols of the state: the presence of the public festival fiesta and the false ideology inherent in the image of the state as a synthesis of the community were swept out of the center, whose new architectural signs exalted the economic power of the ruling class.[34]

In terms of architecture the center is identified with stylistic and technological modernity, the form determined by a high standard of living, one that ritualizes the functions of work, commerce, and leisure as representing the efficiency of the system in which the integrated society participates. The most characteristic aspect of contemporary capital cities is their economic value and their role as consumption center, caused by high concentrations of population and wealth. This explains the importance of commerce in the center; it is one of the few functions that can change the street plan—the proliferation of shopping malls freely introduced into the orthogonal gridiron plan—commerce thus determining the greatest esthetic improvement of the environment. This contrasts with the slight significance of the same function in peripheral zones, except in the shopping centers, created in bourgeois residential areas, that copy the referential signs of the center.

Chaotically, because the iron law of land value does not permit the planned control of the center, there is opposition and competition among the towers of iron, concrete, aluminum, and glass, and the monumental groupings designed by the local creative avant-garde that idealizes its designs based on the objective conditions existing in society,[35] thus opposing the creativity of the national culture to the imitative reproduction of models from developed countries. The Banco de Londres y América del Sud in Buenos Aires, or the Centro Comercial de la Roca Tarpeya in Caracas are efforts toward esthetic urban value in two functions typical of centrality—banking and consumption—that reject the anonymity imposed by curtain wall towers. It is culture manipulated by monopolistic capital, suggesting the existence of human content that is manifest in the architecture but denied by the very essence that is their foundation.

In the center, however, the participation of the state is not excluded; it proposes to generate architectural signs that refer to a code that can be assimilated by society, to replace the cultural autonomy implicit in eclectic public buildings with a language that will integrate elements of national culture and that will signify a functional revitalization of the structures of government, expressed in the growth of social services, that coincides with great social participation in the direction of national politics. There are four outstanding examples of this tendency in Latin America: Mexican architecture in the 1950s, synthesized in the Ciudad Universitaria; the Ciudad Universitaria in Caracas; the symbolic center of Brasília, and the Gabriela Mistral building (UNCTAD) in Santiago de Chile. Each one has a particular communicative purpose—the reevaluation of the national historical past, that is, the pre-Hispanic forms still considered semantically valid within the contemporary architectural context.[36] This synthesis is identified with the murals on Mexican public buildings, with the educational and cultural function granted to an architecture promoting the integration of the arts and relating society dialectically with the contemporary artistic avant-garde as proposed in the Ciudad Universitaria in Caracas, with the creation of nationally significant symbols of the new dynamic of the state as in Brasília, where the desire is to communicate the existence of a nation rediscovering itself, freeing itself from the neocolonial bonds of dependence identified with the coastal cities of Rio de Janeiro and São Paolo.[37] In the Gabriela Mistral cultural center, built by the Unidad Popular government in 1972 for the third Assembly of UNCTAD, a multifunctional complex was established to be utilized by the masses, assuming a symbolic value that would identify it with the beginning of a democratic process of open social and cultural participation that would integrate all levels of society and make them cohesive.

The rare occurrence of cultural formulations or their invalidation demonstrates the close interdependence of social and cultural programs. Architecture cannot hypothesize a superstructural reality without an essential foundation. In contemporary architecture the necessary connection between form and content has disappeared; the polysemiotic character of the constituent elements of the codes means that denotative and connotative significance does not strictly depend on the signifier. Rather, as Umberto Eco states, it lies outside of architecture, in the attributes emerging from the cultural programming imposed by a specific social group through functional everyday life. The one-to-one codification that still existed inthe 1930s when the Nazis identified rationalist architecture with Marxism and fought it, destroying its visible signs or changing the dominant codification, covering the glass surfaces or constructing peaked Gothic roofs over the flat roofs of reinforced concrete, has been superseded.

Both university cities (Caracas and Mexico City) maintain their original function without making a profound impact on the social context: they are still educational centers serving the ruling class. It is an intellectual elite which receives the message of nativist recovery attempted in Mexico City or the integration of the arts created by Villanueva in Caracas. On the other hand, the supposed democratic symbolization proposed by Niemeyer in the Plaza of the Three Powers in Brasília does not contradict the cultural foundations that support the military government of Brazil,[38] demonstrating to the world the progress of the economic miracle and the modernity achieved in that country's infrastructures. Nor is it opposed to the visible class content of the capital's universal layout. The aspiration of Niemeyer—to design a city for free men—was achieved for white-collar workers; the exploited live outside the city in eight satellites; circumscribed by traditional, anonymous, commercial codification, or the products of spontaneous and precarious elaboration, these are bedroom communities where three hundred thousand inhabitants—proletariat and low entry-level employees—live alienated from the architectonic and urbanistic symbolism and distinction of the pilot plan.[39]

Nor does the Gabriela Mistral building endure in its social functionality:

the military coup against the government of Salvador Allende converted it into the seat of the military junta, radically changing its significance and use in the urban context and altering its cultural identification by renaming it Diego Portales. The first Latin American Nobel Prize-winner in literature, symbol of progressive culture in Chile, was replaced by the designer of repressive political bourgeois structures.

Urban Communication and New Contents

The analysis of these topics clearly indicates the obvious stratification of urban messages in Latin America, reflecting the system of values established by the different social groups. Now then, what changes are necessary to recover a homogeneous code in the environment? Is a change in syntax and semantics viable if a change is not generated first in the social programming that sustains a universally recognized code of signs? Can a communicative change be produced by means of architectural elements, or is it necessary to create a system of relationships—social, functional, cultural—that precede architecture? What is the role played in urban communication by the new dynamic factors in the architectural-urbanistic component?

In contrast to the static value of architecture, urban life, forms of be-havior, the interpretation of functions, and the presence and use of mass media become meaningful dynamic movers within the urban context. An in-creasingly important factor is urban graphics, the neon advertisements that form "electrographic architecture."[40] This dynamic superimposition on the underlying architectural base is, in a consumer society, an alienating com-munication of forms, signs, and symbols pointing to a behavior that is to be followed.[41] It is a heterodirected meaning managed by "economic groups," without the cultural elaborations that propose new concepts, or achieve participatory identification in the community, or at least transcend the simple act of possessing the advertised object.[42] However, the repetition and diffu-sion of these visual elements, whose language varies from pop culture to commercial kitsch, allows them to be assimilated by great strata of the population, proposing a visual and figurative education closer to the expres-sions of contemporary culture than that based on the gray and amorphous anonymity of the urban environment.

Partial answers to these questions can be found in the experiences in Cuba which accompanied the revolutionary changes in the sociopolitical-economic structure. Is it possible, once the basic conditions have been created and the inhibiting factors, such as social differentiation, private property, and sec-tional economic interests, have been eliminated, to "resemanticize" urban form, to remove alienating traits, to give a new sense to architectural forms? It is obvious that in a state of underdevelopment the resources available for effecting radical architectural solutions are very limited due to the need for massive investment in the primary sectors; it follows that first priority is given to those changes in content, function, and partisan interests that are meaningful for the social collective. If new housing developments are a point of departure for achieving a new urban configuration expressed in urban structures and in the disappearance of marginal dwellings, greater communicative content is expressed in breaking down the monopolistic compartments created by residential districts. Social mobility brings with it the threat of symbolic "de-sanctification" of the formal and spatial dwelling and of the attributes of a private property that has now disappeared. At the same time, the transformation of mansions abandoned by the bourgeosie into shelters and schools for scholarship students constitutes a change of function that wipes out the ideological implications of those architectural signs.

The urban center has regained its privileged character as a space that encloses the social life of an entire community, recovering its use-value once the motivations that identified it with change-value had disappeared. The exclusive structures of the elite are open to the entire community, and they have lost the ritualizing implications that placed the functions of work and of leisure—two aspects of daily life—on two differentiated planes. This has occurred in La Rampa, in the Vedado district in Havana, whose diverse structures for leisure time permit the formation of a center for popular recreation that replaces the old compulsive centers lacking in services.

It is not the center that requires fundamental change, but rather the periphery of the city, traditionally deprived of elements of distinction. It is necessary to abolish the pyramid in which architectural value coincides with land values that decrease from the center out toward the urban limits. The deterioration of peripheral districts, the lack of services, the progressive and disorderly replacement of the rural by the urban, are processes that can be reversed with esthetic-functional recovery. This can be realized through territorial integration achieved by means of green areas and structures for leisure time—the Bosque, the Parque Metropolitano, and the Lenin Park at the Paso Seco Dam—for example, a dialectical synthesis between rural and urban space, between work centers and recreational centers. This connection between different functions goes beyond the urban context; when secondary schools, traditionally located in cities, are built in rural areas, thus connecting work with education, the urban and rural environments are merged, and the old city-country contradiction is abolished.[43]

The most dynamic level of urban communication is determined by graphics, which have lost their alienating consumerist implications; they send messages that refer to social life, to collective participation in the tasks proposed by the social group as a whole. The graphic code, in a constant state of elaboration, has two fundamental components: thematic significance (the problems and aspirations lived by the community) and esthetic education that affects the entire population. Although the designs are by graphic artists, there is also social participation, a constant attention to the form and content of the messages as well as a popular creativity expressed in the spontaneous graphics that appear freely in the city. In short, to paraphrase McLuhan, the medium is the same but the changes that occur in society change the content of the message.

It is a question, then, of generating the conditions necessary for Latin American architecture and urbanism to recover the values implicit in a homogeneous communication that generates social participation and integration, that is, "the right to the city as a category superior to other rights: the right to liberty, to individualization in socialization, in the habitat, and in inhabiting."[44]

THE ROLE OF SOCIAL PARTICIPATION

Aspects of Contemporary Reality

In analyzing the meaning of Latin American architecture we have suggested some aspects of social participation implicit in the formation of ideological, symbolic, and figurative attributes. But it is necessary to emphasize the importance of this factor conceived of as the social use of architectural structures and the intervention of the user in defining the environment.[45] Participation is manifested on different levels: (1) social intervention in the decisions that affect the total community in the areas of planning and urbanism; (2) the social use of the forms and spaces that define man-made environment; (3) social intervention on an individual scale, that is, the configuration of the microenvironment of the family unit; (4) direct participation by users in the construction of the individual or social environment.

In contemporary society collective community participation in planning for the whole society is not possible, since it requires specialized technical knowledge. On this level of action that shapes surroundings, the basic factor is to achieve some representative of political, administrative, and technical organisms so that their decisions coincide with the interests of the community as a whole rather than responding to the pressures of small groups with economic power. But at the same time the technical collective, although in possession of the information that indicates the social will, cannot rigidly define the design of the environment unless it maintains enough liberty to facilitate adjustment between territorial structures and effecting social functions. It is a question of open planning, applied recently to European city planning,[46] which includes social participation and goes well beyond the coercive schemes of rationalism that had been uncritically accepted in Latin America. Brasilia is a clear example of authoritarian planning of a city with no social participation; this is manifested, however, almost in symbolic protest, in nearby *Cidade Livre* and *Nucleo Bandeirante*.[47]

Another indispensable element in achieving public participation in the shaping of the environment is rooted in the existence of a socially valid culture that will include understanding and legibility of the formal elements that surround daily life. Beginning with homogeneous values, a sign system would appear whose code would reach the entire population in such a way that the transformation produced in the environment would come from a dialectical relationship among the forms, functions, and referential symbols of community life,[48] coinciding with the integration reached in the social functions that would predominate over individual life, and break down the isolation of different groups.

These premises are not being realized in Latin America, as we have already observed in the discussion of communication. Social and economic contradictions impede the coherence of community objectives, of social culture, and therefore of the configuration of the environment. Since collective, communal actions are impossible, studies of social participation have centered on the analysis of individual units—the habitat—products of spontaneous initiative without the intervention of technicians,[49] built by the inhabitants themselves. It is an architecture of impoverished groups, built in the marginal suburbs of the urban centers, the result of internal migration from the countryside to the city. Because of the accelerated process of urbanization, these groups have gained significant importance in the urban characteristics of the city.[50] It is a process that implies the negation of the city as the enclosure for collective participation, and is the product of antagonistic interests, of fragmentary controls, of economic pressures exerted by the ruling elite over other social groups, all of which generate different levels of significance and participation in the form of the environment. State controls tend to safeguard urban functionality—traffic structures and technical equipment, for example—and to shape the economically hierarchized environments in accordance with the participation of the bourgeoisie that imposes this action. The bourgeoisie manifests itself in decisions that affect the community and in the characterization of its own habitat, whose dominant configuration—the custom-built private house —presupposes a decision-making dialogue between constituent and architect. These degrees of participation and freedom are notably reduced for those who do not possess the necessary resources for making their own decisions; they have to settle for a standard environment of repeated prototypes—high-rise apartments or the suburban cottage—forms conditioned by the mechanisms of commercialized housing. This anonymous urban environment causes certain groups to reject society and take refuge in autonomous communities of an unmistakably medieval flavor, in their desire to recover a high degree of participation in daily life and in the definition of the plan and construction of the habitat.[51]

The growing importance of research into the formation of marginal urban nuclei results from a variety of factors: the dimension of the spontaneous phenomenon as opposed to traditional city structures, the dualism shaped in the very heart of urban culture, and the failure of state initiatives throughout the continent to solve the housing problem and to raise the standard of living.

Free to follow their own initiative, the inhabitants of the *callampas, villas miserias,* or *barriadas* structure their forms of life, their communal organization, and their habitat in a spontaneous, constructive, and formal process. The geographical stability of marginal nuclei resulting from the spontaneous occupation of public or private land, and their subsequent consolidation, has changed flimsy shacks into permanent buildings. This phenomenon, as well as the presence of the distinctive cultural traits of the so-called poverty culture, account for the theory that affirms this process as a valid alternative in the solution of the housing problem by facilitating the integration of rural populations into the capitals of Latin America.[52]

The basic theory can be summarized as follows: (1) uncontrolled urban growth and the exodus of the rural population are considered inevitable; (2) the illegal occupation of marginal lands and their rights of possession provide geographical stability and allow the permanent settlement of the new tenants; this is in contrast to the mechanisms of land speculation; (3) prolonged adaptation to the conditions imposed by the city—unemployment and minimal absorption of the unskilled work force—becomes a natural process; (4) the state does not have resources to meet the housing shortage, nor does the adopted standard correspond to the standard of living or the cultural preparation of the immigrants, on whom the models of the urban habitat have forcibly been imposed; (5) the precarious dwelling, on the other hand, provides security by producing the highest degree of participation through three basic liberties: choice of community, personal decision as to the amount of money to be invested in the construction of the dwelling, and design of one's own environment; (6) the conditions of life in the shantytowns are better than those in the country (lack of services) or in the urban slums (overcrowding and unsanitary conditions); (7) the shantytowns consolidate as housing construction develops progressively, and businesses and services appear that transform the primitive, precarious structure into a stable zone of the city; (8) the inhabitants replace the primitive character of their rural traditions with assimilation of the modernity of urban culture.

The confirmation of a factual reality—the existence of marginal populations—does not imply acceptance of that fact with no effort to analyze the causes of the phenomenon—that is, the production relationships and social structures in Latin America. If these are considered to be static, marginality can be assumed to be a permanent fact, but if we conceive of the possibility of a transformation, new possibilities emerge in which marginality has no place. Let us look at some points of disagreement with the previous statements: (1) The uncontrolled growth of Latin American capitals is not a process whose origins lie in needs of internal functionality, but is, rather, the product of adverse conditions created in rural areas by the persistence of latifundistas (absentee landowners) and feudal structures; their transformation—agrarian reform and increased technology—would create new conditions of life and work that would decrease the uncontrolled pressure on the city.[53] On the other hand, the city assumes a negative character through the growth of a service sector that is disproportionate in relation to the national productive forces, and it changes into a parasitic structure.[54] (2) The occupation of land on the urban perimeter—and preservation of permanent rights to it—is a negative factor from the urbanist point of view insofar as it rigidifies an obsolete organization of the land that lacks the services and minimal conditions that one hopes to create for the development of social life. In general, the occupied territories are located in poor areas, and in the city this prolongs the strict division of social sectors, impeding all integrative participation in communal life. (3) The lack of stable sources of work and chronic unemployment, products of the current economic system, impede the cultural, economic, and social development of the marginal tenants, placing obstacles in the way of their assimilation into the higher standard of living in the city.[55] (4) Although the underdeveloped state should channel its scant resources into primary investments, massive construction of housing could be realized by creating national productive structures planned according to the most advanced technology. This would allow the problem to be faced with modern economic methods, without recourse to craft systems, private middlemen, or the ideological and political interference that occurs with foreign aid or financing. The building methods applied would permit the participation of the inhabitants; they would generate urbanistic flexibility and progressive adaptation of the habitat to the cultural formation of the users, a process of transformation that coincides with the use-value assumed by the dwelling that would modify the emphasis on economic factors. (5) The principle of social participation that is thought to be applied is on an elementary level of simple construction, using primitive craft methods; there is no decision-making outside the elementary form of the unit, whose precariousness, poverty of means, and lack of typological and formal experience (in the context of marginality one loses the creativity of the spontaneous rural dwelling) generates an environment of small cultural and human value. It is surprising, therefore, to see the exaltation of the picturesque by apologists for this urbanization process. (6,7,8) The consolidation of the shantytowns is equivalent to the assimilation of the value system of the urban petit bourgeoisie,[56] manifested in the importance given to the principle of private property, and in the elaboration of formal elements—the kitsch interpretation of high architecture—that characterizes the dwellings; the purpose is to differentiate one unit from another, a clear expression of the loss of the rural collectivist sense and its replacement by urban individualism. To this we can add the uncontrolled introduction of services into the gridiron plan, generating squalor in the urban environment and a lack of adequate social centers and green areas. In short, the principle of participation is circumscribed by the limits of the poverty culture. Little of the potential of urban culture is assimilated, as demonstrated by the estrangement of marginal tenants from the center of the city even after they have lived in urban slums for years. It is unquestionably an expression of marginality with origins in the heterodirection imposed on the community by other levels of society—those who create the symbols and signs that presumably represent national culture, but which are alien to great strata of the population.[57]

Proposals and Future Perspectives

In Latin America the complexity of contemporary social life, the superimposition of multiple cultural traditions, the violence of social and economic contrasts give a dynamic, explosive character to certain forms of participation that are manifested in urban centers; the architectural forms become marginal and are converted into passive circumscribers of a space vitalized by a function that was neither foreseen nor imagined. Examples are the religious festival in Mexico (or, as a counterpart, the student uprisings); the carnival in Rio de Janeiro that endows the center of the city with the value of a theatrical and scenographic background to collective participation; the contrasting carnival in Brasília that takes place in the bus terminal, demonstrating the ability of the social dynamic to take over and transform a site and alter the semantics of an architectural form; the communal use in Cuba of an inhospitable and inexpressive space—the Plaza de la Revolución—converted into a center of significant national participation utilized by massive concentrations in revolutionary or festive acts whose social transcendence gives impulse to total integration (for instance, in December 1966 when one hundred thousand people met in the square for supper on New Year's Eve).[58]

The Cuban experience cannot be placed on the same plane as that of the other countries in Latin America. By destroying the stratification of levels imposed by class contradictions, the revolution opened the door to total participation. The principle of balanced integration between the individual and the collectivity, and free participation in community-wide planning, tends to transform the physical environment and determine not only its character but also the methods applied and the resources made available by the state. The opposition between technicians and the public disappears when their objectives coincide and the methods of action are unified; society establishes its needs, the technicians establish the solutions—they form part of the society and interpret the values that operate in it—while the community as a whole participates in the subsequent execution. This has been put into practice in the building of recreational buildings and the green areas enhancing the outskirts of the city of Havana. In the configuration of the habitat there are two alternatives, one immediate, the other long-term. The first consists of confronting both the housing shortage and the limited technical resources available by using traditional building systems with nonspecialized workers. Microbrigades were begun in 1970. These are teams of thirty-two workers in a productive center—industial, commercial, or administrative—who construct dwellings in addition to their normal work load, that is, as voluntary labor. Although participation usually takes the form of execution of actual construction work, in the residential city of Alamar, of four- and five-story blocks and monoblocks of twelve and twenty stories, the microbrigade members discussed urban solutions, the organization of green areas, the color of the buildings, and the finishing of details with the architects, thus gradually increasing the participation of the user in the structuring of housing complexes. Since the builders themselves would be utilizing the dwellings, a social continuity was produced among the stages of execution, use, and maintenance, thus achieving an enhancement of the environment through the social integration of the community. The second alternative, the one that requires greater technological development, refers to the configuration of flexible urban structures in whose interior the living units would assume the dimensions and forms required by the user through the use of light building elements freely chosen and placed by the tenant.[59] In this way continuing and changing megastructures would be achieved whose diversity would be integrated into the planned unity of the environment. There would be coherence of the urban and rural living nuclei, with minimal units converted to a social service utilized by the population in accordance with its needs; there would be great geographical mobility, achieved when the inhibiting and limiting factors have been eliminated that coincide with the principle of private property applied to the dwelling unit.

Social participation cannot give meaning to architecture if it does not correspond to coherent viewpoints—the aspirations of the total community as it assimilates ideological, political, cultural, and esthetic values into daily life. This is a difficult integrative process, but it would recover the unity of social life and shape a coherent environment. It does not mean anonymity or desemanticization; on the contrary, it would create an environment whose signs and symbols transmit valid multifaceted messages assimilated by the social collective. Clearly, achieving these goals implies radical changes in current socioeconomic structures, the destruction of cultural inequities and of the urban-rural antithesis; it implies the utilization of all resources in achieving objectives that are set by the interests of society. If these premises are carried out, participation will then assume another meaning that takes in all aspects of collective life; it would not require integrating compensations for the individual;[60] rather, the configuration of the collective space would prevail, materialized dialectically by technical-specialized structures and the concrete, material actions of urban inhabitants. Communication and participation will, in this way, have a new significance based on a universe of signs capable of generating an architecture that is truly representative of the particularity of Latin America.

Notes

1. Juan Pedro Posani, "Por una historia latinoamericana de la arquitectura moderna latinoamericana," *Boletín del Centro de Investigaciones Históricas y Estéticas,* no. 9, Caracas (April 1968), p. 184. Posani's recounting of various analyses of modern architecture in Latin American corroborates our thesis. We should mention in this regard a recent book on the topic: Francisco Bullrich, *New Directions in Latin American Architecture.* New York: Braziller, 1969.

2. Aldo Rossi, *L'Architettura della città.* Padua: Marsilio, 1966, p. 53: "In fact I tend to believe that persistent urban facts are identified with monuments, and that monuments persist in the city and, in effect, also persist physically. This persistence and permanence are determined by their constituent values: history, art, being, and memory." On this topic see also: Guido Canella, "Mausolées contre Computers," *L'Architecture d'Aujourd'hui,* no. 139 (September 1968), p. 5.

3. Louis Althusser, *Por Marx.* Havana: Edición Revolucionaria, 1966, p. 157.

4. As explained by Hauser, we understand this substitution to be the passage from popular rural culture to the culture generated in urban centers by the mass media. Arnold Hauser, *The Social History of Art.* New York: Knopf, 1951. (The author sites a Spanish edition, *Introduccion a la historia del arte,* Madrid: Guadarrama, 1961, p. 429.) Also see MacDonald et al., *La industria de la cultura.* Madrid: Alberto Corazón, 1969.

5. Henri Lefebvre, *La vie quotidienne dans le monde moderne.* Paris: Gallimard 1968, p. 149.

6. A representative example of the antithesis between esthetic-symbolic values emanating from thematically intranscendent works in contemporary society—disseminated by criticism and historiography—and their real significance within global society, is found in luxury private homes, designed by contemporary architects, a contradiction that is especially apparent in Latin America.

7. Renato de Fusco, *L'architettura come mass-media. Note per una semiología architettonica.* Bari: Dedalo, 1967.

8. It is the intention of this terminology to counterpose the traditional architecture of the elite and the elaboration of a contemporary synthesis that will assimilate the values of popular culture. See Charles Moore, "Plug It in Rameses, and See if it Lights Up . . . ," *L'Architecture d'Aujourd'hui,* no. 135, Paris (December 1967), p. LIX.

9. In this concept there is room for different interpretations, which we will analyze in the course of this essay. The diversity of criteria implicit in the analyses and proposals of Reyner Banham, Robert Venturi, Christopher Alexander, Yona Friedman, or the Archigram Group, have points of similarity among which the most important is the integrative and totalizing concept of architecture, that is, its identification with environmental design, with the total configuration of the surroundings. The persistence of traditional architectural values is still defended today by some critics, among whom Sybil Moholy-Nagy is outstanding. See "En los límites del entorno," *Summa,* no. 16, Buenos Aires (April, 1969), p. 71.

10. A positive effort in this direction is the monumental *Caracas a través de su arquitectura,* by Graziano Gasparini and Juan Pedro Posani (Caracas: Fundación Fina Gómez, 1969). Although it does not refer with any particular emphasis to the problems of Latin America, a recent book on the theory of architecture, published in Argentina, demonstrates the

concern with aspects closer to everyday reality: the importance of the production process and commercial activity for the architectural forms of popular culture: *La estructura histórica del entorno* by Marina Waisman (Buenos Aires: Nueva Visión, 1972).

11. The ordering of concepts that rule semiotic analysis, established by Charles Morris and others, and developed by Ferdinand de Saussure, was transcribed into architectural terms by a group of European authors with the purpose of establishing the bases for a new theory of architecture. See Gillo Dorflles, *Símbolo, communicación y consumo,* Barcelona: Lumen, 1967; Giovanni Klaus Koenig, *Analisi del linguaggio architettonico* (I), Librería Editrice Fiorentina, 1964; Umberto Eco, *Appunti per una semiologia delle comunicazioni visive,* Milan: Bompiani, 1966; Christian Norberg Schulz, *Intenzioni in architettura,* Milan: Leriri, 1967; Manfredo Tafuri, *Teoria e storia dell'architettura,* Bari: Laterza, 1973; Renato de Fusco, Segni, *Storia e progetto dell'architettura,* Bari: Laterza, 1973; J. M. Rodríguez et al., "Arquitectura como semiotica," *Nueva Visión,* Buenos Aires, 1972; Tomás Maldonado, Ambiente humano e ideologia, *Nueva Visión,* Buenos Aires, 1972; Charles Jencks & George Baird, *Meaning in Architecture.* New York: Braziller, 1970; Umberto Eco, *La struttura assente* (1968) and *Le forme del contenuto* (1971), Milan: Bompiani. To this European bibliography should be added contributions from Latin America, particularly from Argentina, where a chair in architectural semiotics was created in the Faculty of Architecture and City Planning of the University of Buenos Aires in 1969. We should point out the theoretical works of M. Gandelsonas, R. Doberti, and J. P. Bonta. See "Arquitectura, historia y teoría de los signos" (mimeographed), a paper delivered by J. P. Bonta at the Symposium of Castelldefels, Barcelona, 1972; J. B. Bonta, *Sistemas de significación en arquitectura,* Barcelona: G. Gili, 1974.

12. A group of designers and scientists, among them Alexander, Gregory, Broadbent, Jones, and Moles, created the essential foundations of the new design methodology. Concerning this, see Christopher Alexander, *Notes on the Synthesis of Form,* Cambridge: Harvard University Press, 1974; Giuseppe Susani, *Scienza e progette,* Padua: Marsilio, 1967; S. A. Gregory, *Progettazione razionale,* Padua: Marsilio, 1970; Design Methods in Architecture Symposium, Portsmouth School of Architecture, 1967, New York: G. Wittenborn, 1969; G. Broadbent, *Design in Architecture:* London: J. Wiley, 1973.

13. Erwin Panofsky, *Meaning in the Visual Arts.* New York: Doubleday, 1955. It is not a question of the existence or nonexistence of *intentio* that would distinguish works that are experienced esthetically from "practical" works conceived of as vehicles of communication, utensils, or apparatus (that is, architectural artifacts). On the "high' as well as on the "spontaneous" level there is an *intentio* with a different esthetic value, characterized in each case by the specific cultural and social context.

14. Ferruccio Rossi-Landi, "Programación social y comunicación," *Casa de las Américas,* no. 71 (March–April 1972), p. 29.

15. Architecture as specific "practice" within the social praxis has different levels of concretion determined by the ruling ideological, social, and economic structures. An exhaustive analysis of architectural practice in contemporary European society has been developed by Jean Aubert, Jean-Paul Jungmann, Arnauld Suger, Hubert Tonka, *Des raisons de l'architecture (l'architecture comme problème théorique dans la lutte de classes),* Paris: Utopie, 1968.

16. The historiography of architecture has made repeated attempts to define the continental or national constants that would characterize a Latin American architecture, but with no positive result. When one concludes that international stylistic currents permeate the architectural figuration of the urban centers, the only viable way to recover national or continental values is to return to popular architecture, rural models considered to be "uncontaminated" by external influences. It is a romantic concept not based on scientific analysis of the relationship between architectural practice and social praxis in Latin America. On this subject see Enrique Neuhauser, Marcelo Vergara, "Arquitectura nacional latinoamericana," (diss.) Facultad de Arquitectura y Urbanismo, Universidad de Chile, 1969.

17.   Christian Norberg-Shulz, *Intentions in Architecture.* Oslo: Universitetsforlaget, 1966.

18.   It is evident that most proposals are still closer to utopia than to immediate realization. I refer to the concept of building environments based on the needs of each individual, proposed by Yona Friedman or the Archigram Group in their "control and choice living." Closer to reality, however, are proposals for achieving dynamic structure for leisure time, which imply social participation: the Fun Palace project of Cedric Price finds a first and timid materialization in the Agora of Dronte, recently constructed in Holland.

19.   Silvio Grichener, "Diseño de vivienda y desarrollo," *Summa,* no. 9 (August 1967), p. 82.

20.   Graziano Gasparini, *América, barroco y arquitectura.* Caracas: Armitano, 1972, p. 22.

21.   Gasparini is opposed to the use of the term *mestizo* architecture, claiming that in Latin America there was no *mestizo* culture that took part in manifestations of Hispanic origin, and that it is more accurate to speak of a process of acculturation rather than of crossbreeding, or *mestizaje.* We believe that the term can be used, without racial connotations or cultural or technical undervaluation, to characterize participation and communication on a regional level, from the response to the functions that integrate the customs or values of the original inhabitants—the open chapels of Mexico—to the application of decorative motifs and local themes to architectural structures of Hispanic origin. This architectural crossbreeding, the result of participation and communication on a local level, is not necessarily identified with popular or spontaneous architecture, usually occurring in rural areas, which we consider to be on another level of architectural production. See Graziano Gasparini, "Análisis crítico de las definiciones 'arquitectura popular' y 'arquitectura mestiza,' " *Boletín del Centro de Investigaciones Históricas y Estéticas,* no. 3, Caracas, p. 51.

22.   This peculiarity, represented by Cuba in the twentieth century, is due in part to her delayed liberation from Spanish colonial domination, which prevented the local bourgeoisie from developing new architectural roles. On the other hand, the elementary quality of the figurative typology of the style conditioned by ecological determinants, made their interpretation by different cultural levels viable without thereby affecting the semantic content of the linguistic signs.

23.   Henri Lefebvre, *Le droit á la ville,* Paris: Editions Anthropos, 1968, p. 5.

24.   Jean Aubert *et al., op. cit.*

25.   Juan O'Gorman wrote in 1936: "Noble technological architecture, architecture that is the true expression of life and that is also the manifestation of the scientific means of contemporary man. . . . Architecture will have to become international for the simple reason that every day man becomes more universal, collective, and educated for the world. . . ." Raquel Tibol, "Juan O'Gorman en varios tiempos," *Calli Internacional* 28 (July–August 1967), Mexico City.

26.   Francisco Bullrich, *New Directions in Latin American Architecture,* p. 18: "It is true that functionalism was a new source of inspiration that freed the architect's concepts from sterile stylistic formulas and engaged its followers in the sincere search for a new architectural expression based on the objective evaluation of the needs of modern man and the new technical means at his disposal. But the socioeconomic circumstances and local cultures differed from those of contemporary Europe. The first rationalist efforts were inevitably an expression of a progressive, isolated intelligentsia rather than products firmly rooted in Latin American soil.

27.   Israel Katzman, Mexico City: Instituto Nacional de Antropolgía e Historia, 1965, p. 150: "In the 1930s there were only three functionalists: Juan O'Gorman, Juan Legorreta and Álvar Aburto. All three had government posts, and identified functionalism with socialist ideas and with a glorification of poor architecture, which corresponded to the conflict between the desires of the government to solve collective problems in housing, education and health, and the scant economic resources available for that purpose. . . ."

28. It is a phenomenon that has become evident in the last decade in the area of greater Buenos Aires despite the forty-year-old warnings of the German city planner Werner Hegemann: "As the building code in Buenos Aires permits unnecessarily high construction in all areas of the city every landowner will think he has the right to speculate, hoping for structures of immeasurable size and fantastic height. *Revista del Centro de Arquitectos,* Constructores de Obras y Anexos, Buenos Aires, November 1931, p. 135.

29. P. Parat and Ch. H. Arguillère, "L'Individuel, rêve, cauchemar; tendences," *L'Architecture d'Aujourd'hui* 136 (February–March 1968), p. 7.

30. John Turner, "Problèmes d'habitat: solutions administratives et solutions populaires," *L'Architecture d'Aujourd'hui* 140 (October–November 1968), p. 1.

31. Henri Lefebvre, preface, *L'habitat pavillonnaire,* H. Raymond, N. Haumont, M. G. Raymond, A. Haumont, Centre de Recherche d'Urbanisme, Paris, 1966, p. 15.

32. Vittorio Gregotti, "Kitsch e Arquitettura," in *Il Kitsch, antología del cattivo gusto.* Milan: Gillo Dorfles, Mazzotta, 1968, p. 268. "The dwelling on horizontal property, the 'palacete,' the one-family dwelling in the suburbs where one finds an obstinate, miserable residue of the sense of private property, of possession as a value—these are kitsch typologies, directly on the level of the relationship between behavior and object."

33. Pierre Bordieu, "Campo intelectual y proyecto creador," in *Problemas del estructuralismo.* Mexico City: Siglo XXI, 1967, p. 163.

34. Henri Lefebvre, *L'habitat pavillonnaire,* p. 45: "On grouping together the decision-making centers, the modern city intensifies and organizes the *exploitation* of the whole society," that is, it is not the passive place of production or the concentration of capital, but the fact that the "urban" intervenes as such in production (in the *means* of production).

35. The Banco de Londres y América del Sud in Buenos Aires is one of the works that illustrates what has been stated. It has been widely written of in all international publications as an expession of Latin American architecture. The designer, Clorindo Testa, states: "The contest took place in 1960. We developed the plans until 1962; then construction took four years. A black period for Argentina: economic crisis, political reaction, liberticidal efforts, fights between generals of opposing factions. All this might have had an influence on us, our morphological inclinations, even though we did not perceive it consciously. Certainly it has weighed on people, stimulating curiosity. An important building had not been realized in Buenos Aires: for years the frustration was notable. Our bank had offered a pretext for rediscussing architecture, particularly with students. At last we had something concrete to argue about." Quoted in Bruno Zevi, "Sette architetti contro una banca," *L'Espresso,* March 5, 1967, p. 20.

36. Israel Katzman, *Arquitectura contemporánea Mexicana,* p. 86: The effort is made to create participation through a figurative means even when in and of itself it may imply no real popular participation in its production. For that reason O'Gorman's statement is purely ideological: ". . . architecture that is produced from below, as a necessary, normal, natural, and logical form to satisfy the needs and to express the desires of the people of Mexico in their struggle for freedom. . . ."

37. Some authors do not share this ideological foundation expressed by Kubitschek at the beginning of the venture. See Eduardo Galeano, "Qué bandera flamea sobre las máquinas," *Cuadernos Americanos,* CLXVII (November–December 1969), Mexico City, 6, p. 14: "Brasília was born, springing up out of a magician's shop in the middle of the jungle where the Indians did not even know of the existence of the wheel; highways were laid and great dams were created; the automobile factories produced a new car every two minutes. Industry grew very rapidly; it was the boom. The doors were opened wide to foreign investment, the dollar invasion was applauded: industrialization, progress, dynamism: Brazil had successfully begun the conquest of the future. . . . According to a bulletin published by CEPAL (1965) no less than 81.7 percent of total investments between 1955 and 1962 came from foreign financing."

38. Norma Evenson, *Two Brazilian Capitals. Architecture and Urbanism in Rio de*

Janeiro and Brasília. New Haven: Yale University Press, 1973, p. 164. "Brasília, with its strong monumental emphasis, was very much in line with military concepts and nationalistic symbols. The new capital, with its regular plan and architectural uniformity, must have seemed an ideal place for administering a new program of discipline and austerity."

39. Lucio Costa, "L'urbaniste défend sa capitale," *Architecture Formes-Fonctions* 14, p. 18: "As for its architectural expression, Brasília obeys an ideal concept of visual purity in which an effort at elegance is always present. Considering that it is a question of a free formal conception ... Brasília, as much for its planning as for its architecture, corresponds to a Brazilian reality and sensibility." The elitist conception identified with a so-called Brazilian sensibility is evident. Also see P. M. Bardi, *New Brazilian Art*, New York: Praeger, 1970, a clear expression of the cultural image-for-export.

40. Tom Wolfe, "Electrographic Architecture," *Architectural Design* (July 1969), p. 380.

41. Henri Lefebvre, *La vie quotidienne*, p. 68: "The city as sign system is associated with consumption because of advertising. Whoever conceives of the city and urban reality as a sign system, implicitly makes them into objects that are integrally consumable as change-value in the pure state."

42. Umberto Eco, *Apocalípticos e integrados ante la cultura de masas*, Barcelona: Lumen, 1968, p. 59.

43. In Havana, the project called Cordón de La Habana has put into practice the theories of the city-as-territory and the integration of urban-rural productive and functional structures. See Roberto Segre, "Presencia urbana del Tiempo Libre en Cuba," *Casa de las Américas* 49, Havana (July–August 1968), p. 28, and *La arquitectura escolar de la revolución cubana*, Havana, 1973.

44. Henri Lefebvre, *La vie quotidienne*, p. 155.

45. Silvio Grichener, "Introducción a la participación," *Cuadernos Summa-Nueva Visión* 29, Buenos Aires, p. 2: "The user of an environment is not a passive consumer of products, situations and/or services designed and produced by specialists, but an actor in and an author of that environment."

46. The method of open planning has been applied in the recent new town, Milton Keynes, establishing a free configuration of residential nuclei within the street plan. The totality of factors that define the planning form part of an imprecise system (cloud like) instead of the precise traditional system (clock like). See Royston Landau, "Thinking About Architecture and Planning. A Question of Ways and Means," *Architectural Design* (September 1969), p. 48.

47. Francisco Bullrich, *New Directions:* This recalls the important question of deficiencies in ex novo planning and dictatorial decisions. A city should not be a unipersonal exhibition, but the result of contributions by other architects and by the public in general; this coordination apparently was missing in Brasília."

48. In the United States pedagogical experiments have been carried out in teaching how to visualize the environment; at MIT and Harvard team efforts at change included students and members of the community. See "Architecture of Democracy," *Architectural Design* (August 1968) and "Environmental Education from Kindergarten on Up," *Architectural Forum* (June 1969), p. 46.

49. It has been calculated that in underdeveloped countries architects participate in 6 percent of the buildings constructed. This statistic demonstrates the importance of "spontaneous urban planning" as the dominant element in the design of the environment. See John C. Turner, "Habitacão, de baixa renda no Brasil: politicas atuais e oportunidades futuras, *Arquitectura*, 68, Brazil (February 1968), p. 17.

50. Roger Vekemans and Ismael Silva Fuenzalida, *Marginalidad en América Latina; un ensayo de diagnóstico*, Santiago: Desal/Herder, 1969, p. 42: "There are now about thirty

million urban marginal inhabitants in Latin America . . . who cannot assimilate into a city because it is not equipped to receive them."

51. This renewal of participation in Argentina is the result of the initiative of certain collectivist groups that try to improve society with the example of their initiatives. See Claudio Caveri, *El hombre a través de la arquitectura,* Buenos Aires: 1967, and Rafael Iglesia, "La reacción antirracionalista en Argentina," *Zodiac* 14, Milan.

52. Various authors have investigated this topic in Latin America; the results are documented in the following publications: Charles Abrams, *Man's Struggle for Shelter in an Urbanizing World*, Cambridge: MIT Press, 1966; William Mangen, "Squatter Settlements," *Scientific American,* October 1967, p. 21; John Turner, "Dwelling Resources in South America," *Architectural Design,* August 1963; "Barriers and Channels for Housing Development in Modernizing Countries," *Journal of AIP,* May 1967; "A New View of the Housing Deficit," *San Juan Seminar Paper,* Puerto Rico, April 1966; "Problemes d'habitat," *L'Architecture d'Aujord'hui* 140, November 1968; "The Squatter Settlement: An Architecture That Works," *Architectural Design,* August 1968.

53. Tenth Congress UIA, *Conclusions de encuentro mundial de urbanistas,* Mar del Plata, Argentina, 1969.

54. Denis Lambert, "Urbanização e desenvolvimento economico na América Latina," *Arquitectura* 75, Brazil (September 1968), p. 27.

55. Victor L. Urquidi, "La ciudad subdesarrollada," *Demografía y Economía,* El Colegio de México, vol. III, no. 2, 1969, p. 145: "Thus, for every middle class building or office skyscraper that is built, there spring up every day thousands of shacks inhabited by five, six or more persons in each room. These people are illiterate, hungry, sick and needy, with few opportunities for advancing economically or socially. According to one study, 90% of the immigrants to Santiago de Chile fail to develop upward mobility."

56. Joaquín Fischerman, "Aspectos sociológicos de la vivienda," Secretaría de Estudiantes, Tenth Congress UIA, Buenos Aires, 1969.

57. R. Vekemans and J. Silva, *Marginalidad en América Latina,* p. 53; "Because they do not participate in the norms, values, means, or division of labor at the social base, the various goods of the total society are not received by the marginal groups; they have nothing to do with them, no matter what kinds of goods they may be. The marginal group does not see any of these resources, nor does it enjoy any of the corresponding social benefits."

58. This points to the possibility of creating dynamic structures within the city that are multifunctional and used collectively by the urban population. The "instant city" proposed recently by the Archigram Group is not so far from our immediate reality.

59. It consists of a building system formed of light modulars—enclosures, interior divisions, and equipment—developed by a team under the direction of the architect Fernando Salinas. Following this concept, although with a projection limited to small nuclei, there is the La Puntilla project by the architect Jan Wampler, and the fishing villages planned by the architect Robert M. Oxman, both in Puerto Rico. See "Annual Design Awards," *Progressive Architecture,* 1968.

60. We refer to the exasperation that leads to the shaping of a personal environment, to sculpting one's own individual cave, a solution proposed by Christopher Alexander in order to escape the universal monotony of the environment. See C. Alexander, "El sistema pared-profunda," *Cuadernos Summa-Nueva Visión* 29, p. 23.

SELECTED BIBLIOGRAPHY

CHAPTER ONE

Adams, Robert McC., *The Evolution of Urban Society: Early Mesopotamia and Prehistoric Mexico*, Chicago, Aldine, 1968.

Aquirre Beltrán, Gonzalo, *El proceso de aculturación*, México, Universidad Nacional Autónoma de México, 1957.

Bagú, Sergio, *Economía de la sociedad colonial*, Buenos Aires, El Ateneo, 1949.

——, *Estructura social de la Colonia*, Buenos Aires, El Ateneo, 1952.

Barnett, H. G., Broom, B. J. Leonard, Siegel, E. Z. V., and Watson, James, B., "Acculturation: An explanatory formulation," *American Anthropologist*, 56, pp. 973–1002.

Bartra, Roger (ed), *El modo de producción asiático: problemas de la historia de los países coloniales*, México, Era, 1969.

Bastide, Roger, y Fernandes, Flòrestan (eds.), *Brancos e negros em São Paulo*, São Paulo, Editora Nacional, 1959.

Beyhaut, Gustavo, *Europeización e imperialismo en América Latina durante la segunda mitad del siglo xix*, Montevideo, Universidad de la República, 1963.

——, *Raíces contemporáneas de América Latina*, Buenos Aires, Eudeba, 1964.

Borah, Woodrow, "America as Model: The Demographic Impact of European Expansion upon the Non-European World," *Actas y Memorias*, vol. 3, pp. 379–387, XXXV International Congress of Americanists, Mexico City, 1964.

Buarque de Hollanda, Sergio, *Raizes do Brasil*, Brasilia, Universidade de Brasilia, 1963.

Comas, Juan, *Relaciones interraciales en América Latina: 1940–1960*, México, UNAM, 1961.

Costa, João Cruz, *Contribuição a história das ideias no Brasil*, Rio, de Janeiro, Editora Nacional, 1956.

Coutinho, Afranio, *A tradição afortunada: o espírito da nacionalidade na crítica brasileira*, Río de Janeiro, Olimpio, 1968.

Crawford, William Rex, *El pensamiento latinoamericano de un siglo*, México, Limusa-Wiley, 1966.

Childe, V. Gordon, *Social Evolution*, London, Watts, 1951.

Fanon, Frantz, *Wretched of the Evils*, trans. by Constance Farrington, New York, Grove, 1965.

Fernandes, Florestan, *A integração do negro à sociedade de classes*, São Paulo, Universidade de São Paulo, 1964.

Foster, George, M., *Culture and Conquest: America's Spanish Heritage*, New York, Wenner-Gren Foundation for Anthropological Research, 1960.

Frank, André Gunder, *Dependencia económica, estructura de clases y política del subdesarrollo en Latinoamérica*, paper given at the IX Latin American Congress of Sociology, Mexico City, 1969 (mimeo).

Freyre, Gilberto, *The Mansions and the Shanties*, trans. from the Portuguese by Harriet De Onis, Westport, Conn. Greenwood, 1980.

Furtado, Celso, *Formação econômica do Brasil*, Brasilia, Editora Universidade de Brasília, 1963.

Gaos, José, *Antología del pensamiento de lengua española de la edad contemporánea*, México, Séneca, 1945.

Gillin, John, "Mestizo America," *Most of the World*, compiled by R. Linton, New York, Columbia University Press, 1949.

Henríquez Ureña, Pedro, *Obra crítica*, México, Fondo de Cultura Económica, 1960.

Ianni, Octavio *Raças e classes sociais no Brasil*, São Paulo, Civilização Brasileira, 1966.

Kroeber, A. L., *El estilo y la evolución de la cultura*, Madrid Guadarrama, 1969.
Lewis, Oscar, *Five Families: Mexican Case Studies in the Culture of Poverty*, New York, Basic Books, 1959.
——, *The Children of Sanchez*, New York, Random House, 1961.
Linton, Ralph, *The Tree of Culture*, New York, Knopf, 1955.
Lipschutz, Alejandro, *El indoamericanismo y el problema racial en las Américas*, Santiago de Chile, Nacimiento, 1944.
Mannoni, Otto *Prospero and Caliban: The Psychology of Colonization*, New York, Praeger, 1966.
Mariátegui, José Carlos, *Siete ensayos de interpretación de la realidad peruana*, Santiago de Chile, Editorial Universitaria, 1955.
Martínez Estrada, Ezequiel, *La cabeza de Goliat: microscopía de Buenos Aires*, Buenos Aires, Club del Libro, 1940.
Murena, Héctor A., *El pecado original de América Latina*, Buenos Aires, Sur, 1964.
Picón-Salas, Mariano, *A Cultural History of Spanish America: From Conquest to Independence*, trans. by A. Irving. Berkeley, Calif., University of California Press, 1962.
Pontual, Roberto, *Dicionário das artes plásticas no Brasil*, Rio de Janeiro, Civilização Brasileira, 1969.
Redfield, Robert, *Peasant Society and Culture*, Chicago, University of Chicago Press, 1956.
Reyes, Alfonso, *Pasado inmediato y otros ensayos*, México, 1941.
Ribeiro, Darcy, *O processo civilizatório: etapas da evolução socio-cultural*, Rio de Janeiro, Civlilização Brasileira, 1968.
——, *As Américas e a civilização: processo de formacão e causas do desenvolvimento desigual dos povos americanos*, Rio de Janeiro, Civilização Brasileira, 1970.
——, *El dilema de América Latina*, México, Siglo XXI, 1971.
Romero, Francisco, *Sobre la filosofía en América*, Buenos Aires, 1952.
Salazar Bondy, Augusto, *La filosofía en Perú*, Lima, 1954.
Sánchez, Luis Alberto, *¿Existe América Latina?*, México, Fondo de Cultura Económica, 1945.
Sodré, Nelson Werneck, *A ideologia do colonialismo*, Rio De Janeiro, Civilização Brasileira, 1965.
——, *Síntese de história da cultura brasileira*, Rio de Janeiro, Civilização *Brasileira, 1970.*
Stabb, Martin S., *América Latina en busca de una identidad: modelos del ensayo ideológico hispanoamericano, 1890–1960*, Caracas, Monte Avila, 1969.
Stavenhagen, Rodolfo, "Clases, colonialismo y aculturación: ensayo sobre un sistema de relaciones interétnicas en Mesoamérica", *América Latina*, 6, pp. 63–104, Rio de Janeiro, 1963.
Williams, Eric E., *Capitalism and Slavery*, Chapel Hill, University of North Carolina Press, 1964.
Zea, Leopoldo, *Do etapas del pensamiento en Hispanoamérica: del romanticismo al positivismo*, México, El Colegio de México, 1949.
——, *América como conciencia*, México, Fondo de Cultura Económica, 1953.
——, *América en la historia*, México, Fondo de Cultura Económica, 1957.
Zum Felde, Alberto, *La narrativa en Hispanoamérrica*, Madrid, Aguilar, 1964.

CHAPTER FOUR

Chueca Goitia, Fernando, Torres Balbás, Leopoldo, and González y González, Julio, *Planos de las ciudades latinoamericanas y filipinas existentes en el Archivo de Indias*, Madrid, Instituto de Administración Local, 1951.
Díaz del Castillo, Bernal, *Historia verdadera de la conquista de la Nueva España*, México, Ediciones Mexicanas, 1950.

Giedion, Siegfried, and Frank, Klaus, *Affonso Eduardo Reidy: Bauter und Projekte,* Stuttgart, Verlag Gerb Matje, 1965.
Kubler, George, *Mexican Architecture of the Sixteenth Century,* New Haven, Yale University Press, 1948.
McAndrew, John, *The Open-Air Churches of Sixteenth Century Mexico,* Cambridge, Harvard University Press, 1965.
Moholy-Nagy, Sybil, *Urbanismo y sociedad,* Barcelona, Blume, 1970.
Toscano, Salvador, *Arte precolombino de México y de la América Central,* México, Universidad Nacional Autónoma de México, 1944.
Toussaint, Manuel, *Arte colonial de México,* México, Imprenta Universitaria, 1948.

CHAPTER SIX

Alexander, Ch., *La estructura del medio ambiente,* Barcelona, Tusquets, 1971.
Bonsiepe, G., *Manual del diseño,* Santiago, INTEC, 1970.
———, "Trazado de una alternativa de diseño", *Summa,* 48, Buenos Aires, April 1972.
DMG-DRS Journal: Design Research and Methods, San Luis, no date.
Fratelli, E., *Il disegno industriale,* Trieste, Universitá degli Studi, 1972.
Gregory, S. A., *The Design Method,* London, Butterworths, 1966.
Hymer, S., *Empresas multinacionales: la internacionalización del capital,* Buenos Aires, Periferia, 1972.
Jones, J. C., *Design Methods,* London, Wiley, 1970.
Katz, J. M., Mallmann, C. A., and Becka, L., *Investigación, tecnología y desarrollo,* Buenos Aires, Ciencia Nueva, 1972.
Maldonado, T., *Avanguardia e razionalitá,* Turin, Einaudi, 1973.
Nelson, G., *Problems of Design,* New York, Whitney Publications, 1965.
Sábato, J. A. *¿Laboratorios de investigación o fábricas de tecnología?,* Buenos Aires, Ciencia Nueva, 1972.
Selle, G., *Ideologie und Utopie des Design,* Cologne, M. Dumont Schauberg, 1973.
Wolf, L., *Ideología y producción: el diseño,* Barcelona, Redondo, 1972.

CHAPTER SEVEN

Auca, 4, issue devoted to prefabricated construction in Chile, Santiago, June 1966.
Bonta, Juan, *Eladio Dieste,* Buenos Aires, Instituto de Arte Americano, Facultad de Arquitectura y Urbanismo, Universidad de Buenos Aires, 1963.
Conescal, 13, issue devoted to prefabricated school buildings, Mexico City, August, 1969.
Faber, Colin, *Candela: The Shell Builder,* New York, Reinhold, 1963.
Morley, Sylvanus G., *La civilización maya,* México, Fondo de Cultura Económica, 1961.
Seminario Internacional de Construcciones Escolares, *La arquitectura escolar de la revolución cubana,* La Habana, DESA, 1973.
Vaillant, C. C., *La civilización azteca,* México, Fondo de Cultura Económica, 1960.

CHAPTER EIGHT

De Fusco, Renato, *L'architettura come mass-media: note per una semiologia architettonica,* Bari, Dedalo, 1967.
Dorfles, Gillo, *Símbolo, comunicación y consumo,* Barcelona, Lumen, 1967.
Eco, Umberto, *Apocalípticos e integrados ante la cultura de masas,* Barcelona, Lumen, *1968.*
———, *La estructura ausente,* Barcelona, Lumen, 1972.

Gasparini, Graziano, and Posani, Juan Pedro, *Caracas a través de su arquitectura,* Caracas, Fundación Fina Gómez, 1969.

Lefebvre, Henri, *La vie quotidienne dans le monde moderne,* Paris, Gallimard, 1968.

——. *La revolución urbana,* Madrid, Alianza, 1972.

Norberg-Schulz, Christian, *Intenzioni in architettura,* Milán, Lerici, 1967.

Pawley, Martin, *Architecture Versus Housing,* London, Studio Vista, 1972.

Segre, Roberto, "Habana r", *Arquitectura/Cuba,* 340, La Habana, 1972.

——, and Salinas, Fernando, *El diseño ambiental en la era de la industrialización,* La Habana, Centro de Información Científica y Técnia, Universidad de La Habana, 1972.

Notes on Contributors

BONSIEPE, GUI

Industrial designer (Glucksburg, Federal Republic of Germany, 1934). Resident of Chile until July 11, 1973. Graduate of the Hochschule für Gestaltung, Ulm, Federal Republic of Germany. Professional work: design of equipment for consumer use, children's recreation areas, toys, electromedical instruments and appliances, food packaging, agricultural machinery, electronic equipment, corporate planning handbooks. Books and essays: *Manual de diseño industrial* [Handbook of Industrial Design] (Santiago, Chile, 1969). About fifty essays in books and professional journals, including *Form* (FRG), *Casabella*, *Marcatré* (Italy), *Cuadernos de arquitectura y urbanismo* (Spain), *Boletín de la Escuela de Diseño Industrial* (Cuba), *Auca* (Chile), *Summa* (Argentina), etc. Teaching positions and activities: professor, department of industrial design and visual communication, Hochschule für Gestaltung, Ulm, FRG, 1960–68; United Nations advisor in Chile for the development of small and medium industrial enterprises, 1968–70; chief of industrial design in INTEC/CORFO, the Technological Research Committee of the Chilean Government Corporation to Foster Economic Development, 1971–73; advisor to the Instituto Nacional de Tecnología Industrial [National Institute of Industrial Technology], Buenos Aires. Has lectured at schools of architecture and industrial design in Chile, Argentina, Cuba, Germany, and Italy among others.

CETTO, MAX LUDWIG

Mexican architect (Coblenz, Federal Republic of Germany, 1903). Graduated from the Technical University of Berlin as architect-engineer. Professional work: planner in the public works department of the municipality of Frankfurt-Main, directed by Ernst May, 1926–31; planner in the studios of Richard Neutra, 1938, and of J. Villagrán García and Luis Barragán, 1939. Beginning in 1949, residential construction in Mexico City; second prize in the international competition for the Berlin Art Museum, Federal Republic of Germany, 1966. Books and essays: *Moderne Architektur in Mexiko* (Stuttgart, 1960; Mexico City, 1961; New York, 1961); contributor to *Knaurs Lexikon der modernen Architektur* (Munich, 1963). Teaching positions and activities: professor of composition, Upper School of Applied Arts, Offenbach-Main, 1928–32; visiting professor, School of Architecture, University of Texas at Austin, 1960–61; visiting professor, School of Architecture, Clemson, South Carolina, 1962; visiting professor, School of Art, Auburn University, Alabama, 1965; professor, National School of Architecture, Autonomous National University of Mexico (UNAM), since 1965.

ESCOBAR LORET DE MOLA, EMILIO

Cuban architect (Lima, Peru, 1934). Graduate of the University of Havana. Professional work: member of the planning team for the School City "Camilo Cienfuegos," Oriente Province, 1963; Basic Secondary School and other projects, Oriente Province, 1963; first prize in design competition, and construction supervision of, the Park of the University Martyrs, Havana, 1965; hotel design, Santiago de Cuba, 1965; director of design team for the Cuban pavilion for Expo '70 of Osaka, Japan, 1968; National Aquarium, Havana, 1970. Teaching positions and activities: chief of planning section, rural housing, INRA [National Institute for Agrarian Reform] 1962; chief of design workshop, Construction Ministry, 1964–66; director, School of Architecture, Havana, 1968–70; chief of the Design Department, 1971–74. Professor of the fundamentals of architecture, basic design, and design workshop in the above school. Has lectured in universities in Mexico, Argentina, and England.

GASPARINI, GRAZIANO

Venezuelan architect (Venice, Italy, 1924). Historian of architecture and restorer of monuments. Graduate of the Central University of Venezuela. Books and essays: *Templos coloniales de Venezuela* [Colonial Churches of Venezuela] (Caracas, 1959); *La arquitectura colonial de Coro* [The Colonial Architecture of Coro (Caracas, 1961); *La casa colonial Venezolana* [The Colonial Home in Venezuela] (Caracas, 1965); *América, Barroco y Arquitectura* [Architecture and the Baroque in America] (Caracas, 1972). Has restored buildings of the colonial period, civil and military, throughout Venezuela. Has carried out archeological research in several countries of Latin America. Teaching positions and activities: professor of architectural history, Faculty of Architecture and Urbanism, Central University of Venezuela, and director of its Center for Historical and Aesthetic Research.

GROSSMAN, EDITH

North American writer, translator, and teacher of Spanish and Latin American literature (Philadelphia, 1936). Has written studies and translations of contemporary Latin American literature. Has taught at the University of Pennsylvania, University of California (Berkeley), Hunter College, Lehman College, Queens College, and New York University. Currently Associate Professor of Spanish at Dominican College of Blauvelt.

KUSNETZOFF, FERNANDO

Chilean architect (Temuco, Chile, 1929), resident in the US since 1973. Graduated from the Facultad de Arquitectura, Universidad de Chile (1952);

Master of Architecture, University of California, Berkeley (1959). Professional work: Team Leader, UNDP Project Hon/74/102 on urban and rural housing in Honduras (1976) Special Mission following Guatemala's earthquake for ECLA-UN (1976). Books and essays: Editor, *Revista de Panificación*, FAU-UCH (1964–68). Some publications in specialized magazines include: "Spatial Planning and Development in Latin America" (1977) and "Housing Policies or Housing Politics: an Evaluation of the Chilean Experience" (1975) both in *Journal of Inter-American Studies and World Affairs*; "Política de Vivienda o Política y Vivienda (1975) *Revista Interamericana de Planificación*; "Aspectos Espaciales en Vivienda y Planificación en Santiago Metropolitano" (1967) Revista PLANDES, Santiago; "Dimensiones de una Política Habitacional para Chile" (1964) FAU, UCH. Teaching positions and activities: Professor and researcher in housing, urban and regional planning at the Facultad de Arquitectura, UCH (1953–1968) Dean of the Facultad de Arquitectura y Urbanismo, UCH (1968–1973); Co-Chairman, Building Commission Universidad de Chile (1968–1973); Visiting Professor, College of Environmental Design, University of California, Berkeley (1974–79); Senior Lecturer at the Departments of Architecture, and of City and Regional Planning, CED, UCB-Specialist, Center for Planning and Development Research, CED-UCB (1979–80).

LÓPEZ RANGEL, RAFAEL

Mexican architect. Theoretician and researcher of architecture. Graduate of the National University of Mexico. Has published essays and articles in various Mexican professional journals. Teaching positions and activities: professor of the history of philosophy, University of San Nicolás de Hidalgo, Michoacán (Mexico), 1960–1965; professor of the theory of design, National School of Plastic Arts, UNAM [Autonomous National University of Mexico], 1971–1972; professor of the theory of architecture in the School of Painting and Sculpture of INBA [National Institute of Fine Arts]. Advisory board member of and contributor to, the analytical architecture journal *Calli* (Mexico City).

RIBEIRO, DARCY

Brazilian anthropologist (1922). First Rector of the University of Brasilia; former Minister of Education and Culture of Brazil. Books: *The Civilizing Process* (Rio de Janeiro, Washington, 1968; Caracas, 1970; Frankfurt, Buenos Aires, 1971; Milan, 1972); *The Americas and Civilization* (Buenos Aires, 1969; Rio de Janeiro, 1970; New York, 1971; Milan, 1973); *El dilema de América Latina* [Latin America's Dilemma] (Mexico, 1971); *Teoría del Brasil* [A Theory of Brazil] (Montevideo, 1969; Paris, 1970; Rio de Janeiro, 1972); *La universidad latinoamericana* [The Latin American University] (Montevideo, 1968, Caracas, Santiago de Chile, 1971); *La universidad nueva* [The New University] (Buenos Aires, 1973). Recent positions: collaborated in the formation of the Centro de Estudios de Participación Popular [Center for Popular Participation Studies] created by agreement between the Peruvian government agency Sinamos and the United Nations.

SEGRE, ROBERTO

Argentine architect (Milan, Italy, 1934), resident of Cuba since 1963. Architectural historian and critic. Graduate of the Faculty of Architecture and Urbanism of the University of Buenos Aires. Books and essays: *Antecedentes de la arquitectura actual* [Forerunners of Contemporary Architecture] (Buenos Aires, 1959), contributor; *Diez años de arquitectura en Cuba revolucionaria* [Ten Years of Architecture in Revolutionary Cuba] (Havana, 1970); *Cuba, arquitectura de la Revolución* [Cuba, Architecture of the Revolution] (Barcelona, Padua, 1971); *La arquitectura escolar de la Revolución cubana* [The Architecture of Schools in Revolutionary Cuba] (Havana, 1973), contributor. Over thirty essays in professional journals including *Arquitectura/Cuba, Casa de las Americas, Pensamiento crítico, Unión, Cuba/Internacional, Revista de la Biblioteca Nacional "José Martí", Revista de la Universidad de La Habana* (all in Cuba); *Auca* (Chile); *Summa, Obrador, Nuestra Arquitectura* (Argentina); *Conescal, Calli Internacional* (Mexico); *Cuadernos de Arquitectura y Urbanismo* (Spain); *L'architecture d'aujourd'hui* (France); *Deutsche Architektur* (GDR); *Op. Cit.* (Italy). Teaching positions and activities: member, Faculty of Architecture and Urbanism, University of Buenos Aires, 1960–1963. Professor of the history of architecture in the School of Architecture and the School of Arts and Letters of the University of Havana. Has taught or lectured in the following universities: Facultry of Architecture, University of Rome; Polytechnic Institute of Milan; Faculty of Architecture and Urbanism, Barcelona; Architectural Association, London; Ecole Nationale de Beaux Arts (University of Paris VI), Paris; Faculty of Architecture, University of the Andes, Mérida; Central University of Venezuela, Caracas, Faculty of Architecture and Urbanism, University of Chile, Santiago and Valparaíso, etc. Chief of the History of Architecture Section and of the Historical Research Group in Architecture and Urbanism (GIHAU) of the School of Architecture of Havana. Editor of the journal *Arquitectura/Cuba*.

VARGAS SALGUERO, RAMÓN

Mexican architect (Mexico City, 1934). Theorist and researcher of architecture. Graduate of the Autonomous National University of Mexico, architect and master in philosophy. Essays: Has published various essays on history of architecture, theory, criticism, and studies of Mexican architecture in professional journals and newspapers in his country. Teaching positions and activities: Has been researcher in the Architecture Department of the National Institute of Fine Arts, and director of the joint governance of the School of Design and Craftsmanship. Has taught courses in ethics, aesthetics, theory of architecture, history of culture, and art history in various divisions of the Autonomous National University of Mexico. Professor of the theory of architecture in the National School of Architecture, and of historical materialism and dialectics in the School of Design and Craftsmanship. Editorial board member of the analytical journal of contemporary architecture, *Calli.*

Index

Specific buildings, complexes and planned cities are listed with architects' names where possible. Cities and states (or republics) are listed separately.